KT-223-688

Murray Walker

MY AUTOBIOGRAPHY

Murray Walker

UNLESS I'M VERY MUCH MISTAKEN

TED SMART

This edition produced for The Book People Ltd,
Hall Wood Avenue, Haydock, St Helens WA11 9UL

First published in 2002 by CollinsWillow
an imprint of HarperCollins*Publishers*
London

1 3 5 7 9 8 6 4 2

A CIP catalogue record for this book is
available from the British Library

ISBN 0 00 766373 0

Set in Linotype Perpetua by
Rowland Phototypesetting Ltd,
Bury St Edmunds, Suffolk

Printed and bound in Great Britain by
Mackays of Chatham, CPI Group

The HarperCollins website address is
www.**fireandwater**.com

Contents

Introduction

Like everyone, I left my [illegible]
idea of what I wanted [illegible]
80 years on, starting [illegible]

Years ago I gave myself [illegible]
amateur racing gathering [illegible]
cluded Rob Walker, [illegible]
Stirling Moss. Rob, one of [illegible]
of the Johnnie Walker whisky [illegible]
worry where his next pay cheque was coming from. I asked
him when he was going to write his life story. He seemed
amazed. "Oh, I couldn't do that, Murray [illegible]
bunking with a bunch of chaps like this but [illegible]
tried to put it all on paper."

"Rob," I said, "if you don't [illegible]
everything you've said [illegible]
committing a crime against [illegible]

Introduction

Like everyone, I left my mother's womb without a very clear idea of what I wanted to do with my life yet here I am, nearly 80 years on, starting to write about it. Why? Who cares?

Years ago I gave myself the answer when I was gossiping at a motor-racing gathering with some great characters that included Rob Walker, friend, mentor and sponsor of the great Stirling Moss. Rob, one of nature's gentlemen, was a member of the Johnnie Walker whisky family and didn't exactly have to worry where his next pay cheque was coming from. I asked him when he was going to write his life story. He seemed amazed. 'Oh, I couldn't do that, Murray. It's one thing reminiscing with a bunch of chaps like this but I'd just dry up if I tried to put it all on paper.'

'Rob,' I said, 'if you don't do it and go to your grave with everything you've said and done still in your head, you'll be committing a crime against motor racing. You *must* do it.'

So I believe I have memories and stories to tell that might interest and entertain those many people who haven't had the good fortune to be where I have been. But how Rob felt is how I feel right now, staring glumly at my laptop. So much done and so much to say, but where to start and how to go about it? All sorts of things motivate me to try though, one of which is gratitude. I've been both lucky and privileged, having had a fabulous life full of richness, variety and satisfaction, with hardly any setbacks. From as far back as I can remember I've enjoyed almost every second of it, basically because I like people and there are usually plenty of them around whose company and friendship I can share.

Normally I'm not much of a chap for looking back; to me the present and future matter more than the past. Life is about making things happen – planning, organizing and getting it done – and I like it most when anticipation turns to realization. But I must be getting old (well I *am* old, though I certainly don't feel it) because I now want to remind myself about who I've known, where I've been, what I've seen and what I've achieved. So I'm writing this book primarily for my own satisfaction, not for the money!

Many years ago in my youth I spent a long time trying to persuade a particular girl whom I was very fond of to marry me, but she finally refused because she said I was too interested in security. We went our different ways, but to this day I have an unashamed horror of being insecure – having a mortgage I can't keep up with, not being able to pay the bills, wondering what would happen if I wasn't earning, or whether the pension would be enough. I've a theory that there are two sorts of people in life: those who work for someone else for a salary and, hopefully, the greater security that goes with it, and others who work for themselves, take risks and can potentially do better, though not necessarily. Well, I'm one of the former. I can think of few really big 'risk' decisions I've made in terms of my career development, and luckily for me those I've had to make all paid off. I've largely reacted to situations rather than initiated them, but things seem to have worked out pretty well. I'd love to be a bright spark who ducks and dives and comes out ahead – someone like Bernie Ecclestone, whom I greatly admire – but I'd hate to be the one who ducks and dives and falls flat on his face. Better to be at ease with yourself than try to be something you are not.

'He's obsessed. If it hasn't got an engine he's not interested,' says my long-suffering wife, Elizabeth. This is not *entirely* true, but I confess that the groaning bookshelves in my study do not include the works of Shakespeare, selections from Chaucer or too many volumes of poetry. Talking of Elizabeth, incidentally, you are not going to hear too much about her in this book. It's not that I do not love her dearly or respect and admire her, because I do all of those things by the bucketful, it's just that Elizabeth's attitude is 'He's public, I'm private'. We met at a London party when I was 34 and although it took me far too long to get around to the subject of marriage I really was smitten at first sight. She is a tower of strength and has an infinitely better brain than me, but whereas I love the limelight and positively revel in it, her idea of purgatory is to have her photograph taken or to appear in public. She wouldn't welcome me banging on about her qualities here either, so I'm not going to do so. It's a marriage of opposites I suppose, but just like it says in the old song: *'We've been together now for 40 years [and more] and it don't seem a day too much. There ain't a lady living in the land as I'd swap for me dear old Dutch.'* I wouldn't have been able to do what I have done without her and she's the one for me.

I have to confess that I'm a workaholic. I'm absolutely useless at relaxing. I get irritated, bored and restless. For about 20 years Elizabeth and I didn't have a normal holiday because I spent all the time either at my job or doing broadcasts. I really enjoyed both my work and what was then my hobby – commentating. Saving for security mattered more to both of us than spending now and maybe suffering later, but neither of us regrets it for we certainly haven't been deprived. It's different now, because we go on cruises to magnificent places and, in my last commentary year, we had a fabulous trip to Australia, Thailand and Malaysia with, hopefully, more to come.

'For God's sake, don't ever retire,' Elizabeth used to say. 'What on earth are you going to do with yourself?' Throughout my life I've had to be *doing* something all the time, whether it's writing, researching my next race, going to it, beavering round while I'm there, talking about it, or travelling home eagerly to await the next one. And that's still the case now that I've retired from full-time commentating. I always reckoned that writing this book was going to take me a good 12 months, after which something else would turn up. It always does.

I've managed to go from one thing to the next with little

difficulty and have always made the best of my lot rather than dreaming up impossible goals. From my beginnings in Birmingham, with the wonderful influence of my parents (had my Dad not been obsessed with motor cycles I may not have had half the life I have); my childhood, passing through several schools; my time in the army, in both war and peacetime, from which I returned far more of a man than before; and jobs with Dunlop – at the time one of Britain's greatest companies – and two major advertising agencies with whom I became satisfyingly successful; not to mention all my wonderful experiences in motor sport: through it all I have never been unhappy with the way things have turned out, whatever the change of direction. It's all been worthwhile, enjoyable and good experience for the rest of my life.

What about the broadcasting though? I thought you were never going to ask. It's difficult to know where to begin because it has been going on for so long now. In fact, it could be a question of heredity. I often wonder whether I would have been so passionately interested in motor sport had I not been born and brought up with it, whether I would have attempted to race motor cycles had my father not been so successful, or whether I would ever have picked up a microphone had he not been as brilliant and gifted a speaker, writer and commentator. It's impossible to tell, but it looks as though I am a chip off the old block and that's very much all right by me; I cannot think of anyone I'd more aspire to be like than my father. After a long and distinguished racing career – of which more later –he became editor of the failing magazine *Motor Cycling*. He turned it round by sheer ability, hard work and personality, matched the sales of the previously dominant competitor, *Motor Cycle*, and also became a much-loved broadcaster.

It must be in the genes: all his siblings were 'arty' in some way. My Uncle Eric was Professor of South African history at Cambridge and Cape Town Universities, my Aunt Elsie was a gifted painter and all the rest were good communicators. In 1935 when Dad had given up racing, the BBC asked him to do their radio commentaries (there was no television back then) for the Isle of Man TT, the Ulster Grand Prix and other motor cycle events. He took to it like a duck to water. In sport there are people who compete at the top level and people who can talk about it entertainingly, but there aren't many who can do both supremely well. In my day James Hunt could and, more recently, Martin Brundle can, but my father was unique. He made you feel as though you were there, with an infectious enthusiasm overlaid by total knowledge of his subject, and he was the BBC's top man on the sport for 31 years.

Those that can, do; those that can't, talk about it, so maybe that's why I ended up where I did. I was reasonably good at trials riding on my 500T Norton – I won a Gold Medal in the 1949 International Six Days Trial at Llandrindod Wells and various other awards – but it was at racing that I wanted to excel. I've always believed that if you want to do anything enough you will succeed, so I couldn't have wanted to race that badly because in 1949 I decided that I was far more likely to get somewhere in business than by trying to set the world's racetracks alight. I retired at the peak of my inconsiderable form after I'd won a 250cc heat at Brands Hatch. Thereafter

I confined my lack of two-wheeled talent to weekend commuting between Dunlop in Birmingham and my home in Enfield, on my Triumph Tiger 100.

At heart I think I'm a bit of a ham, for I've always enjoyed public speaking and was therefore delighted when I got my first chance at broadcasting – albeit on a public address system. The Midland Automobile Club asked me if I'd like to do the PA commentary on a combined car and bike meeting at their world-famous Shelsley Walsh hill-climb in Worcestershire. My father had been due to commentate for the BBC but had to drop out at the last moment, and was being replaced by the man who had been booked to do the PA. The Club asked my father, who'd caused the situation, to recommend someone to take his place.

'Why not try the boy?' he said. 'I think he'll be all right. Even if he isn't it won't be a disaster because he'll only be talking to the spectators and they'll be able to see what's going on anyway.'

I suppose it was nepotism, but I wasn't going to say no. You have to grasp your opportunities where they are offered in this world. And never mind the spectators: as far as I was concerned I was talking to one man at Shelsley – Jim Pestridge, the BBC producer. There was no way he was going to miss me for my voice was blasting out of a battery of loudspeakers right by his side. Now, the way you do a PA commentary and the way you do a radio commentary are quite different. With the former there's no need to talk non-stop as your role is more to give information and announcements than to commentate on the action, which the punters could see for themselves. *The hell with that!* I thought. For Jim's ears I submitted the poor devils on the hill to a non-stop barrage of facts, figures, hysteria and opinion. (Not much has changed!) And it worked. The next week Geoffrey Peck, one of the BBC's senior sport producers, invited me to an audition to commentate at an imminent Goodwood car meeting. And I got the job.

One thing led to another. 'We'd like you to do the second position, Stowe Corner, at Silverstone at the 1949 British Grand Prix,' said Geoffrey after my successful Goodwood stint. *Yes!* I was on my way for what was to be a half-century-plus career doing what I wanted to do, travelling the world, going to wonderful places, working with stimulating people, satisfying my ego and, moreover, being paid for it!

For the next 13 years, in addition to my developing advertising career, I would be my Dad's number two as the only long-term father-and-son sports commentary team the BBC has ever had. That was entirely to do with motor bikes but, as the years rolled by, I would also cover, for both BBC and ITV, anything to do with motor sport: motor-cycle trials, scrambles and races of every type and class, truck racing, power boats, touring car racing, sports cars, rallycross, Formula Ford, Formula 3, Formula 3000, Formula 5000 and, of course, the pinnacle of them all, Formula 1.

It was here that I developed a reputation of being an enormously excitable chap who used colourful phrases but didn't always get things right in his enthusiasm to communicate what he was seeing. Inevitably people remember my amusing 'mistakes' more than the factual comment, but importantly they found them endearing – and that didn't do me any harm! Not so for others though, given my entirely justified reputation for the 'Murray Walker Kiss of Death'. I would confidently predict something was going to happen and, dramatically, it wouldn't. At the 1986 Australian Grand Prix Keke Rosberg came up to me and asked if he could have a word – a highly unusual move for an F1 driver.

'This is my last race, Murray. I'm retiring after it.'

'I know that, Keke, I've been talking about it for ages.'

'Well, this being my last race I'm particularly anxious to do well in it.'

'Of course you are, good luck to you my friend.'

'Murray, if I *am* doing well, for Christ's sake don't say anything about it!'

He was leading the race, I said he was going to win his last event, and he got a puncture and retired.

Similarly, in 1993 the BBC did some technical fiddling that allowed me to talk to Damon Hill while he was actually qualifying on the track. I wasn't going to risk breaking his concentration while he was working but right at the end of the session he took pole position and on his run-down lap I shouted out, 'FANTASTIC Damon! POLE POSITION! Well done! You must be delighted!'

'Thanks, Murray,' came Damon's reply, which was going out to the BBC's vast worldwide audience, but as he went on to say how happy he was and how much he was looking forward to starting from the front in the race, I was horrified to see the word PROST appear *above* HILL on my timing monitor. In my excitement I had failed to spot that Alain had passed the start just before the flag went out and could therefore still do a hot lap that would count. To my acute embarrassment The Professor beat Damon's time by a tenth of a second and snatched pole position from his team-mate.

'Damon,' I said. 'That was the good news. The bad news is that you are now starting second. Alain's just beaten you.'

I conveniently cannot remember what Damon said in the car but he came up to me afterwards and said, 'Murray, do something for me will you?'

'Anything, Damon. What is it?'

'In future just keep your mouth shut, will you?!'

Another Williams success, Portugal 1990, was even more embarrassing. After a brilliant victory ahead of Senna and Prost, Nigel Mansell made his way to the interview room standing in the back of an open car, waving to the crowd, and hit his forehead on a steel beam. He staggered in and sat down as the cameras started rolling. 'Nigel,' I said. 'First of all, will you carefully and slowly take your cap off. You've got an enormous bump on your head. Can you let them see it? Right up there' . . . and stuck my outstretched finger right into the middle of it. It's a clip that's been shown dozens of times and it never fails to raise a laugh. I hope my life story is even half as entertaining . . . and rather less painful.

CHAPTER ONE

A Proud Brummie

People think of me primarily as a commentator and yes, to my continual amazement, I've been one for well over half a century. But for the first 59 years of my life it was very much a second string to my 'proper job' in advertising and to be honest I sort of blundered into it, partly out of desire and partly because of circumstances at the time. Did heredity play a part or was it just the environment in which I was brought up? It's impossible to tell. But of one thing I'm sure. A lot of my characteristics come from my mother and maybe even more from my father.

My mother was the daughter of Harry Spratt, a well-to-do draper and gents outfitter (as they used to call them in the 1920s) who owned businesses in the market town of Leighton Buzzard, Bedfordshire. She had a pretty idyllic upbringing amidst a loving atmosphere in a fine home with servants, horses and stables, and she seems to have wanted for nothing.

She was an extremely attractive woman, both physically and personally, had a very strong personality, was very much the belle of the local ball, very feminine and great fun. But she was also extremely bright, pragmatic and good with money, being a very nifty operator on the Stock Exchange. She created a wonderful home for me to grow up in, I loved her dearly and suspect that her influence resulted in me marrying as late as I did.

Into her life in the 1920s came Sergeant Graham William Walker, despatch rider, Royal Engineers, then convalescing at Leighton Buzzard after having been injured in France in World War One by a German shell. The son of William Walker of Aberdeen, Company Secretary of the Union Castle shipping line, and his wife Jessie, this young, attractive man (*most* attractive, even in hospital blues, according to my mother) was potty about motor bikes. He was also personable, had a highly developed sense of humour and couldn't have done a dirty trick if he'd thought about it, so it's not surprising my mother fell for him. His father, Grandpa Walker, I remember as a kind, gentle man with a fine white beard. His wife, who produced four sons and two daughters, was a dominant woman who ruled her family with a rod of iron and adored my father, her youngest son, probably because he was the only one who stood up to her. Sadly she seemed a rather unhappy woman, and after her husband's death she spent most of her time wintering in Madeira and restlessly buying, moving into and then selling numerous expensive houses.

When my father set about wooing Elsie Spratt it wasn't

long before they were wed. And, the way these things happen, their marriage was followed by the arrival of 9lb 12oz Graeme Murray Walker on 10 October 1923. I was born at home at 214 Reddings Lane, Hall Green, Birmingham, for at that time my father was working there – so, like Nigel Mansell, I'm a Brummie and proud of it. I nearly killed my poor mother: at one point during her immensely long labour the doctor told my father, 'They can't both make it. One of them's got to go. It's the mother or the child. You've got to decide.'

'No question,' said Father, 'it's the child.'

Fortunately both of us survived, but my parents never tried for another. 'I lost the blueprint,' said my father. He subsequently told me that, while he certainly didn't mind being a father, it had never been one of his great aims in life. My mother had always made the running and was keen to have another, but the fear of losing her had well and truly put him off.

I worshipped my father for he was a wonderful man. I called him 'Daddy' to his dying day, when I was in my thirties, but I frankly feel a bit of a twit doing so now. He was kind, generous, as honest as the day is long, a brilliant communicator and an immensely hard worker. Not a demonstrative man but a pillar of support if ever one was needed and never deviating in his loyalty to his beloved wife and son. But he was a terrible worrier. My mother used to say, 'Tim worries if he hasn't got something to worry about because if he hasn't there must be something wrong.' ('Tim' was her nickname for him – don't ask me why.)

His passion was motor bikes. He joined the Royal Engineers as a despatch rider in World War One because of it and they dominated his life. But motor cycles were looked on very differently in those days. Incomes were vastly lower and so was the general standard of living: no central heating, no washing machines, no fridges, no fitted carpets; homes with telephones were highly unusual and television didn't even exist. Cars were rare and for the wealthy. There were no interesting and exotic foreign foods, no wine-drinking and no credit cards. You were somebody if you had a motor bike and very much somebody if you had a motor bike and sidecar. So, as my Dad made an increasingly successful living through racing them and tuning them for others, I grew up in a very comfortable atmosphere dominated by motor bikes.

It was certainly an unusual childhood. Where the fathers of other children went to work in the morning, came home in the evening and were home at the weekends, mine was forever disappearing to race on the Continent, soon to re-appear with some massive trophy, for he was very much one of the top men of his day. That being so you'd think I would either like or loathe what he did, but in truth I was pretty much unimpressed by it. When I think back on it I'm quite ashamed by my apathetic attitude, because he was a great man who achieved an enormous amount in what was far too short a life. He wore himself out editing a motor-cycle magazine and recruiting despatch riders for the army in World War Two, smoked too much and died in 1962 at only 66 years of age.

Conversely, my mother lived until she was a spirited 101.

She had a home in the New Forest fairly near us and not long before she died I went to see her on one of my regular visits.

'Hello, dear,' she said, looking disapproving. 'It's time you had your hair cut.'

'But I've hardly got any left, Mother.'

'Well, what you have got is too long!'

So what did I do? I had it cut.

I'd give my eye teeth to have been with my father at an age of understanding and appreciation when he was racing but as a young and developing child I just didn't realize how lucky I was. To the extent that I thought about it at all, racing motor cycles was what he did for a living. Whereas some boys' fathers were plumbers and others were solicitors or doctors, mine raced motor cycles. But I thought it was great when, as a result of it, I went to places like Holland, Spain, Germany and France to be with him at one of the Grands Prix. None of my friends did that. All this was at a time when 'The Continent' was somewhere that very few people in Britain had ever been. France and Germany were more foreign then than Russia is now. People had neither the time nor the money to travel far from home. Very few had been out of the UK, hardly anyone 'abroad' spoke English and communications were comparatively archaic. There's no doubt that travel broadens the mind and it surely broadened mine.

When I was born my father was a works rider for the fabled Norton motor-cycle company with its legendary Bracebridge Street address which, in truth, was anything but inspiring, being a typically drab 1920s Birmingham factory site. But because of its riders' achievements, its image among racing enthusiasts was all-powerful. It was the start of my father's career and his day was yet to come, but he won countless awards for Norton, including second place to the great Freddie Dixon, about whom volumes could be written, in the 1923 Isle of Man Sidecar TT. In its day the TT was more important than all the rest of the world's races put together so this was quite a feat. In my study I have the actual piston from his side-valve engine. It makes me feel quite spooky when I look at it.

In 1925 the Walker family moved to Wolverhampton, for my father had been made an offer he couldn't refuse – to become Competitions Manager for Sunbeam, 'the Rolls-Royce of motor cycles' as the company modestly described itself. More success led to another move in 1928, this time to Coventry and Rudge-Whitworth, which has long since disappeared but was then one of the world's truly great motor-cycle manufacturers – at a time when motor bikes were a highly desirable everyday means of personal transport for normal people, as opposed to a sporting device for enthusiasts. And that was where my father really came good. Rudge, Norton and the rest of Britain's motor-cycle manufacturers who dominated the world were in a head-to-head battle for sales. The promotional benefits, both at home and overseas, that came from sporting supremacy were immense, so racing success was vital. At Rudge-Whitworth my father was Sales and Competition Director and he got down to it with a will.

In 1928 he came within an ace of winning what was then by far the most important race in the world, the Senior TT, retiring in the lead with only 14 of the 268 miles to go after a titanic scrap with the great Charlie Dodson. Just two months later he got his revenge by becoming the first man to win a motor cycle Grand Prix at an average speed of over 80mph. It was the Ulster Grand Prix and this time he beat Charlie, after an even more epic duel, by 11 seconds in a race where they were wheel-to-wheel for over two and a half hours. And this on the bumpy, gruelling Clady Circuit riding a bike with no rear suspension, almost solid girder forks, hand-operated gear change and skimpy, narrow, bone-hard tyres. No disrespect to the modern superstars but they made them tough in those days.

With the sales office in London and the factory in Coventry my father had constantly to commute from one to the other by way of the A5 in his mighty 4.5 litre Lagonda, with its mammoth Lucas P 100 headlamps which used to impress young Murray so much. It was a stunning motor car. So he said to my mother, 'We can live in the Midlands or in the northern part of London. I don't mind, so it's your choice.' Well, that was no contest for my mother who, as a Bedfordshire-born country girl, detested the industrial Midlands where her son had been born and in which he subsequently lived, worked and thoroughly enjoyed himself.

Off we went then to Enfield in Middlesex, which is where I spent most of my time from the age of five until I married at the ripe old age of 36.

Father raced on for Rudge on bikes whose constant development by the brilliant chief designer George Hack had made them the class of the field. He rode to victory in the Isle of Man in 1931, and received an impressive 15 silver TT Trophy Replicas, which I still proudly have. In 1931, Hack master-minded a new 350cc which had never even turned a wheel until it got to the Isle of Man, but the three works entries finished first, second and third with all three team members, my father, Ernie Nott and Tyrrell Smith, breaking the race and lap records. Mighty days! And that's not to mention umpteen Continental Grand Prix wins. Had there been World Championships in those days, my father would undoubtedly have won at least one of them.

In the meantime I grew up. If my mother had an idyllic youth then I most certainly did. A governess at home started my early education, which was followed by a couple of prep schools in the country before I went to my father's old public school at Highgate to be taught by several of the masters who had taught my Dad. One of them was the Reverend K R G Hunt, whose claim to fame was that he had played soccer for England as an amateur. On one occasion he got me out in front of the class to beat me (as they did in those days) for something trivial like putting sticky seccotine on the board rubber.

'I'm going to give you three strokes, Walker, but before I administer justice have you got anything to say in mitigation?'

'Yes, Sir! I thought you'd be interested to know that I will be the second generation of Walkers you have beaten because you beat my father.'

'Oh did I? Well, I'm now going to give you six for that!'

Which taught me not to be cocky and to keep my mouth shut in difficult circumstances.

I really enjoyed school. I was no great scholar, but a steady grafter; I got School Certificate with Credits (the equivalent of A-levels today) including, believe it or not, a Distinction in Divinity. I needed an extra subject to compensate for my incompetence at Maths and taught myself by learning almost by heart the Acts of the Apostles and the Gospel according to St Matthew.

Within two years of my arrival at Highgate I'd learnt to play the bugle in the School Corps, become a Prefect, mastered the intricacies of the intriguing wall game Fives, proudly won my First Class shot (0.303 Short Model Lee-Enfield World War One rifles with a kick like a mule) and demonstrated a staggering lack of ability at soccer and cricket due to an abysmal lack of hand and eye co-ordination. Then came the 'Phoney War' and with it evacuation to Westward Ho! in glorious North Devon, as the School's governors were convinced that there was going to be a war and that London would be heavily bombed. They were right on both counts but a year early, so we soon returned. In 1939 we were back in Devon again, this time for the duration, and I was there until 1941.

What a life it was! My school house was at the end of a superb beach with the Atlantic breakers crashing ashore just beneath my dormitory window. Hardly affected by the rationing to which the rest of Britain was subjected, it was shorts and shirts the whole year round, weekend cycle rides to Clovelly and Appledore, excitedly staring up at the Avro Ansons of Coastal Command as they lumbered across the blue skies in search of U-boats, swimming in the sea, sunbathing on the Pebble Ridge and the joy of achieving things that mattered to me as I developed. I rose to the giddy height of Company Sergeant Major of the School Corps, pompously marching about shouting commands in my World War One khaki uniform, complete with knee-length breeches, puttees, peak cap, scarlet sash and a giant banana-yellow drill stick with a silver knob on the top. I became Captain of Shooting with the honour of an annual competition at Bisley and even, arrogance of arrogance, an instructor to members of the LDV (Local Defence Volunteers: the predecessor of the Home Guard, or 'Dad's Army'), many of whom had fought in World War One, teaching them how to use a Lewis machine gun. And I loved it.

But then, at 18, and with school behind me, it was time to go to war myself. As Britain unflinchingly suffered the devastating ravages of Hitler's Messerschmitt, Dornier and Junkers bombers, while his seemingly invincible armies raced across Russia, it was also slowly starting to ready itself for the invasion of Europe. My country needed me. Youth does not heed the horrors of war and I was eager to go – but in one particular direction. Conscription was very much in force and if you waited to be called you went where they sent you. However, if you volunteered and were accepted you went where *you* wanted to. I had stars in my eyes and knowing that inadequate eyesight prevented me from going for every schoolboy's dream – fighter pilot – I volunteered for tanks. I was accepted all right but, believe it or not, they said, 'Sorry Murray, you've got to wait. Not enough of the right sort of kit for you to train on. So off you go. Fill in the time and we'll let you know when we're ready.'

What a frustrating setback. It is difficult to convey to today's generation, who are lucky not to have experienced it, how totally involved, intense and patriotically passionate everyone in Britain was about the war. Germany, and everything to do with it, was then regarded as the personification of evil. It is easy now, divorced from the bitter loathing and hatred that war inevitably generates, to accept that the vast majority of its people were (and are) the same as us but there was naturally little appreciation and no tolerance then of the fact that the ordinary Germans had been taken over by an obsessive megalomaniac and the fanatical political machine he had created. Hitler and his minions were doing unspeakably terrible things in the name of the Third Reich and were aiming for world domination. With the enemy literally at the door, Britain had its back to the wall and was fighting for its very survival. There was a gigantic amount to be done and I desperately wanted to be a part of it. I still had a bit of a wait ahead of me though.

'Fill in the time,' they had said. But how? It clearly wasn't going to be long before I was in battledress but, as I have so often been, I was lucky.

At that time the Dunlop Rubber Company, then one of Britain's greatest companies, awarded 12 scholarships a year to what they regarded as worthy recipients and I was fortunate to win one of them. Sadly, Dunlop now exists only as a brand name, having been fragmented and taken over by other companies including the Japanese Sumitomo organization whose country it did so much to defeat in the war. But back then

Dunlop, with its proud boast 'As British as the Flag', was a force in the world of industry with many thousands of employees all over the world. It owned vast rubber plantations and produced, distributed and sold tyres, footwear, clothing, sports goods, cotton and industrial products and Dunlopillo latex foam cushioning.

Its scholarship students were based at its famous Fort Dunlop headquarters (part of which still exists beside the M6 in Birmingham) and had tuition and fieldwork on all of its activities as well as instruction from top people on every aspect of what makes a business tick, from production and distribution to marketing, law and accountancy. It was an invaluable grounding. I had a whale of a time, living in digs at 58 Holly Lane, Erdington with the Bellamy family, spreading my wings and discovering, amongst other things and to my surprise and delight, that girls had all sorts of charms I hadn't experienced at Highgate.

But then came the call via a telegram. 'We're ready for you now, Murray. Report to the 30th Primary Training Wing at Bovington, Dorset on 1 October 1942'. I went there as a boy and rather more than four years later was demobbed at Hull as a man.

CHAPTER TWO

Tanks It Is Then

In August 1939, at the age of 15, I was having the holiday of a lifetime in Austria, accompanying my parents to what was then the most prestigious event in the world of motor-cycle sport – the International Six Days Trial. Sadly, like the Mille Miglia and the Targa Florio, it has long since been discontinued because of road congestion, but then it was exactly what its name implies: a gruelling, and virtually non-stop, road time trial for modified road bikes with tremendously demanding speed stages. Britain excelled in the event and in 1939, following three successive British victories, it was to be held in Austria. Following its annexation by Germany, Austria was totally under the control of the Nazis, who offered to give Britain an organizational rest and to base the event at glorious Salzburg.

It was a superb location amid the glorious Alpine scenery and my father, who knew the event thoroughly as ex-captain of a winning International Trophy team, had been invited by the War Office to give expert guidance to the British Army teams. The political situation was extremely tense with the threat of war between Britain and Germany, and while we were in Salzburg the Foreign Ambassadors of Russia and Germany, Molotov and Count von Ribbentrop, signed the Russo-German non-aggression pact. Hitler was aggressively rattling his sabre at Poland and the inevitability of war was gloomily forecast. In those days international communications were not as they are now, so the War Office said that in the event of, and only in the event of, an extreme emergency they would send a telegram detailing action and instructions.

Unusually for anything German, the Trial suspiciously showed every sign of having been hurriedly thrown together, almost as though they hadn't really expected to be holding it. 'There will be no problem,' said Korpsführer Huhnlein, the Nazi boss of all German motor sport, 'as there will not be a war now that we have signed the pact with Russia.' On day five though, with all the British teams in very strong positions, a telegram that had been delayed for 24 hours arrived from the War Office, reading: 'War imminent. Return immediately.'

Panic stations! While maps were urgently consulted to find the quickest route to the border, my father went to see Huhnlein.

'We're off,' he said.

'Why on earth are you doing that?'

'Because the British War Office has instructed us to go.'

'But there isn't going to be a war and even if there is I give you my personal guarantee that you will all be provided with safe conduct out of Germany.'

'Just one question,' said my father, 'What is your level of seniority in the Government?'

'I am ranked number 23,' said Huhnlein.

'Well what happens if any of numbers one to 22 reverse your promise?'

'That wouldn't happen.'

'Sorry, but we cannot take the risk. We go.'

For me the trip had been wonderful: the long car ride from England to Salzburg in my father's Rover, exploring beautiful, Mozart-dominated Salzburg with my mother, watching the riders race by, the charm of the sun-soaked Alpine scenery, and the quaint Austrian hotels. The dash home through France was full of drama too but shortly after we returned to Enfield Prime Minister Neville Chamberlain announced that Britain was at war with Germany for the second time in 30 years. Not so very much later I would be heavily involved in it myself. But first, back to school and glorious Devon, my scholarship at Dunlop, and, as my time approached, the decision about how I could best get into the war.

If you haven't actually been in one, no matter how much you've read about it, you just don't realize how horrific war is, how brutal, bestial and mindless. My image of tank driving included racing across the desert trailing great plumes of sand, having leave in exotic Cairo and being in my element with something mechanical. It was an ignorant and absolutely pathetic attitude but I was fresh off the farm, full of patriotic fervour, desperately wanting to do something about the evil which then looked likely to overcome the world. So once I got the call on 1 October 1942 I took the train from Waterloo to Wool in Dorset and reported for duty as number 14406224 at the 30th Primary Training Wing (PTW) at Bovington.

Bovington was and is the home of the Royal Armoured Corps and the whole area seethed with tank activity. There were gunnery ranges at Lulworth, the workshops, the wireless schools, the maintenance areas and driving ranges, not to mention the NAAFI – Navy, Army, Air Force Institute – Bovington's centre of social activity and culinary excellence. ('A char and a wad please, dear.') It was a popular belief that they put bromide into the buckets of tea to suppress the libido of the licentious soldiery. If they did it was just as well, for the fraternization between the ATS girls and the lads was frequent and vigorous enough as it was.

My ignorance of life outside my loving family and school friends was compounded by my youth and inexperience so the 30th PTW was an exciting new experience and a huge culture shock for me. As a wet-behind-the-ears army private, I found myself amongst all sorts of people that I'd never come across before. In the bed on one side of me in the barracks room was an incredibly upmarket chap, whose name I have genuinely forgotten and whose general uselessness was well nigh unbelievable. On the other side was a laconically lovely bloke called Ted Nicklin who, if I remember correctly, was a welder from Walsall and as streetwise as they come. I am convinced that living as part of such a disparate mix did me all the good in the world, because it taught me there were other points of view, other ways to speak and more ways than one to skin a cat.

The 30th PTW was all about the beginnings of discipline – what armies win or lose by. 'Do what you're told. Don't question it. Do it!' was the unbreakable rule at the 30th and rightly so. Soldiers in combat must instinctively obey, not argue whether their orders are right. So seemingly endless drill parades, standing rigidly to attention when addressed by anything senior to the regimental goat, kit cleaning, sentry duty, assault courses and physical training were the order of the day, every day. If you were lucky enough to have leave, you had to report to the Orderly Sergeant for inspection before you were allowed to depart the barracks. He would closely inspect the backs of the tiny brass buttons in the rear vent of your greatcoat and the bit between the heel and the sole of each of your boots to make sure they were highly polished. Daft? No, it was discipline. But by far the worst thing as far as I was concerned was sentry duty.

It was winter and very cold and the system was two hours on and four hours off – dressed in full order. Battledress trousers and tunic, webbing belt and gaiters, boots, greatcoat, a gas mask satchel strapped to the chest, rifle and ammunition pouches and, literally, to top it all, a steel helmet. Clumsily clumping off to the sentry position in that lot was bad enough, but then standing in one spot for two hours of freezing night-time monotony was purgatory. But worse was yet to come. When you thankfully returned to the barracks room for an enamel mug of tea and four hours off, you had to sleep on the floor, or try to, without removing any of your kit – including your steel helmet – only to be woken for the Orderly Officer's inspection just as you'd dropped off.

Eventually, as a result of all this marching, cleaning, running, jumping, parading, sentry-going, weapons inspecting, church parading and general hammering into shape I was ready to move onwards and upwards to Stanley Barracks. Not now as a humble Army Private but as a very proud Trooper to the 58th Training Regiment of the Royal Armoured Corps. Still at Bovington – but the first hurdle had been cleared.

Psychologically the 58th Training Regiment was on another planet because now I felt as though I was really on my way to the commissioned rank to which I had always aspired. My army ambition was geared to it and I would have been gutted and ashamed if I hadn't made it. Life was at a higher level and altogether more specialized, in that it was more mechanically and 'tank' oriented with six months of driving, gunnery, wireless and crew commanding instruction.

Learning to drive was great. I was already proficient on a motor cycle, thanks to the 1928 250cc Ariel Colt my father had given me, but driving on four wheels was something new. We had to learn in a Ford 15cwt truck, which had a V8 engine and whose clutch was either in or out; nothing in between and a bit like a Vincent-HRD 1000cc motor cycle. Get it right and you went: get it wrong and you stalled. By the way, I've never taken a driving test in my life, because when I came out of the Army in 1947 you didn't have to – all you needed was a certificate of proficiency from your Regimental Technical Adjutant. As I was the Technical Adjutant I didn't find that too difficult!

So in the 58th it was not just more assault courses, physical training, marching, drill, belt and gaiter blancoing and ghastly sentry-going, although there was still plenty of all of those, but also getting to grips with the rudiments of being a 'tank man' – gunnery and maintenance, tactics and wireless, weapons handling, and enemy tank recognition. I'll never forget the first time I drove a tank. It was a 20-ton Crusader and I can still feel the thrill as I hunkered down into the driver's compartment, with its 340bhp 12-cylinder Liberty engine thundering away behind me. Rev it like mad, clutch up and – GO! With the crash gearbox in top it could do 40mph in the right conditions and, believe me, that felt more like 400mph. In the Crusader you steered by pulling two metal bars like pencils that braked the appropriate track and made the tank turn one way or the other. You felt invincible as the whole thing noisily bucked and plunged, ripped and roared its way ahead. Magic! I've always been grateful for the fact that I was one of the lucky ones: my tank was never hit by an armour-piercing shell from the Wehrmacht's awesome 88mm anti-tank gun, my turret never penetrated by the blast from a terrifying Panzerfaust and I was never hit by mortar fire.

I loved it all at the 58th except two things: Morse code and Corporal Coleman. Morse code was my *bête noire*. I could never get my head round having to tap out electrical sound messages, machine-gun-like, in the form of dots and dashes with a key that moved only a fraction of an inch. But I beavered away at it and became just about good enough to get by. Corporal Coleman was something else though. At the 58th you may have been potential officer material but you certainly weren't yet an officer cadet – or likely to be unless you played your cards right. Officers were gods and Non-Commissioned Officers (NCOs) were all-powerful. A bad report from an NCO could ruin your chances and they all knew it.

Well into my time with the 58th I got a simple cold which I ignored. With all the assault courses, getting sweaty, swimming icy rivers in battle order and other physically demanding things, it rapidly got worse. Like everyone, the last thing I wanted to do was to report sick, because if you had to go to hospital you were automatically retarded. So I didn't . . . until ultimately I could hardly stand up and simply had to. Sick parade meant you had to assemble your kit for inspection by the Orderly Corporal – in a specific way to a very specific pattern. Highly polished boots with their soles upward. Highly polished mess tins alongside them. All your clothing folded and arranged a specific way, millimetrically precise and faultlessly creased. Blankets folded and gas mask, webbing equipment and cutlery all present and correct and spotlessly clean. Then you stood, alone and ramrod-erect, to attention at the end of your bed whilst the Orderly Corporal gave it his minutest attention.

Enter Corporal Coleman. Not, in my admittedly biased opinion, one of nature's charmers at the best of times. Unsurprisingly my kit hadn't been laid out as army-approved as it might have been and it didn't go down well with Corporal C, who swept the whole lot on to the floor, kicked it round the barracks room and shouted, 'Now do it all again – and properly!' Or rather less refined words to the same effect.

Remember what I was saying about army discipline? There was no point in protesting and anyway I was in no state to, so I did as he said. And, having made his point, it was to his satisfaction this time. Then I dragged myself off to see the MO, who said, 'You've got pneumonia. You're going to hospital.'

I'm not a chap who holds grudges but for many years I dreamt of meeting Corporal Coleman again in circumstances where I held the upper hand. But I never did and in spite of my long hospitalization I returned to the 58th, completed my training successfully enough to be selected for my War Office Selection Board (WOSB) and appeared before it. I made the grade and, to my unbounded pride and joy, was told to report as an Officer Cadet to number 512 Troop Pre-OCTU (Officer Cadet Training Unit), Blackdown. *Yes! Yes! Yes!*

It was at Blackdown that Sergeant Major Hayter of the Coldstream Guards and I had a parade-ground encounter that taught me a lesson. Never was a man better named. Picture the 18-man 512 troop, now sophisticated and hardened veterans of drill parades, expertly marching and halting as one, symmetrically wheeling, turning and rifle-bashing their way around the vast black tarmac acreage of Blackdown's drill square, fearlessly and faultlessly responding to the stentorian commands of Sergeant Major Hayter.

'By the left, quick march! Left, right, left, right, left, right, left.'

'Squad 'alt!'

'Quick march! Left, right, left, right, left, right, left. Aybout turn! Left, right, left, right, aybout turn! Left, right, left, right, LEFT TURN! Left, right, left, right, LEFT TURN! Left, right, left, right, *RIGHT* TURN!'

And who turned left? I did.

'SQUAD 'ALT!'

'Officer Cadet Walker come 'ere, SIR!'

(All Officer Cadets had to be addressed by NCOs as 'Sir', which was usually done with great emphasis and heavy irony.)

'We got it all wrong didn't we, SIR?'

'Yes, Sergeant Major.'

'Shall we show them how to do it properly then, SIR – just you and me?'

'Yes, Sergeant Major.'

'Right then. Officer Cadet Walker only. Quick March!!'

I think you've got the drift now and he had me sweating round the square performing obscure drill manoeuvres by myself for a solid 10 minutes. And the lesson it taught me? Listen out, stay sharp and don't assume that everything is going to be as it used to be.

In spite of that I continued really to enjoy the drill sessions. There is something very satisfying about marching proud, swinging your arms high with your back straight and your head up, knowing that, as a unit, you look terrific. We were getting to be *soldiers* now!

Blackdown held no terrors like Corporal Coleman. I reached the required standard without interruption and, in October 1943, it was goodbye to 512 Troop at Pre-OCTU and hello to 115 Troop RAC OCTU at the Royal Military Academy at Sandhurst, the most famous and historic in the world. Sandhurst, as it is known, has been the elite training centre for regular officers of the British Army since the early 1800s and, compared to Bovington and Blackdown, was relatively luxurious. When World War Two broke out it became the Officer Cadet Training Unit for Royal Armoured Corps (RAC) personnel only. We were quartered in the historic buildings and followed the long-established Sandhurst traditions and practices that had made the British Army so dominant and powerful over the centuries. I was immensely proud to be associated with and shaped by them and to be trained in such impressive surroundings.

Some 23 of us started in 115 Troop and six months later 18 of us reached the giddy heights of Second Lieutenant. Sandhurst was enormously enjoyable but it was also tough, because of the ever-present fear of failing what was a pretty demanding mental and physical regime. The whole thing was even more intense than Blackdown with major emphasis on determination, initiative and leadership. The Sandhurst assault courses had some fiendish elements. One of them required you to climb up a 40ft hill in full kit, run off the top of it on to a single narrow plank, clear a gap on to another plank, run across that, jump on to a third plank and then rush down the hill. I've seen strong men stuck with one foot on each plank and a 40ft drop beneath them, transfixed with fear and panic and unable to move. Being put into a room into which CS gas was pumped, but not being allowed to put on your gas mask until you had inevitably inhaled some of the filthy stuff was not a lot of fun either. Nor was having to negotiate pitch-dark shoulder-width underground tunnels while some joker dropped thunderflashes around you.

However I made it, only to experience the supreme test of physical horror – a Welsh battle course.

It started at a Youth Hostel at Capel Curig, in Caernarvonshire, from which we set off to do infantry manoeuvres, sleeping rough and living off the country until we reached Britain's highest mountain, 3500 ft Mount Snowdon. I was the one carrying the 2in mortar and my abiding memory of the whole week was the Troop Sergeant's non-stop screaming to 'double up, the man with the mortar!' But after days and nights of marching, digging slit trenches, attacking seemingly invulnerable positions, sleeping in pig sties and other fun things, we finally got to the lower slopes of Snowdon.

'I want 10 volunteers to climb to the top with me,' said Captain Marsh, our course commander. And, of course, dead keen, I volunteered. It was hard, but we went up a comparatively easy route and had a double bonus at the end. Apparently, it is very unusual to get an uninterrupted view from the top of Snowdon but ours was as clear as a bell and you could see for miles in every direction – magnificent. As soon as we were done we were bussed back to the hostel we had started from – those who hadn't volunteered, in the belief that they would get to the hot baths and beds before us, were made to march there on a compass bearing that got them back, by way of rivers and very rough country, at four in the morning. My respect and admiration for what was known in World War One as the 'PBI' (Poor Bloody Infantry) had increased tenfold and I knew now why it was that I had wanted to serve in tanks – you didn't have to walk and had a roof over your head.

The camaraderie at Sandhurst was wonderful; the tank

driving and commanding and the gunnery fabulous; and the occasional evenings in the pub were great. Even the Church parades were very special because they were held in the RMA Chapel: an immensely dignified and very moving scene of military tradition and magnificence. But of course all good things come to an end. For me that was on 8 April 1944, my passing out day, with all the moving pomp and circumstance at which the Army is so accomplished. My parents and friends were there and the salute was to be taken by that great American General Dwight Eisenhower, Commander in Chief of the Combined Allied Forces which, in just two months' time, would be landing on the coast of Europe to commence its bloody liberation.

On to that magnificent parade ground in front of the Old College, then, marched the entire Sandhurst contingent in proud formation, with heads held high, arms swinging and boots resounding to the drum beat and stirring military marches of the band that preceded them. I certainly felt emotional – even 57 years on I can still feel the excitement and pride. I was now Second Lieutenant Walker, Royal Armoured Corps, wearing the coveted black beret and ready to go to war from a sealed camp at Manningtree, near Harwich, the gateway to the Continent.

My recollections of Manningtree are dim and my recall of the ship I boarded dimmer, but the trip itself was smooth and straightforward. It took quite a long time: we turned right after Harwich and headed south through the Straits of Dover for the Mulberry Port at Arromanches, a wonderful example of British initiative and enterprise. To bypass the heavily defended French ports of Le Havre and Cherbourg, enormous concrete caissons were prefabricated in Britain and towed out to France on D+1, 7 June, to create a brand new port almost the size of Dover. When we were put ashore the whole area was a hive of khaki-clad activity with tanks, trucks, guns and all the other bric-a-brac of warfare flowing out of ships and on to the shore along the floating roadways. I wasn't there long because I was rapidly assigned to a tank transporter column that was to make its way to Brussels. And what a journey that was. As the lengthy convoy of enormous American White tractor units with their massive trailers, each carrying a Sherman tank, slowly churned its way through the recently liberated French countryside into Belgium we got an enthusiastic reception from the population, still euphoric after their liberation from '*les salles Boches*'.

I was very lucky to join the Royal Scots Greys, even if I was rather a round peg in a square hole. First raised in 1678, the regiment was one of the foremost in the British Army and had fought with great distinction in Palestine and in General Montgomery's magnificent Eighth Army from the Western Desert to Tripoli. It had taken part in the invasion of Italy, landed in Normandy, fought its way through France into and out of Belgium and was now at Nederweert in Holland where I joined it.

So, as a young, untried and totally inexperienced new boy I was becoming part of one of the toughest, most case-hardened fighting units of all. When I reported to the tent of the charming Major Sir Anthony Bonham he said to me,

'Welcome to the Regiment, George, we are glad to have you with us.'

Somewhat embarrassed, I said, 'The G is for Graeme, actually, Sir, but my friends call me by my second name, which is Murray.'

'Oh,' he replied. 'I thought Murray Walker was a hyphenated, double-barrelled name.'

I had the feeling that he was rather disappointed that it wasn't, because that's the sort of regiment it was: very Cavalry, very regular, officered by moneyed County gentry, many with Scottish connections, who had been educated at the very best and most expensive schools and who had known each other and fought together for a long time. I was and still am immensely proud to have been a Greys Officer and to have fought with them but I certainly felt as though I was in a club of which I was not a natural member.

Major Bonham told me, 'You will be responsible to Sergeant McPherson, Murray.'

Sergeant? What the hell does he think this Second Lieutenant's pip on my shoulder is – confetti?

'I know what you're thinking,' he said. 'Fresh out of Sandhurst I expect you think you're God's gift to the British Army, but you should know that McPherson has been with us since Palestine. He has forgotten more about fighting and the way the Regiment does it than you'll ever know and when he says you are capable of commanding a troop you will have one.'

He was, of course, absolutely right. So I watched and listened and before long I got my own troop. A few days later we moved to the island between the Waal and Neder Rijn rivers north of Nijmegen where I had my first experience of sentry-go, Greys style. Up all night standing in the Sherman's turret, with the Germans on the other side of the river, thinking that every sound you heard was one of them creeping up to blast you to perdition with a Panzerfaust. This was shortly after the airborne forces' foiled attempt to capture the bridge over the River Maas at Arnhem and to launch the 21st Army Group across the Rhine into Germany. From our positions on the other side of the river we could see parachutes and supply containers for the beleaguered airborne troops hanging from the trees. One night I had to transport ammunition on my tank to troops of the American 101st Airborne Division. It was not a job I relished as, silhouetted against the sky, we slowly felt our way along the dark and narrow road with no turn offs. There was a great deal of heavy and very messy fighting at this time, clearing river banks, woods and other difficult areas and, as ever, the Regiment came out of it with great distinction.

During the actual fighting, we tried to rest whenever and wherever we could – in the vehicles, in barns and even in Dutch homes. On one occasion though, when I was seeking billets for my troop, the door was opened by a completely bald woman whose head had been shaved by revengeful villagers because she had collaborated with the Germans. The time we spent in our winter quarters was really good. I was billeted in a very comfortable Dutch home in Nederweert with the Regimental Quartermaster, Captain Ted Acres, a dry, exact, pedantic and incredibly efficient chap, and Fred

Sowerby, a blunt and cheerful Yorkshireman who ran the light aid detachment. It was Fred who refused to help me out of a difficult situation when I forcibly removed the windscreen of my regimental Jeep. I had done so in a moment of madness when driving across an airfield while a B17 bomber was starting to take off. The chap who was with me said he'd bet I couldn't catch it. I not only did so but clipped the back of its tailplane with the top of my windscreen. 'You did it, you silly young bugger,' said Fred, 'so you can live with the consequences!'

In the evenings though, when the day's training schedules, joint manoeuvres with the infantry, gunnery practice and tank maintenance tasks had been completed, Ted, Fred and I could relax in front of a roaring fire catching up with the very welcome mail from home and listening to the American Forces Network. Frank Sinatra was the man, Peggy Lee was the woman and the big bands of Benny Goodman, Artie Shaw, Woody Herman, Tommy Dorsey and Glenn Miller were and still are my passion.

In the middle of February 1945 the Greys' winter rest period ended. The long-serving personnel had returned from their UK leave and the Regiment was refurbished and refreshed – just as well, for the end of winter heralded some of the bloodiest fighting of the Second Front. The war had now surged up to the very borders of Germany at the Reichswald Forest and the mighty River Rhine. The Greys were heavily involved, co-operating closely with the infantry, and the going was very tough indeed with the Germans resisting every inch of the way with anti-tank guns, rivers, ditches, snipers, blown bridges and Panzerfausts. Their homeland was now being directly threatened and that added extra steel to their resistance. It was here that I had one of the most emotional experiences of my life.

Times arose when we had to let other units leap-frog through our positions so that we could refuel, take on fresh ammunition and eat. You stopped by the supply vehicles and then there was a flurry of activity: humping five-gallon jerricans up to the engine compartment and sloshing petrol into tanks, passing shells and ammo boxes up into the turret, maintenance work – a sort of tank pit stop. Sitting on the turret with my legs dangling inside while my troop was on its way to one of these, I saw a group of four men in army uniform and idly thought that one chap looked just like my father. As we got closer I realized to my amazement that it *was* my father: he may have been in battledress and wearing a khaki beret but his stance was unmistakable and to clinch it he was smoking his inevitable pipe. At the time he was editor of *Motor Cycling*, and had got himself accredited as a war correspondent with the express intention of finding me, which he'd done. Needless to say it was wonderful to see him but there wasn't any time for more than a short conversation because I had to get back into action.

This all happened close to a place called Udem, near the towns of Goch and Kleve which had been completely obliterated by over a thousand bomber raids. I remember having to get out of the tank at one point during the night and thinking that I must be in Dante's Inferno. The road was blocked by rubble, houses all round me were ablaze, there were dead bodies lying on the ground amid a nauseating smell, bemused cattle were wandering about, people were shouting, guns firing and there was the constant worry that somewhere up the road was an 88mm or Germans to let fly at you with a Panzerfaust. With V1 rockets aimed at Antwerp soaring over us, we advanced despite the most stubborn resistance by Panzers and elite Paratroops. The Reichswald was cleared and on 24 February 1945 we crossed the border into Germany.

It is difficult to find the words to express my emotions as I saw the crudely signwritten board saying, 'YOU ARE NOW ENTERING GERMANY'. Since 1939 Britain had been subjected to defeat after defeat in Europe, Africa and the Far East. Our towns and cities had been bombed and torched with incendiaries. Countless thousands of men and women had been killed, maimed and injured on land, sea and in the air and Hitler's U-boats had done their best to starve us out. Standing alone, Britain had been on its knees but it had fought back and now, with the might of America at its side, it was winning.

The British Army's part of the Eisenhower/Montgomery master plan called for the crossing of the Rhine and then a mighty surge towards the Baltic. Now, after the bloody night attacks using 'artificial moonlight' from searchlights, we were on the west bank of the Rhine near Xanten. Looking across its mighty width, it seemed impossible to cross but we knew that it was just a matter of time. On 23 March there was a 3300-gun artillery bombardment of the far shore and beyond which must surely have been one of the most intense in military history, and on the following day the 6th Airborne Division swept into action. I simply could not have imagined what it would be like, and if I hadn't seen it would never have believed it. As the gathering roar grew louder and louder, I stood beside my tank looking up at a vast fleet of hundreds of aeroplanes towing gliders containing troops and equipment. With no opposition from the Luftwaffe, they reached their targets, cast off their gliders and returned for more. It was the most amazing demonstration of military might and how Britain had clawed its way from the brink, rebuilt its forces and turned the tables on its enemy. But it wasn't all euphoria: at one point, to the horror of the forces below, a Tetrarch reconnaissance light tank emerged from its glider hundreds of feet above us and plunged to the ground with its crew still inside. What had happened I do not know, but the story was that with the engine running for a rapid exit, the driver had dropped the clutch while still high up in the air. Whatever the reason, it was a terrifying sight.

On 25 March we crossed the Rhine. Unlike Arnhem, the air drop had been a total success and a bridgehead had been established. German forces were still holding out in Holland, to our left, and the Ruhr, to our right, but between them the way was now open for a charge to the River Elbe and Hamburg. But there was still a lot of bloody conflict before that could happen. Progress was slow and painful. At one point there was particularly bitter resistance from the German Second Marine Division and I remember standing over one of them, who was clearly dying, with a drawn pistol in my hand in case he was bluffing and tried some desperate move.

After virtually continuous fighting, during which I liberated a fine pair of Zeiss binoculars from a German 88mm gunner who had been trying to wipe us out, we reached the crucial River Elbe, south of Hamburg. In a mammoth military traffic jam pouring across the newly constructed army bridges, the mighty Elbe was crossed and now our momentum was unstoppable. With the Russians advancing rapidly towards Berlin from the East and the combined forces of the West pressing forward from the other direction, the Germans were in a vice and their resistance melted. With vivid and bitter memories of the Russian campaign uppermost in their minds, the last thing they wanted was to be captured by Stalin's men, merciless and eager for retribution and revenge. Things became very political as it was vital to the Allies that their forces reached the Baltic before the Russians. The key was Lubeck. 'Get to Lubeck first!' was the stirring order given by the War Office to the 21st Army Group. The Greys and the 6th Airborne Division were instructed to head for Wismar on the Baltic coast, and we went for it. It was an incredible experience. At the rate of some 5000 troops an hour, the German army was heading *west* as fast as possible to avoid being captured by the Russians, while *on the same single carriageway road* we were hammering *east* absolutely flat out. With the British and the Germans going their different ways just feet away from each other there was no fighting, no acknowledgment even. At one point our headlong gallop was brought to a halt by the sheer weight of traffic and, sitting on the top of the turret eating a tin of Spam, I found myself looking down on to a vast open Mercedes-Benz staff car containing four obviously high-ranking German officers. It was hardly the time, place or occasion for a cheery chat: we studied each other dispassionately and not a word was spoken. Then the column moved on, so did they and that was the last we saw of each other.

On 2 May 1945, after an incredible 80-mile dash in one day, the Royal Scots Greys reached Wismar to become the first unit of the British Army to link up with the Russians – in the form of a captured German BMW motor cycle and sidecar carrying an officer on the pillion and a woman soldier in the sidecar, accompanied by a couple of American White scout cars and another mixed bunch of soldiery. The war was over.

The Greys did not stay in Wismar long. At the end of May 1945 we moved to Rotenburg, between Bremen and Luneburg, where I was given a special job to go to the Philips factory in Eindhoven, Holland to collect a load of radios for the Regiment. I was to be allocated a truck and to find my own way. But I wasn't exactly overjoyed when I found the truck was a Morris-Commercial 15cwt that the Germans had captured from us at Dunkirk in 1940 and had been using all through the war.

It was in running order but not in the best of shape, to put it mildly. However, off I set with Trooper Doug Taylor (my personal servent in the army) to lumber back through Hamburg, Bremen, Osnabruck and Munster, retracing our steps amid refugees, columns of troops, tanks and B (wheeled) vehicles as Europe started to reorient itself after over five years of bloody conflict. The gallant old Morris did a fine job and didn't let us down, although it certainly took its wheezy time getting there. But when we got to Eindhoven the news was not good.

'The radios are not ready,' we were told. 'Please come back in three days.'

Well, there wasn't much to occupy us for three days in war-torn Eindhoven so we decided to go to Brussels – plenty going on there. I had a Belgian girlfriend in Brussels from my time at Villevoorde earlier in the campaign, so we fired up the willing old Morris again, and headed off. This was strictly forbidden, of course, for I had no authority to go there and very nearly ended my army career by doing so. We left the Morris in a military park and three days later, after a great time in the big city, Doug and I returned – but there was no sight of the Morris. Eventually, in desperation, we asked the Sergeant in charge if he could help us. 'Ah, yes, Sir,' he said when he saw the receipt. 'We were a bit suspicious about this vehicle in view of its age and when we checked we found it wasn't on the Army records so it has been impounded.'

Oh my God. Stark panic. I was in Brussels where I wasn't supposed to be, I'd been there for three days without authority, my truck had been impounded, I hadn't got the radios and I had no way of getting back to the Regiment in far off Rotenburg. I could see the court martial looming. There was only one thing to do then: find the Town Major, make a clean breast of it and cast myself on his mercy. 'You've been a bloody fool, haven't you?' he said. 'Well, we're all human and it is going no further. Off you go and the best of luck.' And that, thankfully, was the end of that.

During our time at Rotenburg any fleeting thoughts I may have had about signing on with the Army as a regular soldier evaporated and I decided that the life was not for me. Things became more routine with the fighting over. Now a Lieutenant, I was promoted to Mechanical Transport Officer, which meant that I was in charge of all the Regiment's B (wheeled) vehicles and answerable to the Technical Adjutant who was responsible for all the Regiment's vehicles. This, of course, was right up my street.

During this time a friend of mine, Peter Johnson, returned briefly to the UK, sharing a cabin with a couple of British Infantry officers. They were discussing what loot they'd brought back with them. Peter mentioned he'd a German officer's revolver and a Nazi flag.

'Look at this then,' they said, opening a suitcase full of jewellery and gold ornaments.

'God almighty!' says Peter. 'Where the hell did you get all that lot?'

'Well, we're first in anywhere and we go straight to the jewellers' shops.'

It was thieving of course but anything was fair game in those times. For the record I came out with my binoculars, which I still have, a P38 revolver, which I handed in during the arms amnesty, an enormous Swastika flag and a German officer's knife with '*Gott mit uns*' engraved on its blade. Funny that. We thought he was with us.

I was again promoted, in February 1946, to become the Technical Adjutant and to start a running battle that could have ruined my life. It's a long story so a bit of background might be helpful. The Regiment was reverting to its normal peacetime ways, which were totally foreign to me as mine were to them. For instance, I started a motor-cycle club for the whole of the 4th Armoured Brigade and spent a great deal of time organizing trials and scrambles, sourcing machines to be used for competitions and even working with the Regimental Fitters building bikes, none of which were usual activities for a Greys officer and they were undoubtedly regarded as unacceptable behaviour.

Amid this increasingly fraught situation, I should have been promoted long before to the War Substantive rank of Captain. It wasn't happening, though, and I was getting fractious. I am hard to rouse but was outraged that I was not being given the rank, income and status that went with the job. Eventually I was grudgingly given the rank of Local Captain but not the money that went with it or any promise of permanency, which, if anything, made me even angrier. To top that, they tried to cancel the home leave that I'd previously been granted, and which I'd applied for months in advance so that I could attend the first post-war motor-cycle race meeting in the fabled Isle of Man, the Manx Grand Prix. They claimed it was cancelled for disciplinary reasons.

Now the battle was well and truly on. Thanks in part to my father's influence I got my leave and had a wonderful time in the Isle of Man, but when I reported back to the Regiment in Luneburg it was to find that an adverse report on me had been submitted which recommended that I be reduced to the ranks because I was 'unreliable, unsuitable, untrustworthy and a bad example'. My back was up against the wall now for if the recommendation was accepted, the Dunlop Rubber Company (for whom I'd recently had an interview for a job after I left the army) would certainly have thought it a bit odd that the Captain they had interviewed next appeared as a Lance Corporal, quite apart from the loss of self-respect the demotion would have caused me. Fortunately though, army rules being what they are, I was allowed to submit a written response. Knowing that my future literally depended on it, I sat down and gave it my very best shot – five closely typed foolscap pages.

For most of my time with the Regiment it had been part of the famous 4th Armoured Brigade, commanded by one of the most outstanding men it has ever been my privilege to meet: Brigadier R M P Carver CBE, DSO, MC. He was young – in his very early thirties – had a wonderful personality, and was a superb example of all that was the very best in the British Army. He was the sort who would suddenly appear on the back of your tank in the middle of some very unpleasant action and ask you why the hell you weren't further ahead. And now he was to rescue me from this situation that could well have blighted the rest of my life. He came to the Regiment to interview me and told me that my response had been accepted but that it was clearly impossible for me to continue with the Greys. I could not disagree with him for had I stayed the atmosphere would have been intolerable. So you can imagine the relief and pleasure I felt when he went on to say that I was being transferred to become Technical Adjutant of the recently formed British Army of the Rhine

Royal Armoured Corps Training Centre at Belsen, with the full rank of Captain. So I had won without a stain on my character, but it is a battle I would far rather not had to have fought. I was and still am mighty proud to have been able to serve in and fight with such a wonderful regiment as the Greys, but only sorry it ended the way it did.

So to the BAOR RAC Training Centre at Belsen. Not the Belsen of concentration camp notoriety? Yes indeed, but very different by the time I got there in October 1946. The hideous installations of the Nazi death camp had been destroyed, the bodies buried and the thousands of displaced persons moved to other locations. Belsen became Caen Barracks, which had a driving and maintenance wing, gunnery and wireless wings, a tactical wing and its own AFV ranges to provide short-term courses of just about every conceivable type. 'Officers,' says the brochure which I still have, 'should bring their own sheets and pillowslips and may bring their own batmen [personal assistant] with them if they wish but German civilian servants can be provided by the Centre if necessary. Facilities are available for riding, shooting and fishing, football, rugby, hockey and swimming.' A good place to finish one's army career then and a dramatic contrast to the utterly unspeakable place it had formerly been.

The wheel had gone full circle for me. I had started my army career as a humble Private at the home of tanks, Bovington, and here I was finishing it with greatly enhanced status at Bovington's German equivalent. The work was enjoyable and satisfying, the accommodation was good and I had the opportunity for local leave. On one occasion I went to Hamburg to stay at the Officers' Club, which was located at the old Atlantic Hotel, one of the finest in Europe. It was surprisingly undamaged by the many RAF raids, but around it hardly a single complete building stood, however far you looked and in any direction. I remember thinking that there was no way that it could ever be rebuilt, but go there now and you wouldn't think that there had ever been so much as a broken roof tile.

I started to get involved with the motor-cycle racing world again at Belsen. Germany, a centre of motor-sport excellence before the war, was already striving to recreate its racing activities but, banned from international participation as it was and with the country flat on its back, this mainly took the form of enthusiasts talking and planning for what might be. One such group was the Brunswick Motor Cycle Club, right on the east/west border, who got to hear of my existence and invited me to become an honorary member. It was led and inspired by Kurt Kuhnke, who had raced one of the incredible supercharged two-stroke works DKWs before the war. I spent several very enjoyable evenings in their company talking racing and bikes. Just a few months earlier I had been doing my best to rid the world of these people in the sincere belief that they were the ultimate evil but now here I was socializing with them about a common interest. It is indeed a funny old world – a world that was again about to change dramatically for me as, at the end of May 1947, I boarded the ship for Hull where I was to swap my khaki uniform for my post-war civvies.

CHAPTER THREE

A is for Advertising

It was the summer of 1947 and I found myself back home again, aged 23, at 'Byland', Private Road, Enfield, Middlesex with my mother and father after over four years in the army. A very pleasant place to be, too. I had made another sparkling appearance at Fort Dunlop and, on the back of my Dunlop scholarship, had landed the job of Assistant to C L Smith, the Advertising Manager of the Company's major division, the Tyre Group at Fort Dunlop – starting immediately. So my stay in Enfield was short-lived, and it was off to Birmingham and my digs with the Bellamys in Holly Lane, Erdington.

I didn't find it difficult being a civilian again because I guess I had always been one at heart, much as I had enjoyed my time in the army. But this was certainly different. Every morning I set off to 'The Fort', walking the mile or so to the factory, and spent the day ministering to CL's needs. He was a kind, if rather pompous, man who dressed immaculately and spoke with a plum in his mouth. He was easy to work for, but I cannot say that the job was overly demanding. For doing it I was paid the princely sum of £350 a year (roughly the equivalent of £11,000 today), so I wasn't heading for an early or wealthy retirement, but I enjoyed myself.

I often socialized with Dunlop's charismatic Competitions Manager, Dickie Davis – a great character, manager and salesman and also an accomplished pianist, who loved to entertain his mates by playing the joanna in the bar, surrounded by happy people and with a row of gin and tonics on the upright. I once arrived in the Isle of Man for the TT races and, straight off the boat, went to the Hotel Sefton where he was staying. 'Get up, Dickie,' I said to the recumbent form in his bed, 'it's 6:30. Time to go to the paddock.'

'Get up?' he groaned, 'I've only just got into bed!'

I was happy enough at 'The Dunlop' and used to go home every weekend on my beloved Triumph Tiger 100 motor cycle. Seeing myself as next year's Isle of Man TT winner, I used to do the 110-mile journey in two hours, which wasn't bad going in those days of no motorways. Correct bike wear was a massive, ankle-length army despatch rider's raincoat (featuring press studs to enclose the legs), a pair of clumpy rubber waders, sheepskin-lined, heavy leather gloves, a pair of ex-RAF Mark VII goggles and a tweed cap with the peak twisted round to the back. I was regarded as a bit of a cissy because I wore one of my father's crash helmets, painted white. 'If we both fall off,' I used to say to my friends who mocked my headgear, 'I'll be the one who gets up.'

* * *

My mother had always hated Birmingham but I thought it was great. It was the first time I had been on my own, free from school or army discipline and completely my own master. I had a girlfriend who worked for 'The Lucas' and I used to go by tram from Erdington to Snow Hill to see her. The route took in Aston Cross, where there was Mitchell and Butler's brewery, the HP sauce factory and a tannery. On a hot summer's evening the smell was indescribable.

Nearly every morning at The Fort I had to go down the central staircase when the staff started their day's work. On the Sections Accounts floor – about an acre of tables in rows, wall-to-wall – I would see the clerks pushing big trolleys down to the strongroom to collect their vast ledgers. When they got them back to their workstations they would spend the whole day methodically moving dockets from in-tray to out-tray, entering their contents into the ledgers. Mind-numbing work. You'd have been trampled to death if you stood in the doorway at knocking-off time. For them life began when work finished.

Frankly, my job wasn't onerous and, like the Section Clerks, I had most of my fun outside office hours. Renewing my love of shooting, I joined the Dunlop Rifle Club to compete with my 0.22 BSA-Martini. I often visited the Birmingham Motor Cycle Club, to meet people like the famous BSA competitions boss Bert Perrigo, a chirpy Brummie, one of the all-time greats of motor-cycle trials riding; Jeff Smith and Brian Martin, trials and scramble stars of the day; and the amazing Olga Kevelos, who ran a café near Snow Hill station with her Greek father but was far more interested in being

Britain's leading female trials rider. At this time the legendary Geoff Duke, one of the greatest motor-cycle racers of all time, was making a name for himself – firstly as a works trials rider and then, in 1949, by winning the Senior Manx Grand Prix on his first appearance. We used to meet and gossip in the Norton Competitions Department in Bracebridge Street where Geoff worked – like my father so many years before.

Another of my Birmingham friends was the Ulsterman Rex McCandless, who had designed a spring frame for his grass-tracking brother, Cromie, which was blowing the socks off everything in Irish racing. Rex joined Norton as a consultant and the all-conquering Norton 'Featherbed' racing frame came into being. He was an excitable, fun chap but understandably used to suffer fits of depression. We'd get together in the evenings and he'd sound off at me; 'I've redesigned the whole road bike range to use the Featherbed frame and now they've told me that they've got a five-year supply of frame lugs that have got to be used first,' he once told me in despair.

If you were a motor-cycle nut in those days, as I was and still am, the Midlands was the place to be. Norton were based at Aston, BSA at Small Heath, Ariel at Selly Oak, Velocette at Hall Green, Royal Enfield at Redditch, Villiers engines at Wolverhampton and Triumph at Meriden. Now, with the glorious exception of Triumph, they are sadly all names of the past because of management complacency, union intransigence and the enterprise and competence of the Japanese.

It was while I was in Birmingham that my own short-lived

motor-cycle competition career began. Fired up by all the glamour and excitement of my surroundings, I got myself a 500T trials Norton and, with some advice from Geoff Duke about how to prepare it, set out to show my father how a motor cycle should really be ridden, and amaze one and all with my uncanny natural skill. Except that it didn't quite work out like that: despite my father's genes I was no more than a fairly competent club-standard rider and I singularly failed to hit the big time.

At Brands Hatch, then an anti-clockwise grass track, I raced a 250cc dope-engined AJS, which belonged to the famous Arter Brothers, Tom and Edge. Among my fellow competitors were the great Eric Oliver, later to become a quadruple sidecar World Champion, and John Surtees, who went on to win seven motor-cycle World Championships and become the only person in history also to win the Formula 1 World Drivers' Championship. Needless to say I never saw anything of them on the track other than their rapidly disappearing backs. To maximize his prize money, Eric rode in and invariably won both sidecar and solo races. He would arrive with one bike and two engines, 350cc and 500cc, and switch them around in the frame. It was tedious but very effective.

I rode a 350cc KTT Velocette at the fabulous Cadwell Park and I did a lot of trials on the Norton. I even had a smattering of success, including a Gold Medal and Club Team Prize in the 1949 International Six Days Trial at Llandrindod Wells, a First Class award in the gruelling Scottish Six Days' Trial and a one-off appearance in the Southern Experts Trial. But then came the thing that changed my life – that invitation to do the

PA commentary at Shelsley Walsh, which started my broadcasting career and stopped my competitive riding.

I might have become a lot better had I persevered and practised more but I doubt it. It didn't matter enough to me. I couldn't ride well enough to satisfy myself and talking about it appealed a lot more once I had started. I didn't stop riding competitively through lack of time – it's easy to make time for the things you want to do. The brutal truth is that I wasn't good enough to motivate myself to concentrate on it and hopefully progress onwards and upwards to my father's level.

From then on I led a double life which became increasingly demanding as the years rolled by. My business life occupied the weekdays and very often the weekends, while my broadcasting hobby absorbed every other waking moment. Heady stuff you might think, but it wasn't really, for although I had been promoted to Dunlop's HQ at St James's Street in London and was now hobnobbing with the directors and the divisional top bananas, the Dunlop job itself was too boring for words. I was responsible to the PR mastermind, an irascible Scot named John McColl who was a very nice chap but totally incapable of delegating. I had a very impressive office and a charming secretary but damn all to do so it wasn't long before I was agitating for action elsewhere.

'How about joining the Allied Group Advertising Department?' said its boss, Stuart Janes, who was in the same building. Done! The Allied Group comprised everything except tyres and I became Advertising Manager for Dunlopillo Foam Cushioning, the General Rubber Goods Division and the Special Products Division. Much better, for now I had something involving and interesting to do, like supervising all the Company's publicity for its Dunlopillo installations at the rebuilt House of Commons (I have sat in the Speaker's chair!) and the 1951 Festival of Britain. In the days when a trip by train to Liverpool took 4.5 hours, the job entailed regular visits to the Dunlopillo factory at Speke as well as Manchester, Birmingham and other major cities in Britain. I loved it but, not before time, I realized that if I was going to make any money and achieve anything worthwhile I ought to be stirring myself to find a job with better long-term prospects. I had been with Dunlop for some seven years by then and I had itchy feet.

My friend Terry Thompson, formerly a colleague at Dunlop, was working as a copywriter at the aspiring London advertising agency Masius and Fergusson. 'You can write,' he said, 'so why don't I get you a job interview here?' And he did, but to my surprise when I landed the job it was not with Masius but with Aspro, the headache pill company at Slough. Aspro were looking for a copywriter for their own creative department and had asked their three advertising agencies to help them find the right man. Masius had some minor Aspro Group products but not the lucrative analgesic business so were always looking for an opportunity to promote themselves, and their boss, Jack Wynne-Williams, reckoned that I could be the right man.

I resolved to give it a go, although it was going to be a totally different atmosphere than that which I'd been used to at Dunlop. Creating the demand for and selling, by the million, a fast-moving, low-cost product that called for aggressive and hard-hitting advertising – it seemed another world from those expensive mattresses, rubber buckets, conveyor belting and universal joints. But they offered me the job at £1000 a year. I'd made it!

The Aspro offices and factory in Buckingham Avenue on the Slough Trading Estate (next to the High Duty Alloys foundry, whose fine casting sand ruined my new Standard 10's paintwork) could hardly have been a greater contrast to St James's Street and not long after I had joined came a memorable meeting with Chairman John Jamieson that would lead to something even further removed.

One of the vast geographical areas I was responsible for was India, Pakistan and what was then Ceylon, now Sri Lanka. One day the Chairman called me in and said, 'You're responsible for India, Murray?'

'Yes, Sir.'

'Have you ever been there?'

'No, I haven't.'

'How can you do the advertising if you've never been there?'

'I don't make the rules, Mr Jamieson. I just do the best I can.'

'Well, you'd better go!'

'Yes, Sir. When?'

'Next week!'

Soon I was on the plane heading for some of the most memorable and stimulating weeks of my life.

Back in 1954, India to me meant lots of people, Errol Flynn

and Olivia de Havilland in *Lives of a Bengal Lancer*, the British Raj, the Indian Mutiny of 1857, the Kama Sutra, great gallantry in World Wars One and Two . . . and curry. So I had a lot to learn. The 4700 miles to Bombay took over 30 hours on a lumbering BOAC propellor-driven Argonaut Speedbird with countless meals and stops at Rome, Beirut, Bahrain and Karachi. This was followed by more than 10,000 miles by train, plane and car criss-crossing India, Ceylon, East Pakistan (now Bangladesh) and West Pakistan (now Pakistan). I did it all at a leisurely pace and tried to do everything the Indian way: going to Indian films, eating Indian meals, reading books about India, especially John Masters' riveting novels like *Bhowani Junction* and *The Deceivers*. I spent the majority of my time in the villages, because that was where the vast majority of India's inhabitants lived and because Aspro was one of the few modern, all-purpose medicines they could afford. '*Take Aspro for headaches, colds, flu, rheumatism and all your aches and pains. It is the wonder cure!*' we claimed – and it was true, for acetylsalicylic acid (aspirin), which is what Aspro was, is a vastly underrated product. (Sadly, it does not increase sexual power, which was what a lot of folks in India believed, although maybe if you believe it enough it actually does – I've never tried.)

All this was, perhaps, fairly ordinary stuff in today's environment of effortless communications, jetplane travel and adventurous backpacking but for me, nearly 50 years ago, it was a fantastic trip that I wouldn't have missed for all the tea in the plantations I saw. An incredible 14 weeks of different people with very different languages, different lifestyles, customs, beliefs and religions; different geography; different climate, and different food.

No sooner was I in my room in Bombay's wonderful Taj Mahal Hotel than there was a knock at the door. Opening it I found four Indians of various descriptions all proffering bundles of documents which turned out to be testimonials endorsing their supreme competence as manservants. I'd been told I'd need one, so I chose one called John, who started immediately.

'Would the *Sahib* like a bath?'

'Yes, I would.'

So he ran one, elbow in the water to test the temperature. Most professional. Shortly after I had got in it he was kneeling beside me washing my back.

'Just a minute, John. You do the bath. I'll do the washing. OK?'

'OK, *Sahib*,' he said, looking rather crestfallen, but when I got out there he was again with an enormous towel, trying to dry me.

'Oh, and another thing, John. I'll do the drying too.'

It was when I went into the bedroom to find all my clothes unpacked and beautifully laid out and him wanting to powder my feet and help me put on my socks that I realized what he had been used to. If this was the way things were in the old days, I mused, they must have found it very hard going when they got back to England.

Bathed, dressed and powdered, I went to meet the Indian Account Director and the Aspro International Executive, Englishman Jimmy Turner, who was to accompany me on my tour with the local Director, moustachioed, white suited and swagger-stick-carrying Dickie Deeth – a very pukka *sahib*. I had another indication that things were a bit different in India when I went to the Deeths' superb apartment for dinner. We were having an aperitif on the verandah, with the drinks trolley between me and Dickie's wife Betty, when she asked whether I'd like another drink. When I said I would, she clapped her hands and shouted '*RAJI!*'. About 30 seconds later a servant appeared, having padded his way from some remote part of the apartment, and Betty said, 'A gin and tonic for Mr Walker, Raji' – which he served from the drinks trolley between us.

Crumbs, I thought. *Someone else washes them here and they don't serve their own drinks. I've got a lot to learn.*

On 2 November 1954 my magical mystery tour began at Bombay Central Station, starting with the long haul to Delhi in a twin-berth compartment with shower, basin, loo and our own food in vast tuck boxes which would be prepared and served by the resourceful John. It wasn't long after Partition, when the old India had been split into Hindu India and Muslim East and West Pakistan: thousands of Hindus in Pakistan had tried to get to India by rail, while similar numbers of Muslims in India had tried to get to Pakistan the same way, only for the trains to be stopped on the way and everyone on them massacred for being of the wrong faith. Just another example of man's inhumanity to man. But my journey was fascinating and the trips to the villages even more so.

Communication was the problem when it came to promoting Aspro. Newspapers were limited, there were no cinemas in the villages and no television, while commercial radio was booked solid. So we had Aspro Information Units – loudspeaker vans that toured the villages literally broadcasting the advantages and benefits of Aspro and distributing samples. We even contemplated reviving the Aspro Pipers. Bagpipes are popular in India and Aspro had used them to great effect on a pilot scheme which involved Indians in pink and purple Aspro uniforms going to the villages and playing their bagpipes whilst a merchandiser chatted up the bazaar merchants: 'There's going to be a big demand for Aspro here. Not next week, not tomorrow but today. So stock up!' Now if you, in your sophisticated way of life, looked out of your living room window and saw pink-and-purple-uniformed, bagpipe-playing Indians marching about I dare say you'd go outside to see what the hell was going on. In an Indian village where not much happens from one century to the next it was very big time and when everyone had assembled to see the fun a seventh man carrying a folding stand, who had been marching with his chums, climbed on to it and said, Indian huckster-style, 'I'm not here today and gone tomorrow. I'm here to tell you about Aspro the wonder cure!' It worked very well, but it was mighty expensive.

Visiting India is an assault on the senses: the heat, wall-to-wall people thrusting, jostling and shouting, vibrant colours, bright sunshine, non-stop deafening music, sacred cows wandering along in the streets, horns blowing, spice-laden smells and a terrific sense of vitality and overcrowding. Hot, noisy, smelly and congested chaos. And then there was the curry: real curry, and very different from that I'd had at school. Our first stop was at Jaipur, a place that impressed me. The pièce de resistance was the Maharajah's personal white temple to the god Vishnu, with its solid silver doors and panels of awe-inspiring mythological scenes. Then to Delhi, and on to Cawnpore on the holy River Ganges and an incredible religious festival, with thousands of people completely immersing themselves in the holy waters of the river, drinking them, washing in them and bottling them to take away; fakirs lying on barbed wire or with pins through their noses and flesh; dying and horribly diseased people: all human life was there to pay homage. It may seem hard to believe but I was actually working whilst all this spellbinding tourism was going on, finding out what people thought about Aspro, talking to the merchants, evolving media schedules, booking radio time and newspaper space, writing advertisement copy and radio commercials, getting layouts done, commissioning artwork, producing brochures and touring local shops and bazaars.

Constantly on the move as we were, it was a very tiring trip and by the time we got to Calcutta I was ready for a bit of a rest, but it was not to be. On to Nagpur, nearly slap bang in the middle of India, to Bangalore, an ex-British Army military centre, and then to Mysore. Its Durbar Halls were staggering, with a solid gold ceremonial elephant that weighed 3200lb and was more valuable than the economies of many of the countries around it, no doubt. But although I was seeing sights I had never seen before and enjoying every second of it, I was now learning nothing new. From my round-India trip I had found what I needed to know. The reactions I was getting were exactly the same wherever I was. So on to Ceylon.

The reactions weren't any different there, but it was a fabulous experience. Now alone, I landed in Colombo five days before Christmas 1954 where I spent the holiday at the Galle Face Hotel prior to a road trip to Kandy, high up in the centre of the island. It was quite a small place surrounded by beautiful wooded hills and mountains and on the edge of an artificial lake swarming with fish and tortoises, but my objective was Nuwara Eliya, almost the highest point of the island at some 6200 ft. I reached it by way of the stunning Peradinya Gardens, where Lord Mountbatten's South East Asia Command HQ was located during the war. The views were superb and so was the timbered Grand Hotel where I was to stay. I saw virtually the whole of Ceylon because this was long before the current internal conflict began, and I thought it was delightful. Which is more than I can say for Chittagong in East Pakistan. Getting there was a bit of a shaker. I was driven out to the plane at Dum Dum airport and found, to my amazement, that my transport for the day was a World War Two Douglas Dakota which the American forces had left behind them. Worse, instead of the usual seats it had a continuous stretch of canvas running down each side of the plane, above which was the bar to which the airborne troops had clipped their parachute release gear before they jumped! When the distinctly scruffy pilot arrived I became quite queasy: he didn't have a copy of *How to Fly* under his arm, but he looked as though he should have. *If you'd any guts you'd get off this plane now*, I said to myself, but I guess it was like being a conscientious objector during the war – you needed more guts to be one and take the resultant flak than to actually go to war. So I stayed on the plane and of course it was perfectly all right. But Chittagong was awful – with the possible exception of Mexico City, quite the worst place I'd ever visited – dirty, smelly, chaotic and generally repulsive. The Hotel Miksha was all right though and I had a thoroughly redeeming time in the Chittagong Hill Tracts, which included meeting the local head man's wife, who not only wore the trousers but controlled 40,000 members of her tribe – a sort of native Margaret Thatcher, if you can imagine such a thing! Soon though it was time for another flight, but this time in an up-to-the-minute Lockheed Constellation, over the top of India to Karachi.

While I had been away from Slough I had been continually sending cables back to HQ asking for money to be sent to the local Barclays Bank. But when I got to Karachi I found instead a cable that read, 'Enough is enough. Come home.' After 14 weeks away I'd been rumbled. I got back to Slough at the end of January 1955, wrote a massive report on everything that had happened to me, made sweeping recommendations on how to improve things in the various places I had been and sat back to await developments. But to my extreme frustration there weren't any. No one asked to hear my pearls of wisdom until about two weeks after I had got back. But then it was an invitation from the Chairman, John Jamieson himself.

'Have a good trip, Murray?'

'Yes indeed, Sir!'

'Think you know all about India now?'

'Well no, but I know a lot more than I did before I went.'

'Enough to do the advertising?'

'Oh yes, definitely.'

'Well that's too bad because now we are going to put you in charge of Home Market Media.'

All that work, all that travelling and now it was going totally to waste. But at least I was getting promoted, and after a wonderful trip which I would never have been able to make any other way. In fact that job didn't last very long either, as I was soon promoted to Advertising Manager of the Aspro Home Products Division, responsible to the Marketing Director, Tom Peters, a tough and confident Australian who was great fun to work for. Aspro had bought several companies to diversify from the analgesic business, which coined money but was vulnerable to attack from rivals like Anadin. What a rag bag they were: Lifeguard Disinfectant (*'Kills all known household germs!'*); DIP plastic starch, an easy-to-use stiffener for the voluminous knee-high skirts which were then so fashionable and so attractively made women look like women; DISPEL air freshener (*'Just lift the wick to fill your house with glorious fragrance!'*), and Sherley's Proprietary Pet Products. None of the products had much of an advertising budget but one of my three advertising agencies was Masius and Fergusson, who were after the Aspro account and who were ultimately responsible for me being there. It was at this time that I really took a shine to Masius, the company with which I was eventually to spend 23 very happy and successful years; their team was great and I loved working with them, even on this odd assortment of products. While Dispel and Sherley's didn't get me very far, DIP got me to a lot of fashion shoots of stunning women in great clothes, and Lifeguard Disinfectant got me into countless grocers doing the sort of checking I had done in India, but in rather more attractive premises. And I also learned, thanks to a 'Win a House with Lifeguard' competition, how unreasonable people can be.

The top prize of a house or £30,000 (which would buy an extremely nice place in those days) was won by a Croydon housewife and I went to see her with a giant dummy cheque and a photographer to record her surprise and delight when she opened her front door and got the good news. But I might as well have told her she'd won a bag of jelly babies for all the emotion she showed.

'Will you tell me who you bought your winning bottle of Lifeguard Disinfectant from?'

'Why?'

'Because, great news, whoever sold it to you has won a superb Ford Popular car!'

'Well, it was the chap down the road and if I'd known I was going to win I wouldn't have bought it there because I don't like him.'

Charming!

Tom Peters got a message one day to go and see the boss, Bill Lloyd. A few minutes later he was out the door – fired – and was last seen walking down Buckingham Avenue. I wasn't very far behind him, but not for the same reason. McCann Erickson, the world's largest advertising agency, had made me an offer I couldn't refuse. Apart from my work with Aspro, I was now some eight years into my broadcasting career and becoming well known for my motor sport activities. Peter Laufer, then boss of McCanns, reckoned I would fit in well on an automotive account and doubled my salary to £2000 a year.

Aspro had got me up to speed in the proprietaries business – selling to chemists, newsagents, filling stations and every other conceivable type of outlet – but now I was back in the motor world in which I had started with Dunlop, but this time trying to generate demand for motor oil, a product with as little interest for motorists as tyres. McCann handled the mighty Standard Oil business worldwide, with Esso Extra petrol being the lead product. This alone made a lot of the agency's money and Jack Taylor and I, the account executives, would stagger down to Bernard Allen, the Esso Advertising Manager, with not one but 15 campaign approaches in the hope that one of them would ring the bell. 'Why don't you show me the one at the bottom?' he would say. 'That's the one you want to sell me, isn't it?'

This was before the days of motorist incentives at filling stations and catchy, memorable advertising was the name of the day. For petrol the '*Esso sign means happy motoring*' television commercials, with their singing cartoon petrol pump globes and bouncy jingle, worked a treat but Esso Extra Motor Oil was something else. Oil, like tyres, is a necessary evil. No one says, 'Hey, come and see the stunning new Dunlop tyres on my car,' or 'Wow, I feel like a million dollars now my car's filled with Esso Extra Motor Oil.' Or if they do, they need their brain testing. It was hard going.

It was at this time that things came to a head with a girl named Paddy Shaw. I was now 34 years old and still not married. I was certainly interested in girls and I'd had my share over the years, in the army at home and abroad, at Dunlop and at Aspro, but it has to be someone very special indeed if you are to spend the rest of your life with her and it just hadn't happened. Except, maybe, with Paddy.

I often wonder if my parents, and especially my mother, had more of an influence on my life than other people's do. I was certainly very close to and affected by my mother and father and what they thought. When my father had been a member of the Norton racing team in the 1920s one of his team-mates was a genial Ulsterman named Jimmy Shaw and they formed a very close friendship, as did my mother and Jimmy's wife Ethel. The Shaws ran a garage and motor business in Upper Queen Street, Belfast, were the Ulster distributors for Triumph and Lea Francis Cars (for whom Jim used to race) and made a lot of money. Jimmy got the customers: Ethel did the rest. They had a son, Wesley, and five daughters, Maureen, Joan, Paddy, Fay and Barbara. My parents and I used to go and stay with them, and they with us, and as I grew up I progressively fell for first Maureen, who married an American army Captain and went there to live, and then Joan, who married Terry Bulloch, a BOAC Captain. So then it was Paddy and this time I felt it was for real – so much so that when Jimmy and Ethel sold the business and the whole family went to live in the States I felt I had to pursue Paddy there and resolve things.

This happened between my leaving Aspro and joining McCann. Paddy was working at Yellowstone National Park and when the snows came and the park closed down for the winter I flew to Billings, Montana, to drive with her to her winter apartment in La Jolla, California. It was a four-week trip in a Chevrolet Bel Air, by way of Yellowstone's Grand Canyon and its world-famous geyser 'Old Faithful', the wonderful sights of Salt Lake City, across the Utah Salt Flats to Virginia City and its extinct silver mines to Reno, over the Sierra Nevada to Lake Tahoe (just a few log cabins there in those days), across the Oakland Bay Bridge to San Francisco and on to Monterey and La Jolla, which, like Lake Tahoe, was totally undeveloped and an idyllic spot. It was a great trip and long enough for me to find out that it wasn't going to work out between Paddy and I and that it was better to return to Europe and start my new job.

With all the wisdom of hindsight I truly think that a lot of my feelings for Paddy were brought about by huge unspoken pressure from the Shaw family and my parents who felt that their long-standing friendship should, naturally, result in a marriage between one of the girls and myself. There were regrets at the time, of course, but I was later to find in Elizabeth a woman I fell for with no reservations and now, after more than 40 very happy married years together, I know it was all for the best.

I was at McCanns for two years but I have to say that it made very little impression on me. The people were fine and so was the client. The broadcasting was going well and I was still living at home with my parents, contented and seeing no reason why I should do anything else but I felt once again, as I had at Aspro, that I had to move on. Part of the problem was that there seemed to be no connection between the advertising work I was doing and the sales of the product. I had kept in touch with all the friends I had made at Masius, which, as an agency, was booming, and on impulse I phoned Jack Wynne-Williams. He invited me over to come and talk and, sitting in his cosy office overlooking St James's Square, we did the deal that was to take me to the end of my business life.

CHAPTER FOUR

Starting at Masius

The move to Masius wasn't easy. Aspro and Esso had been as different as chalk and cheese and now things were as different again with my new clients at Masius – the Mars Confectionery and Petfoods companies. These were wholly owned by Forrest Mars, an American with a complex personality and an unusual business philosophy. Forrest didn't think or act like other people; he was a one-off maverick and even his own father, Frank Mars, who owned a hugely successful confectionery business in America, found him too much to stomach. Legend has it that he gave his son $30,000 (a massive amount of money in those days) plus the rights to use the recipe for Mars Bars (named after the owner, not the planet) anywhere outside America, and told him to 'germinate your arse to the other side of the Atlantic.' Forrest set up shop in Slough in 1932 and started his business with the Mars Bar which is still, of course, very much one of Britain's leading brands.

In those tough early days Mike Masius would go down to Slough every Saturday for Mr Mars to tell him how much money he could have for advertising the next week. '*Mars are marvellous!*' was the rather plonking claim but great things start small and under Forrest's distinctive and forceful leadership the business became one of the most successful the world has ever seen, eventually taking over that of his late father and, for a long time, being the largest privately owned company in the world. It began with the Mars Bar, led to other brands like Milky Way, Maltesers, Bounty, Galaxy, Spangles and Opal Fruits, and then to the start of an entirely new and innovatory product – canned petfoods.

So in some ways for me this was a similar situation to Aspro: popular, low-cost products with mass distribution through grocers, confectioners and tobacconists and with tough and aggressive competition from talented and experienced organizations like Cadbury, Nestlé and Rowntree. But the Mars advertising philosophy, enthusiastically embraced and promoted by Forrest himself, was entirely different from anybody else's, being incredibly hard-nosed and product-based in comparison with anything I had experienced before. So I had a very steep learning curve amidst some extremely sharp and demanding people, but at last I felt I was where I wanted to be and I relished the stimulating atmosphere.

Mars were based, coincidentally, in the same road and trading estate in Slough where I had worked with Aspro, while Petfoods were at Melton Mowbray in Leicestershire. Both worked to the same unique management philosophy laid down by Forrest Mars: everyone clocked in and out, even the

Managing Director; rather than receiving a bonus for being punctual you got less if you were late; only the man at the top had a private office, and his had no door; everyone ate in the same canteen. There were no status perks, no company cars, and no sports and social club.

In addition, Mars executives were not allowed to accept gifts from suppliers – no matter who they were. Jack Wynne-Williams was a very keen shot and used to return from week-ends in Suffolk with his Pontiac station wagon full of birds, which his secretary, Mona Fraser, then sent to selected clients and agency people. One day she sent some pheasants to 'Mac' McIntosh, the boss at Slough, who returned them with a very nice note, the gist of which was that Mars company policy prevented him from accepting gifts from suppliers, which of course Jack was.

Jack phoned him. 'My god, Mac, do you think that if I wanted to bribe you I couldn't do better than a few pheasants?'

'Of course not, Jack, but you miss the point. If I accept the pheasants from you how could I stop my buyers from accepting a Jaguar?'

The company had a very generous pension scheme and while everyone was threatened with a drop in salary if the company's turnover decreased by £1 million (it never did), they also got a raise each time it went up by that magical figure. There was an occasion at Petfoods when hitting the next million required a railway container of product to leave the factory limits that day – at a time when no locomotive was available. People just rallied round and pushed it out. Every-one was paid far more for their job than they could get anywhere else and the result was that the Mars companies not only got the best people but kept them. They had a reputation of being heartless hire-and-fire organizations but this wasn't true. They were awesomely efficient with operating systems way ahead of their time, knew who they wanted and got them, but they were no more ruthless with their people than any other decent organization. Once you were there it was actually quite difficult to leave because you could only do so by getting a job at least two levels higher and that was unlikely.

Knowing this, during my time at Aspro I had applied for a job as Brand Manager at Petfoods and after two long individual interviews with the Personnel Director and Personnel Manager was told to report to the Washington Hotel in London's Curzon Street – and be prepared to be there for 36 hours. When I arrived I found I was one of the last six of several hundred applicants. After socializing at three meals, more individual interviews, wire puzzles, group discussions, debates and psychological tests which lasted well into the second day, I staggered home. The last thing required of us was to have a 60-minute debate on a subject of our own choosing – 'But not, Gentlemen, anything religious or political for obvious reasons.' There was a rather thick Scotsman amongst the six of us who had been opening his mouth and putting his foot in it the whole weekend and, obviously eager to demonstrate his leadership qualities and quick thinking, he leapt in with, 'I propose that we discuss the significance of the Roman Catholic Church in today's world.' As one, hardly believing our luck, the rest of us said, 'Isn't that religious?' So then there were five. One then quietly said, 'Let's talk about the pros and cons of capital punishment.' It was a chap called Neil Faulkner. He was head and shoulders above the rest of us, got the job, had since become the man most likely to succeed at Petfoods and was now my client contact at Melton Mowbray.

The way Mars and Petfoods evolved their advertising was just as challenging as their personnel selection. They were the first in the UK to work to the USP philosophy, which involved intensive research to find out what potential buyers wanted from the product and from that the creation of a Unique Selling Proposition (not Unique Sales Point as so frequently incorrectly described). Hence, among the brands I worked on, '*PAL – Prolongs Active Life*', '*Opal Fruits – Made to make your mouth water*', '*Liver-rich Lassie gives head to tail health*' and '*Trill makes budgies bounce with health*'. In my broadcasting life after I had left the advertising world, I was constantly described in interviews as the originator of one of the greatest USPs of all time – '*A Mars a day helps you work, rest and play*' – but I certainly wasn't, unfortunately!

I was like a fish out of water when I joined Masius. The total billing was less than £5 million but in the years to come it was to rocket to stratospheric levels. I had joined at just the right time but I didn't realize my good fortune – I was far too busy struggling to keep afloat in this fast-moving organization and trying to give the impression I knew what I was doing: learning the two companies' very specialized operating procedures, working out how best to cope with their very tough and competent but very human executives and implementing what they wanted, or thought they wanted, inside the agency with the research, art, copy, TV, media and marketing departments. All businesses have their internal rivalries but we had them considerably less than most. We were all working for a benevolent dictator whom we liked and respected. The 'Grocers of St James's Square', as we were sneeringly referred to by a lot of advertising people who were later to eat their words, made dynamic progress but the whole business nearly came to a standstill very soon after I joined it.

At the time, Forrest Mars was trying to get Masius to merge with the Ted Bates advertising agency organization in America, but Mike Masius and Jack Wynne-Williams were steadfastly refusing. Just a few weeks after I had joined we were told that Forrest Mars was coming in on the Saturday morning to collect a pair of shocs that he had had repaired (most people with his income would have bought themselves a new pair but Forrest wasn't like that) and that we were all to be on parade, sitting to attention at our desks, in case the great man wanted to address us. Which is where I was when my phone rang. It was Jack.

'Murray, Mr Mars is in reception. Would you bring him to my office?'

There was just one person in Reception – a balding, middle-aged chap wearing a very ordinary blue suit and one of those strange American homburg hats with a wide ribbon and the brim turned up all the way round. *This can't be him*, I thought, *but there's no-one else here so it must be.*

'Mr Mars?'

'Yes, son.'

'Welcome to Masius, Sir, and do come this way!'

Mr Mars not only collected his shoes but, after again failing to persuade Mike and Jack to merge with Bates, demonstrated his displeasure by announcing that he was going to stop advertising his major cat food brand, Kit-E-Kat, and also transfer the top-selling Spangles to another agency.

Those two brands were vital to us and we were very badly hit but Jack just said, 'There's only one way to recover – go out and get more business.' Which we did, and prospered. The happy ending was that Kit-E-Kat, bereft of advertising support, lost sales heavily and the advertising was restored at an even higher level less than a year later.

An example of how Forrest Mars' mind worked differently to other people's was his question about the agency's very successful use of the world-famous American cowboy film star Hopalong Cassidy to promote Spangles.

'How much is this guy Cassidy paying us?' he asked.

'Er, it's not like that, Mr Mars, we pay him actually.'

'Why's that? Just look at all the publicity he gets from us!'

True enough, but needless to say Mr Mars wasn't daft. He did the things he did and acted the way he did to provoke people into thinking. And it worked.

In those days British pets were fed household scraps and the marketing objective was to persuade the owners to substitute canned Petfoods products. This wasn't easy when the household scraps cost nothing and PAL, Lassie, Kit-E-Kat and the rest were not only regarded with suspicion but had to be paid for. Nor was it easy to get a doubting trade to stock them, when it was generally believed the contents were mainly factory floor sweepings. I used to make shop calls with Petfoods sales reps and we would solemnly open a can of Kit-E-Kat before a buyer's cynical eyes and eat some to show how good and wholesome it was. That usually won them over and so it should have, for at the time it was mostly whalemeat, which most of us ate during the war with no ill effects. Eventually we won the day, for who feeds their pets household scraps these days? It says a lot for the vision and determination of Forrest Mars.

One of my brands was Trill, the packeted budgerigar seed, and on a visit to Melton Mowbray I was presented with a unique problem by Tom Johnstone, the Petfoods Marketing Director.

'With Trill we have over 90% of the packaged budgerigar seed market and we very much want to expand what is an extremely profitable business,' he said.

'Yes, Tom, of course.'

'In a static market, the obvious thing to do is to buy our competitors but we don't want to do that because if we did we could well run foul of the Monopolies Commission.'

'Yes, of course, Tom.'

'So what we have to do is to increase the budgerigar population and then we'll get 90% of the extra business.'

'Yes, of course, smart thinking!'

'So that's what we want you to do, Murray – come up with ideas of how we can do that.'

'*YOU WHAT?!*'

'Off you go then and we'd like your proposals within a week with full advertising and budgetary recommendations.'

Back I went to the agency, got everyone round a table, outlined the brief and sat back to worry. Two days later we were all back together.

'Here's the deal, Murray. Most people have just the one budgie, right?'

'Right.'

'Well, what we want to do is to create a guilt complex by promoting the belief that an only budgie is a lonely budgie and thus motivating their owners to go out and buy another one.'

'You what?'

'You heard, Murray, think about it.'

The more I thought about it the more I liked it. It made sense even if I wasn't too sure about whether sole budgies pined for company and what effect multiple budgies would have on their owners. So we worked up a pool of commercials, publicity material and costings and back I went to Melton where I made a sale. It worked – but I never found out what effect it had on the lonely spinsters who kept their bird for company.

Another product that Petfoods and the agency tried to introduce, unsuccessfully this time, was a very high-quality cat food which we decided to brand as 'Minx'. After all the usual investigatory research it looked as though we had a winner. The formulation was nearly 100% cod (humans turned their noses up at it then) but we were looking for something else to give it a promotable health benefit.

'How about we put some cod liver oil in it?' said the Petfoods nutritional experts.

'Sounds great. Cod liver oil has all sorts of health-giving overtones so we'll go with that if the research supports it.'

It did and from that came the USP, '*Minx gives your cat inside satisfaction plus outside protection*'. The commercial researched well and the next step was to sell the product to a limited-area test market. Bill Rudd was the Regional Sales Manager and off he went to the big buyers, starting with one of the major Co-operative Societies. His contact there was a grizzled old-timer, and when Bill had gone through all the details including the advertising and the brand's USP the buyer rang for his secretary.

'Maisie, I want you to do something for me. Go to the chemist and get me some outside protection and then I'll give you some inside satisfaction!'

Consternation in court. In all the time we had been working to develop the claim its double entendre had never struck us. We were too close to the product. So we had to start all over again and think of something else. Pity. It might have sold a million.

Masius was a wonderful place to work. A great location in our own modern office block in St James's Square and a business that was booming. Every year I was there saw a record income and there was a constant buzz of excitement and achievement as new accounts flowed in and very few flowed out. I shared an office and the Mars and Petfoods accounts with a super chap called Ian Pitt who had been a Major during the war and who had been taken prisoner by the Germans. We faced each other across joining desks overlooking the Square and got on like a house on fire. Our job was to underpin and retain the Mars/Petfoods accounts which were of such importance to the agency. We achieved that thanks to help from a lot of fine people. No two days were the same and life was a constant challenge.

In the 1970s Forrest Mars made a further adventurous leap into the unknown when he entered the potato business. As disposable incomes and the desire to spend less time in the kitchen increased, more and more women were buying ready-prepared products like boil-in-the-bag and frozen foods, which needed less preparation. Enter Yeoman Instant Mashed Potato and another new field of endeavour for me. Masius' job was to create the advertising that would pack Britain's grocers and supermarkets with hordes of eager housewives fighting to buy and experience this exciting new product that was going to unchain them from having to hump heavy potatoes home, wash, peel, boil and mash them. Fantastic.

'*Yeoman gives you perfect mash – every time!*' the TV advertising declared but the housewives turned out to be frustratingly apathetic about this sensational new product and it made agonizingly slow progress, not made any easier by Cadbury's 'Smash' that blew us into the weeds.

This was the time that there were a lot of IRA bombings and one day when I was in Kings Lynn I said to John McMullen, the Marketing Director, 'Do you ever have any bomb scares here?'

'Yes, occasionally, Murray.'

'What do you do about them?'

'Do? Nothing. Why?'

'Isn't that taking a hell of a chance? What would happen if there really was a bomb?'

'Listen, Murray, at any time of the day or night we are processing five hundred tons of mashed potato and if the machines are stopped it all goes solid. If you think I'm risking that for a bomb that never was, you're mistaken.'

Brave words. Unfortunately, John wasn't too amused when a processing glitch resulted in vast quantities of Yeoman powder being blown out of the factory on to the homes and gardens of Kings Lynn. Good thing it didn't rain.

Mars were also one of the pioneers of the vending machine business in the UK with a business called Vendepac. We take machines for drinks, cigarettes and confectionery for granted now but food vending was very avant-garde then. To test consumer acceptance, Mars converted the whole of the canteen at Slough to automated food and drink and since everybody, bosses and workers alike, ate there it was inevitable that Vic Hender, the Research Director, would soon be lining up for his automatic lunch. He was not well known for his acceptance of things going wrong and when he stuffed his pre-decimalization half-crown (those were the days!) into the slot for his chicken pie nothing happened. Adopting the time-honoured British procedure, Vic gave the machine an almighty thump, at which point a chap looked out from behind and said, 'Steady on Guv, I'm putting them in the back as fast as I can!'

One of the agency's greatest successes, which was in full gallop when I joined, was the Babycham business. One day four men appeared in front of our receptionist, Dorothy Hickie, and said, 'Our name is Showering. We're from Somerset and we want to talk to somebody about advertising.' Before they knew where they were, the Showering Brothers, Francis, Herbert and Ralph, and their nephew Keith, found themselves in Jack Wynne-Williams' office.

'There's nothing in it, Jack,' said Mike Masius, when he heard that Jack had taken their business on a fee-paying basis. 'It would cost you more to go and see them in Shepton Mallet than we'd get from the fee.' Mike wasn't often wrong but he was this time. For what the Showerings were wanting to market was perry, a drink made from fermented pear juice – a sort of bubbly, pear-based cider. In those days the traditional pub drink for women was still port and lemon, and in those rapidly changing times it was understandably seen as unsophisticated. Masius took the Showerings product and turned it into magic. They put it into small, dark-glass wine bottles with coloured foil tops, called it Babycham, associated it in advertising and promotion with a loveable, animated baby chamois, and provided the pubs with attractive wine glasses carrying the logo and featuring the claim *'You'd love a Babycham!'*

It worked like a charm. The girls could now ask for a seemingly sophisticated, champagne-like, modern drink which wasn't going to cost their man a fortune and which wasn't going to get them legless. The pubs and Showerings had a high-profit winner; Masius had a client which coined us money and which, in time, led to a flood of new business as the satisfied Showerings family introduced new products. The Showerings had regular board meetings at the agency's offices and one December they produced a Christmas-wrapped parcel and said, 'Jack, as a thank you for all you've done at Masius we've brought you a present.'

'Thanks,' said Jack, 'that's very nice of you. It's usually the agency that buys the client presents in this business. I'm very grateful.'

'Aren't you going to open it then?'

When he did he found it contained a car key.

'And Jack, if you take it to Jack Barclay's showrooms in Berkeley Square there's a Rolls-Royce waiting for you to use it in!'

It was an incredible gesture of friendship and appreciation which I've never known to be equalled before or since. Jack subsequently gave mc the job of getting a personalized registration number for his pride and joy – JWW 347.

I was always at my desk in the West End by 8:00 and seldom home less than 12 hours later. My clients were sophisticated, experienced and demanding and although they were all nice people they didn't permit any resting on the oars. Each week I was at Melton Mowbray, Slough and Kings Lynn making presentations, taking briefs, maintaining contact and generally keeping in touch with the knowledge that not only were they among the agency's most important accounts, which our competitors would kill for, but that they were also those that were enabling us to expand outside the UK. From the time I joined in 1959, the mother agency in London was following in the footsteps of the Mars and Colgate organizations by vigorously and successfully expanding, first in Europe and then throughout the rest of the world. As the Mars Empire grew so did ours, for they gave us their business in the new countries they entered on the basis that it was better to use an agency that knew them, even if it didn't currently have an organization in a new territory, than to use another that didn't know their ways and products. It was marvellous for us, because not only were we guaranteed an immediate income in any new country we decided to enter but we could offer interesting and exciting promotional opportunities with very real prospects to our many good people who might have left us.

So Masius opened offices in the major European countries – Germany, France, Belgium, Holland, Italy, Spain, Norway, Sweden, Denmark and Austria – initially to handle Mars and Colgate brands, but which we could use as bases to pitch for other business. Later we added America, Australia, New Zealand and South Africa to this list, until we became not only the biggest agency in Britain (bigger even than the long-time No.1, J Walter Thompson) but an enormously desirable partner or takeover target for the mammoth agencies in America like Interpublic. I was eventually to be visiting most of the Masius agencies outside the UK regularly as my responsibilities increased but meantime I was a very busy part of expanding the business in the UK.

In 1964, five eventful years after I had joined the agency, Jack Wynne-Williams made me a proposition. The agency had been in existence for some 21 years, Jack was now in total command, but the old guard on the Board weren't getting any younger. There was a need to look to the future, for young blood to take over. There were four people whom Jack jokingly referred to as his Young Turks, one of whom was me. None of us were necessarily going to reach the top – in the event only one of us did, and it wasn't me – but Jack had decided that we had enough potential for him to want to keep us all. One by one he had us into his office to give us all the same message.

'I'm going to give you a chance to put your money where your mouth is by offering you an opportunity to buy into the agency. It will cost you £30,000 and Warburg, the agency's bankers, will lend you the money with an annual interest payment of 10% [very reasonable at the time]. You will be obliged to sell the shares when you retire or leave the agency but in the meantime if we continue to do as well as we have in the past the dividends will cover thc interest and, in time, the share value growth should more than enable you to repay the loan with a sizeable profit. But, of course, there's no guarantee. So it is up to you. Think it over and let me know.'

Now, ever since I was a boy my mother, who was very good at playing the stock market, had drummed the basics of it into me. With agency bonuses and other money I had built up a share portfolio of my own and hadn't done too badly, but this was something else. £30,000 then was the equivalent of not far off £500,000 now and putting myself in debt to that extent was not something that appealed to a naturally cautious chap like me. The agency had done and was doing very well indeed, and there was no reason to suppose that it wouldn't continue to do so, but it was a very volatile business – its assets were its people, who could leave at short notice, while any contracts that existed with clients weren't worth the paper they were written on and if they lost confidence in us they would be off like a rocket. On the other hand, the whole of life is a gamble and I was never going to have another opportunity like this.

I talked it over with Elizabeth and in fact neither of us hesitated. The next morning I went back to Jack and said I was on. He told me I'd made a wise decision and he was sure I wouldn't regret it. I certainly didn't. From then on there were occasional other share offers as directors retired and sold up, and I bought every one I was offered. My faith and good luck paid off because the agency prospered greatly and everything that Jack had prophesied came to pass. I certainly never made a better financial decision.

Before very much longer I was elevated to the Agency's small Management Committee and became a theoretical prospect for Managing Director but for very good reasons that was where my agency progress ended. One of those reasons was the fact that my double life as an agency executive and an increasingly busy broadcaster meant that I'd have to give up the latter and devote all my time to the business and there was no way that that was going to happen – I liked my other life too much. But I also had no illusions about whether I was going to be able to reach the top: it mattered more to others than it did to me. I had a very happy life: a happy marriage, a fine home and a broadcasting hobby where I was making consistent progress and which could go on long after I had retired from the business. Things were going very well for me, and as it happened I was about to make a massive change of direction in my agency life.

CHAPTER FIVE

Goodbye Mars, Hello Wheels

Masius was booming, with new business pouring in as a result of its ever-growing reputation. The Imperial Tobacco brand Embassy, with its coupons and gift catalogue, was proving hugely successful, Nescafé ('*Coffee with life in it!*') was a major acquisition and so were many others like Aspro, Woolworths, Wilkinson Sword razorblades, Weetabix and the Beecham Proprietaries' brands Phensic and Phyllosan ('*Fortifies the over-forties!*'), which I looked after. But now, after some nine years working on fast-moving packaged goods, it was as though my first love was calling me home.

Up until now Masius had a foot in all sorts of major product fields but there were still several missing from its portfolio – most notably the car business, which was already sizeable and clearly going to get bigger. So when Vauxhall Cars contacted the agency and invited it to have a look at its business a shiver of excitement went through the building. Vauxhall was not only one of the UK's leading car brands, it was the British arm of General Motors, the world's biggest business. If we made a success of Vauxhall, heaven knows what might come of it.

'I want you to look after this one, Murray,' said Jack, and I didn't need a second invitation. This was perfect for me and hopefully the credibility I now had as a motor-sport television and radio personality wouldn't do our bid any harm with a car manufacturer. We put together a team of the agency's best research, creative, television and media people and went at it absolutely flat out. After making the best possible presentation we sat back to await the result. And when the call came from Vauxhall Sales Director Geoff Moore at Luton it was good news – we were in! Euphoria all round and for me a pair of engraved gold and ruby cufflinks as a token reward. The joy of knowing that I was going to head up the account was tempered somewhat by the sadness that I would have to come off the Mars/Petfoods business which I had enjoyed so much, but I was looking forward to the new challenge ahead.

It wasn't easy to do well for Vauxhall, for their cars were seen as dull and Americanized rust buckets. The Viscount was the top model, an upmarket version of the six-cylinder Cresta and, to me, the ultimate soft-suspension, personality-free Squidgemobile. It had everything: plenty of smooth power, automatic gearbox, power brakes and power steering, electric windows, leather upholstery, multi-band radio, the lot. You may get all these things in virtually any car now, but you didn't then, and the Viscount oozed along with effortless smoothness – but absolutely zilch in the way of automotive charisma. Elizabeth loved it for its luxury, comfort and lack of

At three years old I fancied myself as a snappy dresser in my Fair Isle sweater and racy beret.

Cheer up, Murray! World War One uniform as a Sergeant in the School Officer Training Corps. The sleeve badge was for shooting at Bisley.

Very proud but shy in the Isle of Man paddock with my father after he had finished second in the 1931 250cc TT.

Above: Passing out parade day for 115 Troop at Sandhurst. An officer at last!
I am second from the left in the back row.

Below: My childhood friend Flight Lieutenant John Arthur came to Sandhurst for my big day. Like me he got through the war, and he later became a Judge.

Below: Lieutenant Murray Walker, Royal Scots Greys, complete with medal ribbons. Note the cavalry whistle and leather buttons. The cap proudly carries the word 'Waterloo'.

The amazing day my father (on the left) found me on the battlefield in Germany. I had liberated my Walther P38 pistol from a German officer.

In my Sherman tank turret just prior to the 1945 Rhine crossing. The tank suits were excellent but I didn't like the army glasses.

Just a fraction of the superb Isle of Man circuit. My father leads the great Jimmy Guthrie at Creg ny Baa in the 1931 Junior TT.

I stood in the slip road for my first TT commentary in 1949, virtually immobilised by the microphone harness and wiring.

Interview time at my first TV job in 1949 – a motor-cycle hill climb at Knatts Valley, Kent. Look at the size of the camera!

Getting the score from BSA's Harold Tozer, the all-time great of sidecar trials. BBC's trilby-hatted Horace Saunders-Jacobs listens intently.

Above: This is what I tried to do on my Norton – ride feet-up through the observed sections. Unlike me the great trials soloist Hugh Viney (AJS) made it look easy.

Below: At the 1957 Senior TT I commentated from the Keppel Hotel as John Surtees vainly pursued winner Bob McIntyre (Gilera). The noise was fabulous!

Action! Action! For me, motocross is the most exciting motorised sport of them all. BSA star Jeff Smith leads the pack.

How the viewers loved Dave Bickers! And so did I because, on his 250cc Greeves two-stroke, he was an incredible spectacle.

Dour and gritty Yorkshireman Arthur Lampkin was the man during the TV scrambles boom. On his BSA he gave me and the viewers endless delight.

drama but it didn't suit my gung-ho self-image at all. I felt 40 years older every time I got in it and in an effort to make it sportier, which it was never meant to be, I had it fitted with a set of the ultimate Pirelli Cinturato radial tyres – the sort that Ferrari used. They didn't make the slightest difference and since it was designed for crossplies they might even have made it worse. However, I convinced myself that it now steered as though it was on rails.

'*Vauxhall – the big breed!*' had been the blanket theme of our successful presentation and soon after it had been concluded Arthur Martin, the Advertising Manager, said, 'Let's go to my office, Murray, and talk about what we are going to say in the advertising.'

Completely poleaxed, I said, 'Arthur, we've been busting our braces for three months to work that out and that's what we presented.'

'Oh no, we can't possibly say that,' said Arthur, and so after the usual arguments off we went again. It's when you have to agree with the client that the going can get tough in the agency business. We ended up with '*The Vauxhall breed's got style.*' As part of the advertising campaign we were asked to make name recommendations for a new saloon and came up with 'Ventura'.

'Like it!' said Vauxhall, only to come back weeks later saying, 'Can't use it. There's already a Pontiac Catalina Ventura model in the States and the Model Names Committee has given it the elbow.'

'Hang on,' I said. 'You can't buy a Pontiac in the UK so what's the problem?'

'Don't confuse us with the facts,' said Vauxhall. 'Try again.'

So back to the drawing board and a stroke of inspiration. We rounded off the U of Ventura and called it 'Ventora'. The faceless men in Detroit accepted it and that's what it was called: '*Vauxhall Ventora – the lazy fireball!*' It did quite well too: I had one and with its high-torque, easy-going engine it fully lived up to the advertising.

With the agency workers concentrated on the UK I set about getting the Vauxhall business in Europe, such as it was. This was a big mistake, because it wasn't worth having and with hindsight was never going to be. The Continent was Opel territory and Vauxhall sales there were very small beer. We had an excellent Masius agency in Amsterdam and after I had met and got to know the Vauxhall boss in Holland, John Czarski, we made a successful presentation for what turned out to be an account well worth having. This was more than could be said for France: we presented for the business in Paris and got it, only to find that the previous year's sales of Vauxhall in France had totalled 47 cars – all of them at greatly reduced prices to GM employees!

It was not a very good start and it didn't get any better. When I appeared with missionary zeal in Stockholm to present for the Swedish business (which we got), Hugh Austin, the American boss, said, 'Come with me, Murray, and I'll show you the sort of problem we have with Vauxhall.' He took me to the Service Department where there was a factory-fresh Victor with drum brakes on one side and disc brakes on the other. If I hadn't seen it I would never have believed it.

* * *

While all this was going on in work, the rest of my life became increasingly hectic. My parents had moved down to Beaulieu in Hampshire for my father to help Lord Montagu develop his newly founded Montagu Motor Museum and were living in the East Wing at Palace House, in the beautiful New Forest. What started with just a few historic cars in Palace House became the present collection of wonderful vehicles in their own custom-built premises and one of the finest automotive museums in the world. My father was particularly responsible for the motor-cycle section, which I still visit regularly to relive old memories, but the whole collection is well worth the trip, particularly the new exhibition, which I had the honour of opening recently.

Elizabeth and I bought our first house in 1960, the base for my uniquely divided life. Monday to Friday belonged to the agency – and a lot of weekends too when we were working on new business presentations. But almost every weekend was either the BBC's or ITV's because for years I worked for both of them on motor-cycle scrambles.

It was non-stop. On Friday evening I would leave the office in St James's Square, meet Elizabeth and our boxer dog, Sheba, and head off in the car to wherever that weekend's scramble was taking place. Usually they were somewhere in the Midlands or the North and in those days there was no M1 motorway, so it was a long slog up the A5 and onwards to arrive at a hotel late at night and then be on parade at the track first thing on Saturday. If it was ITV's *World of Sport*, with Dickie Davis hosting the programme from London, all the races were repeated for the regional network the next day at the same track with the same riders on the same bikes, then it was home again, starting at about 5pm if we were lucky. Trying to get a good meal late on a Sunday afternoon was a major challenge but eventually we were saved by the advent of the Chinese restaurant, one of which was always open and always good. Then it was another long drive and into the office on Monday morning.

I was a glutton for work and in the winter of 1963 wrote most of my book *The Art of Motor-Cycle Racing*, which I co-authored with the great Mike Hailwood, by the light of a flexible reading lamp in the passenger seat of our Austin A40 with Elizabeth at the wheel. Our record was 13 consecutive weeks doing alternate broadcasts for ITV and the BBC in the appalling snowbound winter of 1963, which was when my appendix suddenly packed up. I was climbing down from the commentary box after a scramble meeting near Stratford on Avon when I collapsed in extreme pain. I'd been seeing a specialist so Elizabeth rushed me home and got him over to look at me. Half an hour later I was in an ambulance on my way to King Edward VII Hospital for Officers in London's Marylebone Road and the next morning I woke up in a mini-ward with a General and an army chaplain.

The agency continued to expand, with already great accounts joined by the Co-op, Nationwide, Ever Ready, the Government's Central Office of Information (for whom we did the memorable '*Don't ask a man to drink and drive*' and '*Clunk, click – every trip*' campaigns), W H Smith, Danish Butter and Bacon, Crown Paints, Daily Express, Brooke Bond, Ski Yoghurt,

Golden Wonder Crisps, Hoover, McDonald's and many others. But in 1968 a second major automotive company contacted the agency – my old employer Dunlop.

We got the business with a fairly conventional approach but once we had made ourselves acceptable to the Dunlop management we proposed a humorous, truly innovative and memorable campaign based on a whimsical and endearing made-up animal – the Groundhog. (Only much later when I was in Canada for the Grand Prix at Montreal did I find that there is actually an animal there that they call the groundhog.) Our make-believe, animated cartoon Groundhog had a stumpy body, big eyes, floppy ears and wheels instead of legs and was a natural for television. It was a massive success in terms of public awareness, the commercials were brilliant but there was a problem. The Groundhog tyre was a crossply and they were rapidly becoming yesterday's product as the far superior radial, pioneered by Michelin, increasingly penetrated the market. Radials gave motorists what they really wanted – much higher mileage as well as superior performance. So we had great advertising for the wrong product. After a messy attempt to make it all things to all motorists, poor little Groundhog died and so did our attempt to keep Dunlop on the map, for it too was starting down the long road to oblivion.

The end was far from nigh for Masius but sadly it was also getting very close for our work with Vauxhall. The American influence at Luton became greater and greater, and one of the resident Americans whom I got to know was the styling boss Wayne Cherry, a man whose vision and drive worked wonders and who subsequently became the styling boss for General Motors worldwide. But everything was increasingly being centralized and things got ever tougher for us in the diminishing Vauxhall outpost of the General Motors empire. Sadly, despite all our efforts and enthusiasm from Luton, the business was lost to Interpublic. We had failed to adapt from the grocery products we knew so well to service a world-wide car business controlled from America and, in short, we weren't doing a good enough job. Ultimately, that was my responsibility.

There have been precious few people in my life with whom I have totally failed to get on, but one of them was Desmond Skirrow, the Creative Director at Masius. We were poles apart in attitude and disliked each other intensely, although for no real reason – neither of us had ever done anything reprehensible to the other – it was just a chemistry thing. In 1973 there was pressure from the States for us to present against rival agency Campbell Ewald to retain the Vauxhall account and our animosity did not help the cause. I had been to America to study how McCann serviced the Buick account and was very impressed. At the time we were negotiating to merge with another General Motors agency, D'Arcy MacManus (which subsequently happened), and I went to their offices in Bloomfield Hills, Michigan, to mastermind what was going to be a joint presentation from both agencies. We lost the battle and it was a very bitter pill for me to swallow because I had been enormously proud of having gained the business. I was deeply ashamed at having lost it and very low. While it wasn't the first account we had lost (nor would it be the last) the advertising agency business, like Formula 1, is tough and ruthless and a lot of agencies would have got rid of me. Fortunately for me, Masius wasn't like that and I lived to fight another day. And I've still got the cufflinks.

Dunlop's proud boasts were '*As British as the flag*' and '*Great oaks from little acorns grow*' because it had been a Belfast vet, John Boyd Dunlop, who in 1888 had wrapped air-inflated, rubberized canvas around the wheels of his son's tricycle to make the first pneumatic tyres. The company had grown beyond recognition and had prospered enormously, seemingly unbeatable and unbreakable. But it wasn't. The recruitment of an energetic and industrious marketing manager, an innovation for the company, did little or nothing to stop the rot. He was Keith Pybus, and he and his wife were great opera lovers. I thought Glyndebourne would appeal to them, so organized tickets to hear Kiri Te Kanawa in *The Magic Flute*. We drove there in separate cars and, opera ignoramus that I am, I was a bit startled to see the two of them get out of theirs with an enormous book.

'I hope it's not going to be as boring as that, Keith,' I said.

'What do you mean, Murray?'

'The book,' I replied.

'It's the score,' said Keith witheringly and they sat following it intensely while I morosely tried to work out the plot with its Italian-sung dialogue.

Full of fire and vim, Keith set about a very sophisticated segmentation of the tyre brands, including allocating some of them to an up-and-coming agency which we had used in the past as a creative hot shop. Its name was Saatchi and Saatchi and it subsequently went far, but it was able to do no better than we did with Dunlop. Sadly, Keith's segmentation policy did not work because there were neither the funds nor the sales to support it. For other reasons, Dunlop slid further and further beneath the waves until this once mighty giant of British commerce, a world leader of a great industry, was no more. With its allied companies sold off and the tyre division firstly bought out by Sumitomo and currently a part of the American Goodyear empire, Dunlop is now just the name on the side of a tyre. The site of the commercial offices where I had been a student and where the management strutted their stuff is now occupied by a supermarket and the mirror-image Base Stores right by the M6 motorway were the background to an enormous Ford Mondeo banner the last time I passed. How are the mighty fallen.

My agency ventures into the world of wheels weren't going too well then: two tries and two failures. Time would tell whether it'd be third time lucky, but meanwhile the agency was in a state of major upheaval. As a group we were now the largest agency in Europe that was neither owned by nor affiliated to an American agency network, and we were just as anxious to expand into America as non-global American agencies were to merge with us. It seemed a mutually fruitful situation if only we could find the right partner. We had bought a small agency in New York and I had been over there to help introduce them to Masius and its ways but it was proving to be hard going.

I went to the Mars headquarters in Washington touting for

business and was told I could have a look at the Puppy Palace organization. I'd never heard of it.

'It's our franchise business to sell thoroughbred puppies and everything that goes with them. Why not go to the Long Island outlet and have a look?'

I found an immaculately clean, supermarket-style set-up, with tiled floors, lively and healthy puppies in stainless steel cages along the walls and gondolas stuffed with doggy accessories.

'Hi, I'm Hal,' said a chap in a shining-white, high-collared, Doctor Kildare outfit. 'How can I help?'

I explained who I was and why I was there. Hal couldn't have been more helpful.

'Murray, let's say you're a typical customer. I'll take you through the deal. Here's how it goes.

'You come in and I leave you alone to look around for a while and then, like I did with you, I say "Hi, I'm Hal. How can I help?" So you say you want to buy a puppy. "You're in the right place, then," I say, "and who am I talking to?" "My name's Murray Walker," you say. "Well, Murray, tell me about yourself and your family so that I can make sure you get the right puppy." We're very good at that here in the States, Murray, and you'd say something like, "Well, Hal, I work for Westinghouse as a Development Engineer, I'm married to Margie and I have two wonderful kids, Pete who is seven and Mary-Lou who is five. Pete's a spunky little rascal but we're a bit worried about Mary-Lou 'cause she's very shy." "That sounds like a great family situation you have there, Murray, and we have just the fella to make it complete. What you need is a loveable puppy for Mary-Lou to bond to, but one that's lively enough to stand up to Pete. So, hey, look at this cute little cocker spaniel" – but, Murray, it could just as well be the Irish wolfhound in the next cage. Then I get the puppy out of the cage and give it to you to cuddle. "Say, Murray, I can see that you're really taking a shine to each other. So you know what I'm gonna do? I'm going to put the two of you in the Puppy Loving Parlour!"'

'You *what*, Hal?' I said.

Hal took me to the end of the shop where there was a series of 10ft by 10ft areas with waist-high plywood walls and little doors, and said, 'I put them in one of these and say, "OK, folks, I'm gonna leave you to get acquainted", and after about 10 minutes I go back. You're on the floor and the puppy's so goddamn pleased to be out of the cage he's licking your face like crazy. "It loves me! It loves me!" you say, "I must have it!" "Good choice, Murray! Now where are you going to keep the little critter?" "Don't know," you say, "under the stairs I guess." "Uh huh. In that case, Murray, you'll be needing a mattress for it. Would you like one of these lumpy straw-filled sacks or one of our luxurious, supercomfort, two-inch foam resting pads which are specially made for dogs? The puppy's had its health shots but what about exercise? You know of course that it is a State Ordinance that dogs have to wear a collar and be on a lead? We have a variety of both at all prices. Plus, naturally, water bowls, puppy foods, grown dog foods, medicines, nail clippers, grooming kits, balls, rubber bones, training books, whistles and winter coats. We even have rubber bootees for wet-weather walkies. In fact anything you might need for your new friend, Murray. I guess the kids'd want the best wouldn't they?"

'In short, Murray,' continued Hal, 'I haven't done my job properly if I haven't sold the customer at least the dog's value in accessories by the time he leaves the shop. It's a great business!'

'Hal,' I said, 'I'm truly grateful. This has been a revelation.'

And I wasn't kidding. But not for us, I thought, and I made my farewell to Mars and flew home.

I was telling this story about American salesmanship to a couple of General Motors people some time later and when I'd finished one turned to the other and said, 'It's the optional extras deal isn't it? Sell 'em the basic car, then the alloy wheels, the leather upholstery and all the other things that really make the money!'

After endless sparring and transatlantic meetings, Masius and US agency D'Arcy MacManus decided they liked and respected each other enough seriously to consider joining together. Merging any two organizations with different historics, personalities and attitudes is seldom easy because it almost invariably involves one side losing its identity and people losing their jobs. With our two organizations, of like size but with very different accounts and from countries separated by a common language, it seemed particularly difficult – the only thing we really had in common was that we were both in the advertising business.

So why did we do it? Because in business if you don't go forward you go backward. Inevitably there would be battles for power at the top but Jack Wynne-Williams, no longer a totally fit man, was determined to make it work. Fortunately for all of us the business continued to prosper and each year's billing continued to exceed the last so there were no financial pressures. For the proud Masius element, though, the end was in sight.

In 1973 we landed yet another really big one – the British Rail InterCity account. At the time British Rail was very much a nationalized industry, having been put together, for largely idealistic reasons, from the great traditional railway companies like Great Western, Southern, London and North Eastern and London Midland and Scottish. With lack of investment and low public esteem things had not gone swimmingly and the successful businessman Peter Parker, later knighted for his work, had been appointed to breathe some entrepreneurial life into the system. One of the many things he turned his attention to was the advertising and we won the day with some bright and breezy proposals based on the concept '*Have a good trip – it's easy*' (which was not inconceivable then) and a catchy Cliff Adams jingle.

As the Account Director it was obviously fundamental that I should have some personal experience of the entire system, so I got one of the BR people to plot an itinerary for me that would put me on to every type of train and route of the entire network. Together we then started on a seemingly endless trip. From Euston we took the main line to Crewe, where we joined the night sleeper to Inverness. Breakfast at the Station Hotel and back to the same platform to catch a local train which chuntered through the Highlands to Aberdeen;

then on to something more impressive to Edinburgh by way of Dundee. Across to Glasgow to sample the service between Scotland's two largest cities, and immediately back again to catch a train to Newcastle. Then Leeds for an overnight stop at the Queen's Hotel and off early the next day to Leicester, London and a swoop down to Exeter. The furthest south we got was Cambourne, just in time to rush across a bridge for a train to Bristol and back to London. If you've ever flown to Australia with just one stop you'll know the feeling I had when I got home – only multiplied several times over.

In my time on the British Rail account, which I enjoyed enormously, I found its people to be the salt of the earth. Many of them came from generations of railwaymen, thought of little else than the railways and worked very hard indeed in extremely difficult circumstances to give the best service they could. Underfunding and trying to get different systems to meld together seemed to be their main problem, although I did once have one of them say to me in all seriousness, 'We could run a damned good railway, Murray, if it wasn't for the bloody passengers!'

Working on the account mainly involved meetings at the tired, faded and run-down British Rail headquarters at Marylebone House, which had started life as the Marylebone Station Hotel and which, after massive expenditure on restoration and conversion, is now the superb Landmark Hotel at which I have often stayed. The advertising didn't work miracles and was never likely to but it was fairly successful and, in conjunction with the client's considerable efforts, InterCity's image improved despite the fact that almost anything we did was greeted with public scepticism and suspicion.

Most of the money went into TV advertising to promote the '*Have a good trip – it's easy!*' theme and I can hum the jingle to this day. One of the commercials featured a frock-coated maitre d'hotel, played by Frank Thornton (Captain Peacock from *Are you being served?*), showing a couple to their dinner table in a grand restaurant where they were served with an appetizing-looking meal at a table set with fine china and cutlery. The camera then pulled back to reveal that they were all in an InterCity dining car and although the whole thing was shot in an actual carriage, using only BR settings and food, the result looked so good that it was greeted with howls of derision.

Correcting adverse images takes a very long time and if the product does not live up to the promise the advertising can do more harm than good. But in general we kept ahead. We also gained the Eastern Region's business, as a result of which I not only had a very personal tour of the magnificent Railway Museum at York but was able to add another gem to the list of prestigious seats on which I have sat – Queen Victoria's personal loo in her Royal Train!

We had the British Rail account for some eight years before it moved on to another agency when the management changed – one of the hazards of agency life. It is often virtually impossible to assess to what extent the advertising is helping your business, hence Lord Leverhulme of Sunlight Soap's famous remark, 'I know I waste 50% of the money I spend on advertising but unfortunately I don't know which 50%!'

So when a new broom arrives at a company a very good way to demonstrate decisiveness and leadership is to fire the agency. It makes a big impact and probably does not do much damage. But during our tenure of BR we had suffered what I have always believed to be the agency's mortal blow when, in 1979, Jack Wynne-Williams died. With his ebullient personality, cheerful gregariousness and the business load he carried he had lived life hard both at work and play and in the end it sadly caught up with him. Jack survived open-heart surgery but not very long afterwards, having willed himself to stay alive until the merger deal was done, he passed away.

Now the agency that was so much a part of us all started to change. It was 1979, I was 56 years old, had been with Masius for 20 years, had got as far as I was going to and was doing more and more broadcasting as the BBC had just decided to cover all the Formula 1 Grands Prix as well as the other motor sport I was doing. Looking back I simply do not know how I was managing to do it all but, as a matter of pride, I was reluctant to leave the agency before my official retirement age of 60. I loved the life I was leading, had a wonderfully tolerant and understanding wife and soldiered happily on. Maybe I should have stopped though, for now I got the bed of nails.

It was the Co-op, one of the agency's most important accounts and certainly its most demanding. The size, complexity and scope of the organization was difficult to grasp, its politics were daunting and when I took the account over I felt confused and rudderless. There were the Co-operative Retail Society (CRS), the Co-operative Wholesale Society (CWS), hundreds of self-governing individual societies with anything from one to dozens of shops, the Co-operative Farms, the massive milk business, the funerals service that buried one-third of Britain's dead every year, the very bright and successful Co-op Bank, food factories, the tea business, a very big travel section, a car sales organization, eyecare and shoe shops – and those are just the parts I can remember. It was a massive sprawl loosely integrated by a common ideology that was like a handful of fine sand – very difficult to get hold of and it interfered with the machinery.

Our actual client was the Co-operative Wholesale Society, with its headquarters at New Century House in Balloon Street, Manchester, which was split into two divisions, Foods and Non-Foods. The Foods section was managed by a clever and astute, but abrasive, chap called Barrie Silverman, whilst the Non-Foods part was the responsibility of a bluff, cheerful, no-nonsense Lancastrian named Ken Goodwin. Ken was very much my cup of tea but Barrie wasn't and to say that the two of them didn't get on with each other would be understating things.

My job was to try to get the whole CWS bit to pull together and to work with the societies in advertising terms and it was a job for my lifetime and beyond because it was unachievable and a nightmare. Our efforts were aimed at creating a warm, friendly and desirable image for the Co-op as a whole, allied to aggressive and punchy price-oriented press and TV advertising for special offers. I could write an entire book on the hassles we had about how to position the Co-op, agreeing the merchandise that was to be included and the problems of getting all the societies to take part in promotions.

As the years rolled by and times and attitudes changed the Co-op's enormous strength gradually faded in spite of everyone's well-intentioned efforts. The advent and growth of supermarkets was making the Co-op look ponderous, old-fashioned and irrelevant. The need for it was no longer there, the public was voting with its feet and the whole thing was withering as society after society closed down. Even those that were left seemed to be ashamed of their parentage and started masking their Co-op roots by giving their supermarkets names like 'Beehive' and 'Pioneer'. It is good to be able to say that, having hit bottom, the Co-op now seems to be looking up a bit, but my time on the account was nearing its end.

The advertising was certainly memorable. The original concept, which ran for years, was '*It's all at the Co-op now!*' and that was replaced by '*Your caring, sharing Co-op!*' a claim which was once contested with me by a very senior Co-op chap at a sales conference. 'You're wrong there, Murray. We don't bloody care and we don't bloody share!' Charming! The thing to remember if you have anything to do with the shops business is that 'retail is detail' and there is an enormous amount of it. Fortunately for my sanity I had an absolutely superb Account Director on the Foods business, Francois Neckar, who dealt with the fractious Silverman brilliantly, and two others, Richard Fishlock and Colin Kelly, who similarly had a strong grip on the Non-Foods side. Which was just as well for I had other accounts to look after, in the form of the shops owned and run by Eastern Electricity and a long-running attempt to get the business of a retail chain in Italy called La Rinascente.

In our St James's Square building I had a quite magnificent office but now, in 1982, I had very little to do in it. For only the second time in my life I had a job that was giving me no pleasure or sense of achievement and in which I felt I was neither needed nor pulling my weight. I was bored rigid, felt I was wasting valuable time and wanted to get on with something else worth doing. I was yesterday's man – no shame in that, it happens to all of us eventually. There is only room for one at the top, and while I knew it wasn't to be me at Masius I didn't mind as I genuinely did not want it anyway. I wanted to move on and develop my broadcasting career, which was getting to be more than I could cope with as well as the agency. I only had some six months to go before I was 60 and would have to retire.

So I went to see my friend Dave Lee, with whom I had progressed through the agency, who now occupied Jack Wynne-Williams' position and sat in what had been Mike Masius' office when I had joined 23 years before.

'I'm off, Dave,' I said.

'Oh yes? Going to Manchester are you?'

'No, no. I've reached my sell-by date. I'm leaving.'

Dave understood and there was no real discussion. There didn't need to be. Masius gave me a wonderful sendoff and my full pension, I sold my shares for rather more than I had paid for them and, without regret, set off into the sunset to start my new life as a self-employed freelance.

CHAPTER SIX

My Second Life

I know well enough *how* I started commentating but for the life of me I cannot remember *why*. It's not the sort of thing you just drift into but I certainly don't remember feeling that my life would be incomplete until I had a microphone in my hands. I had only been at Dunlop for a year or so; I was commuting to Enfield at weekends, was very involved in racing the AJS at Brands Hatch and doing a lot of one- and six-day trials riding, so I couldn't have been at a loose end. But the urge must have been there or I wouldn't have leapt at the Shelsley Walsh opportunity or been so eager to take up the BBC's subsequent offer of an audition at Goodwood.

The audition went well and before I knew it I was in the elevated rabbit hutch of a commentary box at Silverstone's Stowe Corner as No. 2 to Max Robertson at the British Grand Prix on 14 May 1949. It wasn't Formula 1 then, for that didn't begin until 1950, and it was radio, not television, but that was very much the medium in those days. Television coverage of sport was in its infancy, although my first TV commentary, on a motor-cycle hill climb at Knatts Valley in Kent, was also as early as 1949. The cameras were the size of a shed and a very youthful Peter Dimmock, who went on to become one of the BBC's greats, was the producer.

I still have recorded extracts of that British GP at Silverstone and I doubt that either Max Robertson or I would get the job today. Max commentated on tennis for BBC Radio and later went on to present its antiques programme *Going for a song*. Motor racing was not his forté and on radio he sounds ill at ease while I sound plummy and stilted. Switzerland's Baron Toulo de Graffenried won the race in a Maserati CLT and I had my first unnerving wake-up call when John Bolster lost his ERA in a big way, came barrelling down the Hangar Straight end-over-end and deposited himself in a bleeding mess at the foot of my box. *Blimey,* I thought, *they didn't tell me what to say about something like this*, and accurately, but understatedly, I said, 'Bolster's gone off!'

I thought he was dead but he recovered, later to become the BBC's outspoken car-racing pit-lane commentator. I must have rung some sort of a bell at the Beeb though, because only 12 days later I was in the Isle of Man to commentate from the TT grandstand on the British Racing Drivers' Club's Empire Trophy and Manx Cup car races. A youngster called Stirling Moss was sensational, creating a record lap and leading by a country mile in his 998cc Cooper-JAP until it broke down. I'd be seeing much more of him in the years to come. There weren't nearly as many race meetings then, so I must have thought all my Christmasses had come together when, only a week or so after the BRDC meeting, BBC Radio producer Geoffrey Peck contacted me again.

'We liked your stuff on the British Grand Prix and the Empire Trophy. We need an extra chap in the Isle of Man for the TT motor-cycle races. Can you help us out? We know that they're very different from the cars you've done well but would you like to have a go at them as part of your father's team?'

Motor bikes were, and still are, very much my first love so I didn't hesitate to accept. I don't know how I got the time off from Dunlop but it was back again in early June to Mona's Isle and the Castle Mona Hotel on Douglas Promenade, where I had stayed so many times in my youth, for the first of some 26 years of magical visits. I loved the place, and TT week had a charisma and atmosphere like no other motor-sport meeting in the world. Le Mans and the Indy 500 might come close, and I'm sure the Mille Miglia and the Targa Florio did too, but sadly both the latter are history and I never achieved my ambition to see them.

The Isle of Man is only about 30 miles long by 10 miles wide but it has some stunning scenery, excellent roads and its 37.73-mile TT circuit is unique. All public highway that is closed for the races, it twists and turns, rises and falls, climbs up and over 1400ft Snaefell, includes superb flat-out sections that are miles long and is the supreme challenge for motor-cycle racing. Every mile of the circuit has a story to tell. From 1907 to 1976 the best in the world raced there and it is still an unequalled motor-cycle racing festival, although no longer part of the World Championships.

I was lucky enough to see it at its best, when my father was racing there with such distinction and later as part of the BBC team. When I rode my motor bikes endlessly round the TT circuit to learn the course I used to revel in the fact that I was flying along the same road on which heroes like Alec Bennett, Jimmy Guthrie, Stanley Woods, my father and so many others had raced. So I was awestruck when I took up station at my 1949 commentary point for the 350cc Junior TT at the Ballacraine right-hander, 7.5 miles from the start at Douglas. My father was at the grandstand on the Glencrutchery Road overlooking the enormous scoreboard, the refuelling pits and Douglas cemetery; Alan Clark was at Kirkmichael Village, 14 miles out, where they blast through the narrow streets absolutely flat out; Richard North was at Ramsey, 9 miles further on and just before the start of the mountain climb, and Alan Dixon was at Creg ny Baa, the 35-mile point. There was no commentary box for me though – I just stood in the middle of the escape road clutching my clipboard, festooned with wires, harness and headphones and with microphone at the ready, eager to give it plenty. When Les Graham arrived at thunderbolt velocity on his works 7R AJS and overshot the corner he nearly disembowelled me with his clutch lever. But it was a great day and on Senior TT Friday it was that same Les Graham who broke down on the last lap, losing a commanding lead on his innovative AJS 'Porcupine' twin (so-called because of the cooling fins on the cylinder head), letting through Harold Daniell to score the last TT win for the old 'Garden Gate' Norton.

Whenever Norton won a TT, which was frequently in

those days, they had a wonderful party at the Castle Mona Hotel and that night's was a cracker. It was presided over by Gilbert Smith, who had been a storeman at the Bracebridge Street factory when my father was there and who had said to him that one day he'd be the Managing Director. And now he was. During some part of the evening I vividly remember trying to do 30 consecutive press-ups whilst holding a beer bottle in each hand. I got to 22.

Part of the uniqueness of the TT is that the meeting lasts for two weeks, with practice the first week and racing on three days of the second, leaving the other days clear in case of bad weather – usually mist on the mountain – which often makes racing impossible. It's depressing and demotivating to arrive at the Grandstand knowing that things are delayed indefinitely, and one year I spent every day of race week in the commentary box as on Monday, Wednesday and Friday the mist would not clear, so the races were held on the Tuesday, Thursday and Saturday. By the end of the last day I felt as though I had lived there all my life. The BBC transmitted a filmed pull-together of the whole TT week as part of *Grandstand* on Saturday afternoon, which meant a frantic gathering of all the Friday race material, getting it to Manchester for overnight editing, to be shown the next day. So when the Friday races were cancelled the producer (Alan Hart, later head of BBC1) phoned the boss of *Grandstand* (Paul Fox – now *Sir* Paul Fox), and the conversation went like this:

'Hello, Paul. The Senior TT has been postponed until tomorrow because of the lousy weather.'

'So?'

'Well, it means that we won't be able to get it into the programme.'

'It's in the *Radio Times*,' said Paul, and put the receiver down.

All hell broke loose. Despatch riders were hired, an aeroplane chartered, and as soon as Saturday's race was over the film was collected from the cameramen around the course and rushed to Ronaldsway airport. I had shot out of the commentary box as soon as the race finished and motored like Jehu to the airport and when Alan and I, plus the film, got into the little one-engined plane that was to take us to Croydon (then a grass-strip airport), there was impenetrable fog ahead.

'I know it's okay above the clouds,' said the intrepid pilot, 'and I'm prepared to take off but it's your responsibility.'

'Anything is better than the wrath of Paul Fox. Go!' said Alan.

The pilot was right, no problem when we got above the clouds and when we landed at Croydon there was a despatch rider waiting for us. The film was edited in treble-quick time and literally loaded into the projector as the studio presenter was making the on-air introduction. I did the commentary live on the film, which I hadn't even seen, and as far as I know there were no complaints from the public, who little knew how close a call it had been. And not a word of gratitude from Paul Fox either.

If you were a motor-cycle racing freak like me the TT was pure magic. You got up at 4am on practice days, went to the paddock, drank hot cocoa in the Cadbury tent and talked to the riders, watched them start one at a time as soon as it was light enough and then rode off through the side roads to see them in action. It was spine-chilling to stand at the bottom of Bray Hill or Barregarrow as they hurtled by in a blur of concentrated noise and action; to hear them approach and then blast past you flat out along the long Sulby Straight; to watch them sweep round the double left-hander on the Mountain at the 33rd milestone on their way to plummet from Kate's Cottage towards Creg ny Baa. Then there were the social functions, the horse trams on the promenade, walking round Douglas to chat with the teams while they prepared their bikes, often in little back-street garages and lock-ups, and the euphoric atmosphere of the prizegiving at the open-air Villa Marina. In Douglas the weather always seemed to be brilliant and if there was a lull there was the lure of the circuit itself, inviting you to blast round its unrestricted roads. They were wonderful times. Unless I'm very much mistaken, I commentated on some 188 TTs plus at least 50 Manx Grands Prix, which are held in September and are, in effect, the Amateur TT. I wouldn't have missed a second of any of them.

Over the years I did my TT commentary from several places, including a GPO telephone box at the Highlander, a pub about five miles from the start where the bikes would crest a rise at about 120mph, fly straight through the air towards me, land a yard or two from my feet and then peel off for the next corner while I shouted at them excitedly. That would never be allowed now. For years I stood on top of a roadmender's steel-wheeled mobile hut in a pub courtyard at Parliament Square in Ramsey and for years more on the pub verandah at Creg ny Baa amid the vast crowd looking up the long hill to Kate's Cottage. If I live to be 100 I shall never forget the thrilling noise of Bob McIntyre's four-cylinder Gilera and John Surtees' MV Four, in first and second places on the last lap of the 1957 Senior TT, as they wailed their way up through the gears towards Brandish Corner. 'Just listen to this!' I said and stopped talking – words were superfluous. That was the historic race in which the great Bob McIntyre became the first man to lap the island at over 100mph.

It is not unfair to say that of the five commentators only my father and I were knowledgeable and enthusiastic about the sport. One of the others was the suave and immaculate David Southwood, a BBC presenter whose speciality was a film review programme called *A Seat in the Circle.* David commentated from Creg ny Baa for some time and one year my father said, from the Grandstand:

'And now race leader Geoff Duke is due at Creg ny Baa within seconds, so over to David Southwood.'

'Perfect timing, Graham! As I look up the hill I can see Geoff, crouched over the tank of his Norton, hurtling round the bend at Kate's Cottage, racing down towards me. And now I can see the sun glinting on his famous helmet . . . Oh, it's a seagull!'

Thank you, David. We'll let you know.

In 1962 my father died at the tragically early age of 66. After his retirement from the editorship of *Motor Cycling* in 1954, when he started helping Lord Montagu at Beaulieu, he suffered a heart condition, which I have always blamed on a life of stress and too much smoking. One day in September 1962 he returned home early and said to my mother, 'I feel tired. I'm going to bed for a rest.' He died that evening and we will not see his like again. I took his place in the Grandstand at the Isle of Man and the other commentary positions but I would not aspire to filling his shoes. The motor-cycling world had lost a colossus and my mother and I were plunged into grief. I have never heard a harsh word said about him for he was a loving, kind, generous and considerate husband, a wonderful father and, in his sporting and business life, a much respected man with a great sense of humour who led from the front and was revered around the world for the warmth, passion and knowledge of his BBC commentaries.

The Isle of Man, which he loved so much, was, and remains, hallowed ground for me. The TT broadcasts were enormously demanding because the competitors started one at a time at intervals and were not seeded. The races were time trials, so you could have the leading riders separated by seconds on corrected time but minutes apart on the road. In 1951, for instance, Geoff Duke, the winner, was No. 1 and Bill Doran, who was second on his AJS 'Porcupine', was No. 68, so they started some 11 minutes apart. Before each race the five-man commentary team would meet to forecast the lap times of the next day's top riders and would then, with their own timekeepers, have to work out each rider's estimated arrival time at their commentary point on each of the seven laps. The producer and master commentator at the Grandstand had to keep on top of where everyone was and hand over to the other commentators round the course as the leading riders approached them. With retirements, changing weather and different speeds it took non-stop mental and arithmetical acrobatics to keep up with it all, quite apart from the commentary words, but it seldom went wrong and the entertainment results were outstanding.

Radio was the medium then and the BBC used to devote a couple of hours of its *Light Programme* to the TT every race day. The audience figures were huge. I know I am biased, but most of the magic that vibrated over the airwaves was because of my father. From his years of race-winning experience he knew every bump and turn of the TT circuit, he had an electrifying voice and delivery, he knew everybody and he had the priceless ability to generate excitement.

The 1950s and 60s were the TT's post-war golden years. At their beginning the British Nortons, Velocettes and AJSs were supreme in the larger capacity classes, with riders like Artie Bell, Geoff Duke, Harold Daniell, Les Graham, Freddie Frith, Bob Foster and sidecar ace Eric Oliver winning everything in the Isle of Man and on the Continent. When they retired or moved on their places were taken by riders of the calibre of John Surtees, Giacomo Agostini, Bob McIntyre, Phil Read, Jim Redman and the greatest of them all, Mike Hailwood. Tens of thousands flocked to see them, British prestige was high and, as a result of it, British motor-cycle sales boomed. All was not well, however. Continental manufacturers like Mondial, Benelli, NSU and MZ had dominated the 125 and 250cc categories since the races had recommenced after the war, but then, from 1952, the advanced four-cylinder bikes of Gilera and MV blew away the old-fashioned

British singles to gain supremacy in the 350 and 500cc classes.

The *coup de grâce* for the British industry came when a Honda fact-finding mission arrived from Japan in 1958. No one had ever heard of Honda and although the war had been over for some time the Japanese were far from popular. However, when they appeared in Douglas studiously photographing everything in sight – engines and gearboxes, frames and forks, brakes, tanks, the lot – there were those of us who thought it was time to turn the other cheek. Speaking slowly and loudly (the time-honoured British conversational approach to foreigners), the discussion would go something like this:

'Where are you from?'

'We from Ondamotocumpny.'

'Honda Motor Company? Oh yes, and what do you do?'

'Make motocycles.'

'Aha! And why are you here?'

'Next year we race TT.'

'Oh, with the Kamikaze Special I suppose? And will Harry Kari be riding for you? First to the bottom of Bray Hill the winner?'

Very funny we thought and with Japan's image as a nation of copyists we expected them to return with rather inferior replica Nortons. But when Honda turned up in 1959 with beautifully engineered, four-valve, double overhead camshaft, twin-cylinder 125s we stopped smirking, especially when they won the team prize first time out. The next year they came back with four-cylinder 250s which turned over at 16,000 revs and, on his Honda debut in 1961, Mike Hailwood won both the 125cc and 250cc races for them (as well as a record third TT win in one week on a 500cc Norton). Honda were followed by Suzuki, Yamaha and Kawasaki and soon Japan ruled the racing roost, as it still does today.

The TT lost favour because the Continental riders were unhappy that it took time to learn the uniquely long and demanding Mountain Circuit. They also regarded it as excessively dangerous and its demands rapidly wore out delicate two-stroke engines. What's more, they had to spend two weeks in the Isle of Man: in that fortnight they could ride in two far shorter Continental meetings, wear out their bikes less and earn far more money. When even British stars like Barry Sheene and Phil Read, a multiple winner, shunned the TT its World Championship status was lost and these days it is no more than a glorified national meeting, albeit a tremendously popular venue and a wonderful motor-cycle event. It's very sad but, I suppose, inevitable.

I console myself with the knowledge that, having commentated on well over 200 Isle of Man races, I saw the best of its stars when they were at their prime. My top 10 solo riders (for the Sidecar TT was a stunning spectacle too) of my TT years were, in no particular order, Mike Hailwood, Geoff Duke, Giacomo Agostini, John Surtees, Bob McIntyre, Jim Redman, Phil Read, Carlo Ubbiali, Luigi Taveri and Tarquinio Provini. Speaking as a patriot, the fact that four of them are foreigners is a real tribute to their skill. Any selection is bound to be controversial and I do not expect mine to be any different so, apart from saying that in my opinion Mike Hailwood was the greatest of all time, I will not try to argue a logical case for my choice. It is, though, obviously affected by personal feelings and prejudices.

I had a very close involvement with Mike for many years, just as I was to have with Nigel Mansell and Damon Hill in my later Formula 1 career. I was at Oulton Park on 27 April 1957 for the 17-year-old's first race when he rode craggy Bill Webster's MV to 7th place in the 125cc event. I watched, marvelled and commentated on his meteoric rise to stardom in which, in only his second year of racing, he won three of the four British championships in 1958 and then, the following year, the whole lot: his first TT win in 1961 and his first of nine World Championships the same year. I commentated on every one of his 12 TT victories for Norton, Honda and MV as well as countless short circuit wins until his first 'retirement' from motor-cycle racing in 1967. I also wrote a book with him and he was a very dear friend. Mike was a natural-born genius in the saddle, a hell-raiser out of it, a modest and easy-going man completely free of pretentiousness and great fun to be with. But, rather like me, he would never have made it had it not been for his father.

Stan Hailwood was a self-made multi-millionaire (he built the Kings of Oxford chain of motor-cycle dealerships); he was astute and quick witted, could be absolutely charming, was a brilliant publicist and a demanding, aggressive and ruthlessly ambitious man. As an ex-racer himself, he quickly realized what a one-off he had in Mike and poured money and resources into developing his son's talent. Bikes, mechanics, transporters, the best tuners of the day, specialized workshops, factory support – Mike lacked nothing and the 'Ecurie

Sportive,' as Stan named it, was much resented by a lot of his less-well-off rivals. But although he undoubtedly owed his success to Stan's money and support, it was down to Mike once he was on the bike and there was just no one to touch him. When there was a race at Silverstone Stan used to invite my father and I to stay at his magnificent home at Nettlebed, near Oxford. It was great but I never had any illusions about why he did it – it was to get the BBC commentary team on Mike's side as much as possible.

On one occasion when I arrived there Stan said to me, 'Mike came off the 500 Norton heavily at Stowe Corner in practice today, Murray.'

'Is he okay, Stan?'

'Well, I'm worried because he's done his leg a bit of no good but he's insisting on riding tomorrow. Why don't you go and see him?'

So I went up to his room and there he was half-lying on his bed with his leg heavily bandaged, playing his clarinet (at which he was very good).

'Hi, Mike. Sorry to hear about the fall but what's this about riding tomorrow?'

'It's not too bad, Murray, and anyway the old man says I've got to so I suppose I will.'

Two contrasting stories, then, and I know which one was right. The next day, with a pusher to get him going, Mike started from the back of the grid against a class field and won the race. He was very much my hero and always will be. Eleven years after his retirement he made an amazing come-back to win two more TTs in 1978 and 79, only to be killed less than two years later in a road crash for which he was totally blameless. Those that the gods love they take early, and they took Mike far too soon. I will always remember him with great warmth and affection, and not only for his uncanny skill as a rider or being the man who won the 1967 Senior TT, the most exciting race I have ever seen.

In all those great years at the TT there are two in particular that stand out for me. The first was 1957, the Jubilee year of that glorious series of races that began in 1907. Although it was the start of the decline of the TT it was also a landmark in terms of works support and technical profusion. In the 125 and 250cc races there were Italian MVs, Guzzis and Mondials, plus NSUs from Germany and Jawas and CZs from Czechoslovakia. The 350cc Junior race had four-cylinder MVs and Gileras, the superb horizontal, single-cylinder Guzzis and the British Nortons, AJSs, Velocettes and BSAs. But it was, as ever, Friday's Senior TT that drew the crowds and the most impressive bikes.

I was at Creg ny Baa and I sat in my commentary position on the pub verandah, surrounded by an eager crowd of knowledgeable enthusiasts who were no less excited than I was. We were about to see the best in the world riding the all-conquering Gilera fours and their four-cylinder MV rivals; the incredible eight-cylinder Guzzi; the sturdy BMW Boxer twin; the British mainstay of the entry, the ageing but still quick Norton, and Matchless, BSA and AJS singles. All would be slugging it out on the most demanding circuit in the world. And the historic race more than lived up to our expectations.

With the great Geoff Duke out through injury, it was dominated by his Gilera team-mate Bob McIntyre, who defeated John Surtees' MV. At the end of the year the rot started when Gilera and Guzzi withdrew from racing but, sad as that was, there were still very great times to come with the advent of the Japanese manufacturers, whose four-stroke and two-stroke machines became ever more complicated, technically advanced and astonishingly fast.

The TT always seemed to rise to the occasion and the 1967 Golden Jubilee Senior race was truly an unforgettable race of the Titans. Just consider the scenario: there was the 27-year-old Mike Hailwood, Master of the Isle of Man and a racing phenomenon, and his great Italian rival Giacomo Agostini, also the son of a millionaire, whose swarthy film-star looks, cheerful personality and riding brilliance made him almost as popular with the crowds as his English rival. This was to be Hailwood's last event on the magical island before retiring when Honda withdrew from racing at the end of the year. He had won 11 TTs, including that Wednesday's 350cc event – at record speed and with an incredible record lap faster than the 500cc record – and five of the last six Senior events, and this despite the indifferent handling of the ferociously powerful Honda. Famed for his ability to learn courses quickly, Agostini had confounded everyone with his speed on the island when he first competed in 1965. Now he was the reigning 500cc World Champion on the three-cylinder MV which, ironically, had been developed by Hailwood in his years of unparalleled success with the Italian concern. The MV was as quick as the Honda but it handled immeasurably better and

Ago was very nearly the equal of Hailwood. It was his 25th birthday and a victory over Mike on the master's home ground would be the best possible present he could give himself – better even than a World Championship.

I was at the nerve centre of the BBC's coverage of the TT, the main commentary box at the Grandstand, looking straight down on the starting grid in ideal weather. In rather tatty old leathers, Hailwood, No. 4, bump-started the Honda into life and blasted off down steep Bray Hill at enormous velocity, followed 30 seconds later by No. 9, Agostini. The other 37 competitors might not have existed for all the attention they got: it was all focused on the two superstars. In the main Grandstand on the Glencrutchery Road everyone's eyes were fixed on the scoreboard indicator clocks that show where all the riders are on the 37.73-mile lap; stopwatches were working overtime to record the time gaps between the two rivals at the various checkpoints. When Ago raced past the Grandstand flat on the tank at the end of lap one and disappeared from view down Bray Hill he was a sensational 11.8 seconds ahead of Hailwood on corrected time, with a searing new lap record of 108.38mph from a standing start. Wrestling with the unruly Honda, Hailwood speeded up on lap two to close the gap to 8.6 seconds (with another lap record of 108.77mph which was to stand for eight years) but then the tension became almost unbearable as they each came in for their refuelling stops at the end of lap three – half distance. Hailwood stopped first and he was now a mere two seconds behind Ago on corrected time. The stop was going to be crucial.

The frenzied crowd shouted '*Mike! Mike! Mike!*' and '*Ago!*

Ago! Ago!', but Hailwood was in trouble. The twistgrip on his right handlebar, which controlled the power, had worked loose. Never an engineer, he yelled to his crew for a hammer and pounded away at it, with me incandescent with excitement in the commentary box above him, but when he finally heaved the unwieldy machine into life it looked as though he was defeated. His stop, 48 seconds to Agostini's 37, meant he was now 10 seconds behind the Italian with three laps to go.

At the start of the fifth lap Ago led by an increased margin of 11.6 seconds but this was where Mike's grit, strength and experience paid off. At Ramsey, 23 miles out and the start of the Mountain climb, he was in the lead by a single second, but Ago got the news from his signalling station there and speeded up yet again to lead by 2.5 seconds at the Bungalow, 32 miles out. But then disaster – the MV's chain came off as Ago rounded Windy Corner. Amazingly, he coasted down and pushed in to his pit, but his race was over after an inspired ride. No more inspired than Hailwood's though, on a bike that only he could have mastered and which was not worthy of his talent. It was a fantastic race made all the more so by the unique time-trial nature of the TT – and I was like a limp rag at the end of it.

At that time I was involved with the production of long-playing *Sound Stories* records of the TT races, with all the actual sound effects as they were made, and I sometimes get out the one of that fabulous race and play it. It never ceases to stir me. I'm pleased to report that Mike and Ago partied together in the evening – a very happy ending to a memorable day. Hailwood went on to race cars and Agostini to dominate the TT and World Championship races until he retired from motor-cycle racing in 1977, but it was the end of an era.

The TT and the Manx Grand Prix were a long way from being my only broadcasting commitments though: with my father or alone, for the BBC or for circuit PA, I worked over the years at nearly 20 other circuits and it was hectic fitting it all in around my regular job. There were occasional trips to Holland for the superb Dutch TT at Assen; to Northern Ireland for the North West 200 at Portrush and the Ulster Grand Prix at Dundrod; regular commentaries at Brands Hatch, Scarborough, Silverstone, Thruxton, Snetterton, Oulton Park, Cadwell, Blandford (another telephone box job), Boreham, Anstey, Kirkcaldy, Crystal Palace, Mallory Park, Aberdare and Ibsley – and those are just the ones I can remember. A wonderful apprenticeship it was too. Whenever anyone asks me how to get started in commentating I always tell them to try to do the public address at a race meeting: it is like being a cub reporter on a local newspaper. You learn to be on time, how to interview people, what the rules are, who the competitors are, what their strengths and weaknesses are; you learn about the cars or bikes, the history of the sport and how to string it all together in an informative and entertaining fashion. In short you learn by experience in a situation where it is not the end of the world if you make a mistake. Not that I have been immune from doing that from time to time!

I was, of course, exceptionally lucky in being able to serve a long apprenticeship as No. 2 to my father, before taking over his position as the BBC's top motor-cycle racing commentator after his death. I vividly remember our joint BBC radio commentary on the 1959 Thruxton 500-mile race for production machines. Dad was in the elevated commentary box and I was in the pit lane as roving reporter with a 30lb radio pack on my back for a race that was to last nearly 7.5 hours.

'Here comes McIntyre into the pits and Murray Walker is down there.'

Murray was and reported on the stop. Minutes later:

'And here's Tony Godfrey! What's the problem, Murray?'

Needless to say, Godfrey's pit was at the other end of the pit lane from McIntyre's but Murray was there and told it like it was. My old man, looking down on my exertions from above, had me sweating up and down the pit lane for the whole race. When it finished I jumped straight on to a charter flight to Paris, where I was met by the BBC's Ronnie Noble in a Renault Dauphine and driven to Le Mans to commentate on the closing hours of the 24-hour car race. We got there at about one in the morning and I was talking until the end at 4pm. It was worth the effort though, for the race was won by Carroll Shelby and Roy Salvadori in an Aston Martin with another British Aston in second place. The moment the race was over we drove back to Paris for me to make an in-vision report on television. So including Thruxton I was on the go non-stop for some 48 hours. I couldn't do that now.

The national motor-cycle meetings in Britain where I worked on the PA and for the BBC were very different to the Isle of Man. They were short, sharp races of maximum intensity, enormous fun and a very different atmosphere to today's high-pressure, big-money professionalism. The bike crowd are still a lot more friendly than those in Formula 1, but then it was even more so: people found the time to talk to one another even though the racing was just as fierce. Those were the days of John Surtees being almost unbeatable on his self-prepared Nortons and Derek Minter making his name as a superlative short-circuit rider; the time of Hailwood, McIntyre and all those other aces overlapping each other as they raced wheel-to-wheel, passing and re-passing and thrilling with every turn of their wheels; the time of the Race of the Year at Mallory Park on TT Sunday, with its then mammoth first prize of £1000, and the three-circuit Easter Holiday Transatlantic Trophy Series at Brands Hatch, Oulton Park and Mallory Park, where the best of Britain took on the best from America with often surprising results (it was, for instance, where Kevin Schwantz first made the headlines in the UK).

While Mike Hailwood was my all-time motor-cycle hero he was run a pretty close second by Geoff Duke who, like Mike, was a legend in his own lifetime. Geoff's bright and shining image was intensified by the fact that he burst into prominence just after the war when the nation was hungry to get back to normality. And he was a very special person. After being a member of the Army's Royal Signals motor-cycle display team he got a job with Norton at Bracebridge Street as a works trials rider, but he really wanted to be a racer. An accomplished engineer and extremely determined, he created a sensation by winning both the 1949 Senior Clubman's TT and Senior Manx Grand Prix, the latter at record speed.

Norton's race chief, the fabled Joe Craig, knew a winner

when he saw one and signed Geoff for the works race team. The next year, 1950, at a time when the TT was more important than all the Continental Grands Prix put together, Duke won the Senior TT first time out at record speed and with a record lap. The impact of this fresh-faced and modest newcomer vanquishing the established aces of the day was enormous, but to add to the glamour of the occasion he did it on a revolutionary works Norton (christened the 'Feather Bed' on account of its advanced frame construction) and wearing an innovative, slimline, one-piece leather suit made to his design by glove-maker Frank Thomas, from Geoff's home town of St Helen's.

Geoff became an instant hero and started a brilliant but unhappily short career which won him six TTs and six World Championships between 1950 and 1957 riding for Norton and Gilera, plus countless short-circuit victories. It's not as impressive a record as those of Hailwood, Agostini and John Surtees, perhaps, but unlike all of them Geoff won many of his international honours on a bike that was inferior to the opposition's. When he joined Gilera to ride their four-cylinder 350s and 500s he was supreme and it was very sad when the Italian concern withdrew from racing and effectively terminated his career.

I was working with Dunlop when Geoff was at Norton and used to see a lot of him at the Bracebridge Street factory and subsequently became friends with him when he made his name. With his first wife Pat he owned and ran the Arragon Hotel between the airport and Douglas in the Isle of Man and Elizabeth and I used to stay there. When he switched to cars, with great success in testing and his initial races with Aston Martin, it looked as though he was going to become another Nuvolari or Rosemeyer. But things conspired against him and he never did. He remains very much at the top of my mind as one of the very greatest.

After the withdrawal of the European manufacturers except MV in the late 1950s the TT, and motor-cycle racing as a whole for that matter, was saved by the Japanese, albeit at the expense of the British industry. For them success in the Isle of Man was essential for publicity and imagery, and in the furnace-heat of competition they produced a seemingly never-ending series of brilliant designs and employed the very best there were to ride a staggering variety of mechanical marvels in some superb races. The noises they made were fantastic: 50cc twin-cylinder bikes with nine-speed gearboxes whose engines revved at 20,000 rpm; 125, 250, 350 and 500cc machines with engines of two, three, four, five and six cylinders; they were all there and it was a golden age.

The competition was as good as it had ever been but in 1974 when all the works bikes had disappeared and when even Giacomo Agostini, who had reigned supreme in the major classes since Hailwood, had stopped going to the island, so did I. The place was still wonderful and so was the spectacle but it had lost the magic of the superstars on works bikes and by then I was heavily involved in motor-cycle scrambling and rallycross, touring cars and all sorts of other four-wheeled sports. But the Isle of Man remains the place I enjoyed more than any other and I look forward to returning there. I wasn't finished with bikes, though. When the TT lost its World Championship status in 1977 Britain's place in the series was taken by the newly instituted short-circuit British Grand Prix and I was in the commentary boxes at Silverstone and Donington Park until 1993. When the motor-cycle Grand Prix clashed with one of the Formula 1 races, usually the German event at Hockenheim, Simon Taylor took my place in F1 and I would do the bikes, which meant that I had to keep on top of everything that was happening in the bike world as well as the cars. To my intense irritation I was once accosted in the pit lane at Donington by a very stroppy chap who demanded, 'What the hell are you doing here? You're a car man.'

It was hard work but worth it because this was the era of my friend Barry Sheene, Kenny Roberts, Randy Mamola, Eddie Lawson, Freddie Spencer, Wayne Gardner, Kevin Schwantz, Wayne Rainey and the start of the spellbinding career of the very greatest of his time, Mick Doohan. This period also saw the very rapid development of the big bike two-stroke era, with Honda once again taking the lion's share of the honours over the years. What a fantastic company it is: in 2001 it celebrated an unprecedented 500th Grand Prix win in less than 40 years of competition. They were wonderful times and wonderful races, although I was obviously not as deeply into it as I had been before, simply because I wasn't there as often.

Was the racing as good in my years with the bikes as it is now? Yes, of course it was – but different. Where the competitors used to turn up and live in trucks and clapped-out vans, they now have luxurious motorhomes and the very best of everything; where the sport had limited coverage on radio and almost none in the press, it is now seen by the world on television and reported at length in the rest of the media; where the riders used to do most of their own mechanical work, they now just ride the bikes with a fleet of engineers, mechanics, fuel and tyre experts, computer technicians, fitness gurus and business managers looking after everything else. In place of the pudding-basin helmets and Mark VII goggles, they now wear sophisticated full-face helmets with anti-mist ventilation; those bulky and heavily padded black, two-piece leather suits with not a graphic on them have been superseded by multicoloured one-piece garments covered with sponsors' logos. And good luck to them – they are still supermen who put their lives on the line in wheel-to-wheel combat, riding to the very limits of safety and often beyond every time they get on the bike, and they still produce the most exciting and closely combated motor sport in the world. They are heroes every one as far as I am concerned, and after a lifetime of being so closely associated with the sport and 43 continuous years of talking about it, I do miss it. But you can't do everything in this life.

In my early days the BBC had delusions that I could become a general-purpose all-round commentator and presenter. Heaven knows how I would have found the time to do it all if they had been right. As it happened I didn't need to make the effort; 1950 was the beginning and end of any aspirations the Beeb may have had to turn me into a sort of minor Richard Dimbleby.

Their first attempt was the Military Tattoo at White City. It was the usual very impressive scene: military displays, the Royal Signals motor-cycle display team (of which Geoff Duke had recently been a member), marching bands, all that sort of stuff. I did my homework diligently, talked to anything that moved in my search for knowledge and even discovered the name of a regimental goat mascot before pouring out a torrent of explanatory words to accompany the pictures on the night. The next day I eagerly bought a copy of the *Evening Standard* to see if they had anything to say about my tour de force and there it was, on the TV review page written by the eminent Milton Schulman:

'Last night's TV was a very garrulous affair,' he wrote. 'It started with a wordy play and was followed by the White City Tattoo, which was dominated by a non-stop commentator. Anyone who can, as he did, overcome the combined efforts of the United States Army and Air Force bands deserves a Purple Heart [the American forces award for those wounded in action].

Never mind. On to the next thing – the Serpentine Regatta. Now, with hindsight, I think it would actually be quite hard to find anyone *less* suitable than me to commentate on rowing. It is quiet and calm; I am not. (Strangely enough I have always wanted to commentate on snooker and do it my way, but that's another story.) Anyway, I once again did the research and duly did my stuff. I can't pretend it was difficult but, every man to his taste and, fine sport as it is, rowing is not to mine. It was not the most successful of days, and it wasn't helped by my disparaging remarks about a lot of elderly chaps who were walking about in pink blazers and schoolboy caps and who, I later discovered, were senior members of Leander, the *crème de la crème* of rowing clubs.

But my final non-motor sport event was the best of all. I was sitting in my office at Masius one Thursday when the phone rang. It was the boss of *Grandstand*, the redoubtable Paul Fox.

'Doing anything on Saturday, Murray?'

'Nothing in particular, Paul. Why?'

'I want you to go to Bristol and commentate on the Great Britain versus The Commonwealth Weightlifting Championships. And don't say that you don't know anything about weightlifting because nor does anybody else and you've got until Saturday to find out.'

Paul is not the sort of chap you say no to so I put down the phone and thought, *Bloody hell, what do I do now?* But then inspiration.

'Annette,' I said to my secretary, 'can you bring me the telephone directory that covers the letter B?'

Something told me that there had to be a governing body of the sport and that it would be the 'British' something or other. Sure enough, it was the British Weightlifting Federation. So I got on the phone and asked who was in charge.

'Oscar State,' replied the voice. 'I'll put you through.'

'Mr State, you don't know me but my name is Murray Walker and I'm doing the BBC TV commentary at Bristol on Saturday. I wonder if there is a handbook [every sport has a handbook] and if there is whether I could have a copy?'

'I'll send one over,' said Oscar.

'Great! And tell me, how are you getting to Bristol?'

'I'm going on the train.'

'Well, I'd be delighted to give you a lift if you'd talk to me about weightlifting.'

'You're on. I never talk about anything else anyway.'

When the handbook arrived I had a quick look at it and phoned home.

'Have we got a broom handle?'

'Yes, of course we have,' said Elizabeth, 'but what on earth do you want one for?'

All was revealed when, supervised by her, I practised the Press, the Snatch and the Jerk, which are the three lifts in the sport. I mugged up the rules and regulations, listened to Oscar every inch of the way to Bristol and talked to all the contestants, most of whom were West Indian railwaymen from Reading and one of whom, Precious McKenzie, went on to do great things in his sport.

The actual event went off extremely well but that was the last of me commentating on anything without an engine. I've no regrets though: jacks-of-all-trades can easily end up masters of none and motor sport was where my heart was. There was plenty of that ahead of me.

CHAPTER SEVEN

The Rough Stuff

Motor-cycle racing is easy to understand. With the exception of the Isle of Man, everyone starts together and the first rider to go the distance wins the race. It happens on special road circuits, it makes sense and you can watch it in relative comfort and understand what is happening. However, motor-cycle trials, which held me enthralled in the late 1940s, are about as different from that as it is possible to be. They are a challenge for man and machine to overcome rough and demanding cross-country terrain, the bikes are highly specialized and useless for anything else, their riders are a breed apart and you have to be a masochist to spectate because trials riding is a winter sport that entails struggling to inaccessible places and then standing around, wet and cold, waiting for something to happen, without a clue about who's doing well and who isn't. But enthusiasm conquers all and there is a special kind of pleasure to be had from watching supremely talented people make the difficult look easy.

As a competitor at my level such talent was sadly lacking. Trials were about sweating and cursing while you resolutely wrestled, bullied, coaxed and cajoled your bike, against its better judgement, up muddy hills, along slippery tracks, over rocks and through rivers to negotiate tortuous marked sections non-stop without putting either foot on the ground. But, believe it or not, this was the most enormous fun. It got you out of the house, gave you a lot of exercise and fresh air, put you among good-hearted people in a highly competitive environment, showed you stunning countryside you would never have seen any other way and gave you a colossal sense of achievement if you got it right. I rode in trials on an alloy-engined 500T Norton and with its long-stroke engine it was ideal for the job, but in the winter of 1949, flushed with success after my awards at both the International and Scottish Six Days events, I stopped riding and started talking about it instead – but not without memories. Blasting along the Tregaron Pass in the Black Mountains of Wales against the cream of the world's riders, or slogging my way through the scenic majesty of Scotland around Fort William, Ben Nevis and the Lochs of Linnhe, Leven, Alsh and Ailort were experiences not to be forgotten in a hurry. On a trials bike you could get to places no car could reach and cover distances that no hiker could. There's just nothing else like it.

At the time I was working at Dunlop and BBC Birmingham had a popular Saturday evening programme called *Sport in the Midlands*. It was the usual pull-together of what had happened in the area that day and predictably centred on football, but one day the producer, Horace Saunders-Jacobs, called to ask whether I could do a report on the Manville Cup motor-cycle trial at Fillongley the following Saturday. Off I went to be greeted by an unlikely sight: an enormous BBC Humber Super Snipe limousine drew up and out of it – and into the glutinous mud – stepped a tall, elegant, grey-haired man with aquiline features and a military moustache, dressed in a navy-blue suit, long Crombie overcoat, trilby and shiny black shoes. At least they were until he got out of the car. This was Horace Saunders-Jacobs, for whom I was to do many programmes and who was about as suited to motor-cycle trials as I was to ballet dancing. Before long, and I suspect with no regrets, he retreated to the studio and left me to my own devices.

Recording equipment was in its infancy then, without the foolproof portable units there are now. The massive microphone we used was attached by cable to a turntable in the rear compartment of the Humber, so the drill was for me to get the car as close as I could to the observed section – which was never very close as it was large, ponderous and no Range Rover on mud – and then slip, slither and slide to a vantage point, mike in hand. The driver was also the engineer and when I told him I was ready to record he'd drop the turntable's pick-up needle on to a rotating blank wax disc into which it would cut sound grooves as I commentated. (Yes, really!) When the event was over we'd rush back to the studio in Birmingham and I would write and deliver a script into which the recorded extracts were played. It's obviously archaic compared with today's slick procedures, but it worked well.

With the Midlands being the centre for Britain's then very successful motor-cycle industry, to whom the publicity was important, the programmes were very popular and I certainly learned a lot doing them. Amongst many great events, they took us to the Victory and D K Mansell trials amid the glorious Shropshire scenery at Church Stretton, and the Cotswold Cup. Petrol rationing was still in force so the trials courses were only some 35–40 miles long but with the severity of the observed sections and the difficulty in getting to them they made a great day out. Legendary names like Hugh Viney, Bill Nicholson, Arthur Ratcliffe, Jim Alves, Johnny Brittain, Geoff Duke and Bob Ray were the solo stars on AJS, BSA, Matchless, Triumph, Royal Enfield, Norton and Ariel works specials, with the weight pared down to the minimum, super-low gear ratios and low compression engines for 'plonking' through the mud and winkling their way through the twisty sections. The 'combinations' – trials solos attached to high and narrow-bodied alloy sidecars to make a three-wheeler crewed by two people – were no less impressive. Harold Tozer (BSA), Frank Wilkins (Ariel), Arthur Humphries (Norton) and Frank Whittle (Panther), plus their gallant and athletic passengers, were the top men at battling their way through the sections on three wheels that I would have found difficult on two.

I knew and made friends with them all, had some wonderful times at the socializing that followed the event and felt very privileged to have been a part of it. Trials and what happened at them were far closer to the public then than they are now because far fewer people had cars then and they were much more aware of and affected by motor-cycle sport. Today's trials bikes are a far cry from then – while those of my day were heavy, single-cylinder four-strokes, those of today are featherweight two-strokes, and where the sport in the 1950s was essentially British it is now truly international and has developed almost into trick riding – in indoor arenas as well as outdoor venues. How things have moved on.

For some eight years after I began commentating I did a great deal of public address work at motor-cycle race meetings all over England, particularly Brands Hatch, but comparatively little national radio work for the BBC. The work I did for them in the Isle of Man and Northern Ireland, the English circuits and those trials events in the winter was very enjoyable and provided satisfying 'hobby' relaxation breaks while I beavered away at my job. But then, in 1957, came scrambling, which not only dramatically increased my broadcasting tempo but got me heavily involved with television for the first time. I think it also made a major contribution to my commentary style, because scrambling is the most exciting thing I've ever seen on two wheels and it demands commentary to match. Scrambling, or motocross as it was called on the Continent ('moto' for motor cycle and 'cross' for cross-country), is yet another sport that originated in Britain and at which we now fail to lead.

I don't know what it is about we British but we seem to be brilliant at inventing and developing new sports like cricket, soccer and rugby only to let our foreign rivals catch us and then beat us! It's the amateur spirit I suppose – '*it's not the winning, it's the taking part*' – but what's the point of taking part if you don't do everything you fairly can to win? To me we seem, as a nation, to lose the plot by failing to support our sports people properly. For instance, although Britain is the home of motor sport with more cash-rich Formula 1 teams than any other nation, sadly very little sponsorship comes from British companies. Yet they could benefit enormously from the global coverage and massive worldwide following that the sport now enjoys. For potential Nigel Mansells, struggling to progress from karting to Formula 1, British financial support is notoriously difficult to attract: embarrassingly, it is to impoverished South America that we have to look to find countries that wholeheartedly support their emerging motor-sport talent. From Argentina and Brazil the great Juan-Manuel Fangio, Froilan Gonzalez, Emerson Fittipaldi, Carlos Reutemann, Nelson Piquet and Ayrton Senna, all, to their eternal credit, found the funds to leave their far-off homelands, compete in Europe and make their names. And now Colombia's Juan-Pablo Montoya is a potential World Champion. But the British don't seem to like promoting their own: do other sports like rugby, tennis, athletics and skiing do any better? I'm no expert but my impression is that they do not.

Anyway back to scrambling, which is to motor cycles what steeplechasing is to horses. It started in Frimley, Surrey on 23 March 1923 with an event called the Southern Scott Scramble, a version of the historic Scott Trial in Yorkshire where chaps on bikes competed in a long-distance time trial over a crucifying cross-country course with observed sections. 'Let's do the same thing,' a bunch of Southern enthusiasts decided, 'but make it a cross-country race without the observed sections. Don't know what we'll call it but it'll be a right old scramble!' So began what is now a major worldwide sport that has its own World Championship and which annually creates sales of many thousands of very specialized bikes, most of which are Japanese. Some of us still call it scrambling, but its modern name is motocross.

Motocross is fast, furious, noisy and enormously spectacular, but not particularly dangerous and considerably less expensive to compete in than other top motor sports – which isn't to say it is cheap! As television developed in the post-war years you didn't need to be Einstein to work out that scrambling was ideal for the box: exciting, cheap and cheerful, there was lots of it readily available and it was eager to promote itself. In the mid-1950s the BBC dabbled with it but ITV were the first really to give it a go with an event at Bentley Springs in Yorkshire, masterminded and driven by my old friend Dennis Parkinson, a very talented road racer and five-time winner of the Manx Grand Prix. He's the one that coined that memorable catchphrase 'the undulating straight', which never sounds the same without his broad Yorkshire accent.

Dennis was a huge enthusiast and wanted to put scrambling on the map. As Secretary of the Wakefield Motor Cycle Club he badgered away at David Southwood (he of the infamous 'Oh, it's a seagull!' commentary at the TT), who was now Head of Sport of ABC TV, the Northern and Midlands contractor. The Bentley Springs event went down very well with the public and I was contracted to commentate on a whole series of future meetings. There was no reason why I shouldn't: I wasn't exclusively contracted to the BBC and was really keen to do it. It was something different, great fun and it was my breakthrough into television. I had done the odd thing on the box for the Beeb but now I was to do it on a very regular basis for ITV and it was terrific. For over 10 years until 1968 it was a major part of my life and one which raised my profile with the public, because scrambling became as much of a must for Saturday and Sunday sports viewers as all-in wrestling with Kent Walton, snooker with Whispering Ted Lowe and darts with Sid Waddell. The top riders of the day – Dave Curtis, Geoff Ward, Les Archer, Dave Bickers, Arthur Lampkin, Jeff Smith, Vic Eastwood and John Banks – became national sporting heroes as people talked about their thrilling battles, which undoubtedly had a major effect on the way I commentated. There was no way I could be dispassionate about the way they rode. Fast and exciting action demanded fast and exciting words to describe it and that suited me fine.

When you are doing radio commentary you are talking to people who cannot see what's going on. So for all-action sports like car and motor-cycle racing you have to maintain a virtually non-stop flow of words to inform and, hopefully, entertain the listener with a verbal picture of what you see happening. You can't say, 'Not much happening at the moment, folks. I'll give you a shout when something does,' and leave them in silence wondering what the hell is going on. But with television the viewers see what you see – often better, in fact, for the cameras follow the action and if you take your eyes from the monitor momentarily to look out of the window or at your notes you can easily miss something the viewer has seen. TV doesn't actually need the word-intensity of radio and can often be better without it, but by the time I got there my style was set. And anyway, the sport excites me and when I saw something that fired me I got caught up in it and let things rip. Australia's favourite son Clive James said I commentated as though my trousers were on fire and with noisy, exciting and dramatic sports like mine that wasn't surprising. I liked to tell it like I saw it and it didn't seem to do me any harm, for people used to say that what they liked best was my enthusiasm – which came from the heart by way of a lot of words. 'Pause, Murray, pause!' my BBC TV producer Jim Reside would say to me over the headphones during Formula 1 commentaries, and I would manfully try to give it a rest, but when you're bursting to tell people about all the riveting things that are happening before your very eyes it is very difficult for anyone with a temperament like mine to dry up.

The winter scrambles for ITV were pretty rugged. We did the long haul from London the night before an event as there were still no motorways between us and Yorkshire, where most of them occurred. On arrival, Elizabeth and I would find ourselves on the often wet, muddy and cold outskirts of somewhere like Thirsk, Clifton, Ripon, Leeds or Wakefield. I'd spend as much time as I could in the paddock talking to the riders, officials and anyone else who could add to my knowledge and then we'd disappear for the rest of the day into a rudimentary and often open-fronted commentary box containing just a TV monitor and a microphone.

Dennis Parkinson was my co-commentator and Elizabeth my hapless lap-scorer, charged with working out who was who and what lap they were on as the unrecognizable, mud-plastered apparitions blasted past us. The transmissions went on all afternoon and together we would embark on a voyage of discovery as the events unfolded around us. Rider identification was often virtually impossible and cynically I had the assurance of knowing that if I didn't know who was in the lead the viewers certainly wouldn't, but I wasn't worried for I hardly ever knew who I was talking to anyway. Only some of the ITV companies took the scrambles coverage and they seldom had the same transmission times. Just as we were getting to the climax of a race I'd hear, 'Say goodbye to Westward, Murray,' in my headphones from Andy Gullen, my producer; when I'd done so he'd be back again with, 'Welcome viewers in Tyne Tees, Murray, and Anglia has now left us.' It was a very moveable feast but we managed and built a big audience.

It was all exciting stuff and in the heat of the moment the words sometimes came out the wrong way. Arthur Lampkin, a very tough and determined Yorkshireman of few words but much action, was one of the top men riding a works BSA, very much the bike to have if you intended to win. The courses were fast, rough and bumpy so the rider stood on the footrests to let his knees absorb the shock, with his backside thumping the foam-rubber 'bum pad' on the rear mudguard. At a race near Leeds airport Arthur was hurtling over the bumps at enormous speed when his bike took off and his feet left the rests as he shot into the air, grimly hanging on with just his hands. As he landed with his legs splayed open his groin crunched down between the saddle and the bum pad and I shouted excitedly into the microphone, 'My god, he's trapped his knackers!' Except that, while the words were actually on the way from the brain to the mouth I said to myself, *They're not going to like this, Murray*. What I actually ended up saying was, 'My god, he's trapped his *knickers*!' Not a very good line I admit, but as a result of my verbal gymnastics I kept my job.

They were great days with ITV but frankly it wasn't top-quality stuff. Those pioneering early events were primarily low-cost time-fillers with mainly club riders plus a sprinkling of stars. The whole thing was a bit ragtime and went on far too long for everyone except the truly dedicated. I once did three successive weekends where the transmissions lasted for over five hours but they pulled the viewers, the appeal was very much there and the BBC was getting envious.

In those days BBC's *Grandstand* was the TV sport colossus, with ITV's *World of Sport*, fronted by Dickie Davis, a mere also-ran. As someone who spent so many happy and fulfilling years with BBC TV Sport I find it very sad that it is now a pale shadow of its former great self. For whatever reason sport as a whole became of less importance to the BBC hierarchy and it has lost sport after sport to ITV and the satellite channels. It can huff and puff as much as it likes about the great events it still covers but the fact is that its overall coverage of sport seems small beer in comparison to its glorious past. Although I did very well from my move to ITV, who in my opinion cover Formula 1 far better, I regret the BBC's fall from grace. It was, however, the Corporation's own fault: it had great people, superb facilities, unrivalled experience, historic dominance and enormous ability but it lost its grip. In my opinion, the men at the top got their priorities wrong and the Corporation has certainly suffered as a result. I hope I am wrong, but with the competition from today's proliferation of channels I cannot see a programme like *Grandstand* ever regaining its previous dominant position.

For me things came to a head in the winter of 1962, when the weather was so appalling that virtually all outdoor sport was cancelled – except scrambling. For weekend after weekend we would motor north to do yet another ITV event with national coverage into *World of Sport* on the Saturday followed by ABC TV's regional coverage for the North and Midlands on the Sunday. ITV got the ratings, the BBC didn't and they didn't like it. If you can't beat 'em, join 'em, so the Beeb did just that with an all-star event of its own on *Grandstand* from Naish Hill near Chippenham.

Brian Johnson, with whom I subsequently spent many a scrambling weekend, was the producer and Dave Bickers was the sensation who fired the nation. Dave, a laconic and dry-humoured chap from Coddenham in Suffolk who is now one of Britain's leading film stunt organizers, was riding his famous 250cc two-stroke Greeves against other established stars. At the start he stalled his engine and lost a full lap before he could get going but when he did he absolutely flew, full-on over the bumps with giant leaps and impossible speed through the twisties, hurtling past his rivals until, as the last lap started, he was second and gaining hand over fist on the leader. 'This is bloody marvellous!' shouted the new-to-it-all *Grandstand* director Alex Weeks over the wires from the gallery in London. 'Tell them to do another lap!' Well we couldn't do that, obviously, but the coverage was an enormous success, which increased the BBC's resolve to have scrambling on its screens. And this was exactly what the Competitions Committee at the Auto Cycle Union (ACU – the governing body of the sport) was after, for they rightly wanted to change the public perception of scrambling from that of ITV's localized mud bath 'club' meets into one of slick and impressive professional events featuring the stars.

There was nothing wrong with that, but it inflamed the feelings of the Northern clubs that had pioneered ITV's successful coverage and who saw the ACU Committee as a bunch of Southern upstarts who were trying to steal their thunder by kidnapping their creation. All political hell was let loose as the two sides locked horns amid outraged Northern declarations about mutiny and organizing pirate events. It was 'The North' and ITV against 'The South' and BBC TV. For a while I worked for both channels and on two occasions was on both at the same time, with my live commentary for BBC TV clashing with an event I'd recorded previously for ITV. There was no getting away from me! But it couldn't last and unsurprisingly the BBC and ACU bosses won the day. The Beeb was given a contract to run events on *Grandstand* while the Northern clubs and ITV were left fuming on the sidelines.

While all this was going on, BBC TV's Head of Sport Bryan

Cowgill, a dominant and forceful Lancastrian, caused me to appear before him at his office.

'We like this scrambling, Moorie, and we're going to have it. We want you to do it so I'm offering you a long-term contract. Now of course, Moorie, I know you work with ITV and I want to make it quite clear that this contract in no way prevents you from carrying on with them. Should you do so we'll continue to use you – for as long as it takes to find a replacement.'

It wasn't until the very last word that I realized that this was the end of my happy days with ITV. Until 1997 that is, when the boot would be very much 'on the other Schumacher' and ITV's crushing revenge would be very sweet as it took Formula 1 from the BBC. But that was some 35 years ahead of me.

The BBC did a superb job with scrambling. It is really a summer sport when the ground is hard, the grip is good and the spectators can watch in comfort but the winter scrambles had given it an entertainingly slapstick image of an exciting and spectacular high-speed mud bath on wheels. The *Grandstand* series still went for winter dates, with classes for 250cc and 500cc machines that earned the winners fame plus a superb silver model of a BBC TV outside broadcasts camera; but it also covered summer fixtures like the British Grand Prix and special international events featuring Great Britain versus Russia, Czechoslovakia, Belgium and the historic meeting at Beaulieu in 1963, which gave the viewers who regarded Britain as the best a very nasty jolt. In snow-covered conditions more suitable for reindeer than motor cycles the Swedish Husqvarna riders Torsten Hallman and Rolf Tibblin, both World Champions, made their rivals look like a bunch of amateurs. I was amazed at their skill and superiority and had the embarrassing job of commentating on them as they joined hands to ride across the finish line for a dead-heat victory.

The BBC events weren't only in the North as they had been with ITV; there were more than 20 different locations all over England and Wales and the Beeb put all their very considerable resources behind the sport, with Brian Johnson, one of their best outside broadcast producers, heading up a very talented team. The ACU appointed the tough and experienced Harold Taylor, known as 'The Colonel', to act as liaison man between the clubs, the riders and the BBC. Harold, an ex-sidecar trials rider of no mean talent, was a very forceful man with only one leg. He dotted about on his famous aluminium crutch, exploding in every direction as he masterminded the proceedings, and as he knew what was needed the whole thing worked extremely well. The *Grandstand* series gave the sport the impact, respectability and image it deserved and if multiple World and British Champions Jeff Smith and Dave Bickers were famous before, they now became TV superstars. Jeff worked for BSA, built his own bikes at the Small Heath competitions department and was a wonderful Brummie character. In my opinion he is the greatest all-round scrambler and trials rider that Britain ever produced and he deservedly did well financially.

Motocross took off in a big way on the Continent after the war, especially in France. With well-organized, well-promoted big-money meetings nearly every weekend during the summer, British riders flocked there and pioneers like Harold Lines, Brian Stonebridge and Basil Hall (whom I once raced against at Dunstable, failing dismally even to stay on the same planet) did very well indeed. But, as so very often happens, I regret to say, the rest of the world rapidly caught up to do it better. With more sponsorship, well laid out permanent courses, excellent facilities, aggressive promotion, great professionalism and massive public support they closed the gap and before long the Belgians, Swedes, East Germans and Czechs were as good as, and then better than, their British rivals.

One of the main international events was the Motocross des Nations team contest and I went to Sweden as early as 1953 to do the commentary for a film that my then employer, Dunlop, was producing. At that time Sweden was officially a teetotal country and you needed a permit to buy alcohol, but I've never seen so many drunks in my life. If you ban things people will always find a way to get them. After being met at Malmö off the boat from Copenhagen I was taken to an uproarious dinner party at Jönköping, where endless toasts were drunk to the English guest and during which one of my hosts quietly slid under the table, where he was completely ignored. I stayed at the home of a local carpenter at Skillingaryd and was amazed at his family's high standard of living, with a fine double-glazed and centrally heated wooden home, car, TV, washing machine and other things which were then unattainable to most people in post-war Britain. I'm glad to say that, in front of over 30,000 wildly enthusiastic spectators, Britain won the event with Les Archer (Norton), John

Draper (BSA) and Geoff Ward (AJS). In my time it continued to do so with monotonous regularity until, significantly, Russia was victorious in 1968.

Fitting it all in was my problem. Working at Masius during the week, and often the weekend too if there was a new business presentation on the go, meant that sometimes the scrambles trips didn't get the administrative pre-planning they deserved. Dashing out to work one day during the 1964 season I said to Elizabeth, 'We're at Hadleigh for *Grandstand* this weekend, can you get us into a hotel and phone me at the office?'

'I've found what sounds like a super place,' she said when she rang. 'It's called The Swan and it's at Lavenham.'

'Great! I've heard Jack Wynne-Williams talking about it. It's near where he lives in Suffolk and apparently it's a fourteenth-century place that had something to do with the wool trade.'

When we got there on the Friday evening it was superb and everything I'd imagined, but when I woke with a start on Saturday, the day of the event, it was with a ghastly feeling that we were in the wrong place. With a sense of mounting panic I woke Elizabeth and said, 'How far away is Hadleigh?'

'Relax, it's only a few miles.'

'Hadleigh, *Essex*? We're in *Suffolk*.'

'You didn't say anything about Essex!' she said.

Nor had I, for I didn't know that there are two Hadleighs in England. Fortunately for me they aren't all that far apart and I ought to have realized for Hadleigh, Suffolk isn't far from Manningtree where I had sailed to war in 1944. We were out

Same man, different clothes. Now with non-existent hairline, executive spectacles and a sharp suit, I was delighted with the fun-filled Dunlop Groundhog advertising.

With some heavy hitters at Beaulieu. Left to right: Dave Potter, Geoff Duke, Geoff Shepherd (Duckhams Oils), Mick Grant, John Surtees and Sammy Miller.

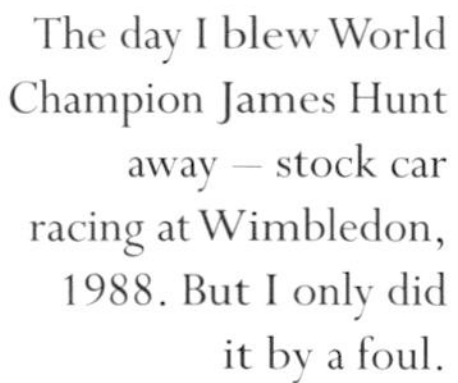

The day I blew World Champion James Hunt away – stock car racing at Wimbledon, 1988. But I only did it by a foul.

All friends together at champagne time. James Hunt, Simon Taylor and Barry Sheene have a laugh while I spray the crowd.

of the lovely Swan Hotel faster than light and into my Vauxhall Ventora – the one we at Masius had called 'The Lazy Fireball'. Fireball it certainly was on its trip from Lavenham to Hadleigh, Essex – but there was nothing lazy about it. We arrived in the BBC TV compound 15 minutes before we were due to go on the air.

All good things come to an end and that is what happened to the BBC *Grandstand* motocross series in the late 1960s. The spectacle was no less exciting but seeing the same people weekend after weekend dulled the public appetite, just as over-exposure was to do with snooker, all-in wrestling and darts. You can get too much of a good thing. The BBC carried on with coverage of the prestigious British Motocross Grand Prix, part of the World Championship series, for a long time and I was to have the very real pleasure of commentating on Honda riders Graham Noyce and the great Dave Thorpe as World Champions, but those exciting early glory days of regular scrambles transmissions were over and so was Britain's domination of the sport it had started in the 1920s.

My mother, God bless her, used to say to me, 'Always remember, dear, that, in life, when one door closes another opens,' and she was right. When the BBC decided that scrambling had run its course on the box they switched to the same sort of thing on four wheels – rallycross – which turned me from being primarily a motor-cycle sport commentator into mostly a car-sport commentator. It was such a gradual process that I hardly realized it was happening but I was very happy with it although, with motor bikes being closest to my heart and the riders and their followers being such a great bunch, I really did miss being a part of their scene when I had time to think about it. Thankfully this wasn't very often for my life certainly wasn't about to slow down as its direction changed.

CHAPTER EIGHT

Hell on Wheels

For me the mists of time have shrouded exactly how BBC TV came to replace its *Grandstand* coverage of two-wheeled motocross with four-wheeled rallycross, but it was an inspired decision because this spectacular sport might have been made for the box. It is rough, tough, full of high speed action and very simple. Men – and the very occasional woman – race each other in cars that bear a passing resemblance to those you see every day on the roads, on short circuits that are part cross-country and part tarmac.

Rallycross had its origins at Brands Hatch in 1963, when a series of special stages were organized by BBC TV for would-be competitors in the RAC Rally, which had been cancelled due to appalling weather. Although the resultant programme was a success nothing much came of it until 1967, when a similar event was held at the Lydden Hill circuit near Canterbury. This decided the BBC, in 1968, to cover a winter series of meetings there sponsored by Imperial Tobacco's Embassy cigarettes, the advertising for which was coincidentally handled by Masius, for whom I was then working. It's no exaggeration to say that TV made rallycross and, without wishing to sound big-headed, I like to think that I had a part in its success because, like motocross, my crash, bang, wallop commentary style fitted its all-action happenings perfectly.

Like motocross, rallycross is really a summer sport but its TV emphasis was during the winter. Where, for years, Elizabeth and I had motored north to work at those pioneering TV scrambles that made household names of Dave Bickers, Jeff Smith and Arthur Lampkin, we now had a much easier time after work on Fridays, driving south to the Chaucer Hotel in Canterbury weekend after weekend to be at Lydden the next morning. We did some 40 meetings there over the years. Motor cycles may have been replaced by cars but the winter conditions were much the same and the meetings were no less fun. There was a wonderfully matey atmosphere at Lydden despite, or maybe because of, its facilities – which were about as basic as they could be. The race cars and their support vehicles were jumbled together on a grassy hillside paddock alongside the boomerang-shaped, chalk-based track, which was about a mile long. You parked where you could and you took your own food. The trackside headquarters of the excellent Thames Estuary Automobile Club (dominated by the irascible but loveable Sid Offord) was a Portakabin and the toilets were ramshackle, all-friends-together affairs at the end of the paddock, with just a canvas screen between the men and women's sections. (On our side there was a handwritten notice saying, '*Gentlemen keep your voices down – the ladies can hear every word you say!*') With morning practice followed immediately by the afternoon racing there was non-stop activity. The buzz was great and it made superb TV.

There is no such thing as cheap motor sport – even children's karting costs a small fortune these days – but, again like motocross, rallycross was certainly a lot cheaper than most other forms of motor sport. The competitors were mostly associated with the motor trade, with access to know-how, parts and at least some sponsorship, and many of the much-modified cars they turned up with were extremely impressive. In the early days the ubiquitous Mini was the hot favourite: widely available, inexpensive, easy to modify and possessing superlative handling, it was ideal for the job and a lot of the top men used them until more ambitious and much more expensive machinery sent them to the back of the field. My very first event at Lydden was won by the personable Suffolk apple farmer Hugh Wheldon, who subsequently did consistently well in the *Grandstand* meetings. This caused a lot of political correctness problems with the BBC, whose highly cultured Director General had the same name. There were those – who had better be nameless – who unbelievably felt that I should not be talking about Hugh the competitor by name in case the Director General might not like to be associated with this brash, noisy and dirty sport. But when I asked them how they would like me to identify the top man without mentioning his name they backed off.

* * *

You name it in the way of production cars and they were there in rallycross: front-wheel drive, rear-wheel drive, four-wheel drive; normally aspirated and turbocharged; Ford Escorts by the factory load, rear-engined Hillman Imps, VW Beetles (one driven with great verve and success by Jenson Button's father John), Saabs, Ford Fiestas, Renault 5s, Golfs, Porsches, BMWs, Volvos, Skodas and DAFs. *Yes, DAFs!*

Rallycross is very definitely a man's sport but some of the men were even more manly than the rest. The Dutch De Rooy brothers from Eindhoven, for instance, must have been made from solid testosterone. Chunky Jan and Hunky Harry, who ran a trucking business in Holland, looked like packing cases on legs and drove seemingly ordinary household, four-wheel drive DAFs with their unique stepless transmission. (One lever: push forward to go and backward to reverse.) It was the car that silver-haired old ladies used to bumble along in the middle of the road – not the most suitable device for muck-or-nettles rallycross, you might think, but you'd be wrong for the ones that Jan and Harry drove had 240hp Ford BDA engines and went like stink. Saying that the De Rooy's on-track behaviour was forceful is a bit like saying Bernie Ecclestone is well off. They were animals and while they made great television as they tore round, through and over everyone else, their tactics were not always appreciated by their rivals – or the organizers for that matter, which led to their being banned for dangerous driving.

They weren't the only spectacular ones though. Craggy-faced John Taylor was an outspoken ex-National Hunt jockey who had switched to rallycross with great success in, of all things, a Volvo Amazon. By the time I came across him he drove a Ford Escort with a Cosworth BDA motor and was very much the man. And it proved to be some meeting.

'We've fixed for you to go round with John,' said BBC producer Ricky Tilling at Lydden one day, 'and we'll wire you up for commentary. Bit of a first. Should be good!'

Little did I know what was to come. There was no passenger seat in the Escort, so I had to sort of crouch alongside the forceful Taylor, hanging on to the roll bar with one hand while the other alternately stuffed the microphone inside my helmet and gripped the door pull as he proceeded to go berserk. A rocket-propelled, up-through-the-gears start led to a full lock, flat-out slide round greasy Chessons Drift, full chat along the bumpy Dover Slope, off the grass-covered infield and on to the tarmac, up Hairy Hill and then down again at breathtaking speed into Paddock Bend, which we exited in a colossal full-on drift to be faced with the dreaded Mabbs Bank, which would overturn a car as soon as look at it. Three laps of this we did and as we began the last I felt an agonizing pain in the side of my chest. As I babbled away about how riveting it all was I thought I was going to faint, so when I finally fell out of the car I tottered off to the circuit doctor.

'You've broken a rib,' he said matter-of-factly. 'Nothing I can do about it. It'll get better in time but it'll be a bit sore.'

Thanks, John! Commentating that day wasn't easy and I've never failed to remind him about it. Not that it gets me anywhere – he's a hard man! In 1973 he deservedly became the first-ever European Rallycross Champion, for by then the Continent had woken up to this exciting British innovation and had embraced it as successfully as it had embraced motocross.

Rallycross was full of great characters. Ron Douglas, super-extrovert Barry Lee and jovial Rod Chapman were but three of many. Rod drove an Escort and later a 3 litre, 250hp, four-wheel drive Ford Capri that was built by the works especially to exploit the very high viewing figures that rallycross was getting. Like all of them he made his living elsewhere – oddly from landfill – but seemed to do very well out of it, for he used to turn up at Lydden in an enormous motor home with bedroom, bathroom and swish living accommodation.

Excitable and mustachioed Martin Schanche was the most incredible of them all though. From Trondheim in Norway, he was not only a brilliant engineer who built amazing cars, like his turbocharged 420hp Ford Escort, but he was also an extrovert showman. When he won he would do a victory lap standing on the door sill with only one foot inside the car to operate the accelerator and if anything happened to offend him, which it frequently did, he would erupt into a flood of outraged protests in perfect but heavily accented English. His driving was sensational and it was Martin who motivated me to produce one of my more memorable 'Murrayisms'.

'The car in front is absolutely unique,' I shouted, as Schanche spectacularly led the way, 'except for the one behind it, which is identical!' How on earth, you may wonder, can anyone say anything as daft as that? Well, here's how. The heats at Lydden were very quick-fire. As four cars blasted off the line for their four-lap sprint the next four lined up ready to go as soon as those on the track finished their race. Sometimes, though, a car would drop out as they moved up to start, in which case the fastest car from the next batch would immediately take its place. Which is what John Welch did in his Schanche-built Escort, identical to Martin's, as someone dropped out of Schanche's batch ahead of him on the grid. So during the race as I was enthusing about Schanche in his, I thought, unique Escort, I produced the words, 'The car in front is absolutely unique' – but while I was actually saying them I realized to my horror that John Welch, who was meant to be in the next batch, was right behind the master. So I hastily added 'except for the one behind it, which is identical.' All very understandable under the circumstances don't you think?

John Welch was one of Britain's top drivers and famous for his frequent battles with Yorkshireman Tony Drummond, another give-no-quarter character. At Lydden in 1980 when Drummond was literally within yards of becoming British Champion he emerged from Chessons Drift side-by-side with Welch, both refusing to give way. As the inevitable high-speed collision happened and they plunged into the bank together I shouted, 'That's it! Bang! Bang! They're off!' Exciting stuff.

Lydden invariably made for great viewing, which usually involved something violent. The big entries often included people I had never heard of so I used to pitch up in the paddock early in the morning as soon as scrutineering began and talk to as many of them as I could with a mental check list. 'How old are you? What do you do for a living? Have you had any success? Is there anything special I ought to know about the car?' – that sort of thing. So one day there I am talking to a Mini driver called Stan Hastilow, who was new to me.

'Nice to meet you, Stan. Tell me how old are you?'

'I'm 32, Murray.'

'What do you do for a living, Stan?'

'I'm a computer programmer.'

'Oh, that's interesting,' I said, trying to make it sound as though it was. 'Any success with the racing?'

'Not really, Murray. It's just a hobby but I've had my moments and I get a lot of fun out of it.'

'Yes, of course. And tell me, Stan, is there anything special I ought to know about the car?'

'Glad you asked that, Murray, because if you look closely you'll see that it has a Perspex windscreen into which, using my skill and experience as a computer programmer, I've drilled a lot of holes of different diameters to a random pattern, as a result of which, wherever any mud lands, I've got a hole to look through.'

'Thank you, Stan, we'll let you know,' I said and set off for the next chap, little realizing how significant this information was to be. For later on, during what was a processional race with no drama, I suddenly realized that there was an opportunity to be grasped. Stan was in the lead.

'Here's something interesting! Race leader Stan Hastilow – who, by the way, is a 32-year-old computer programmer – is doing so well in these ghastly conditions because, using his skill and experience, he's drilled a large number of holes of different diameters to a random pattern in his Mini's Perspex windscreen, as a result of which wherever any mud lands there's a hole he can see through.' As I said it he shot off the circuit, hit a bank, took off, plunged through a hoarding and disappeared from view. And the commentary went '. . . there's a hole he can see through. *WHAT AM I SAYING?*'

At that time one of BBC TV's most popular programmes was *Sportsnight with Coleman* in which David had a request item every week. Anything you wanted to see again, you phoned in, and if there were enough requests they'd repeat it. My Stan Hastilow blunder was the most requested of all and ran for six consecutive weeks – perhaps not the greatest claim to fame but a lot of fun.

Then there was the Keith Ripp incident. Keith, another of the many characters of rallycross, a five-star driver and multiple British Champion, was not a chap to hang about and came rocketing down Hairy Hill in his very special Mini, took Paddock Bend in a too-wide slide and hit Mabbs Bank at full speed.

'Ripp's in trouble,' I perceptively observed; and then, 'He's in *REAL* trouble!' as he took off, flew through the air, landed at undiminished speed and rolled end-over-end with the whole car literally disintegrating around him. I could hardly believe my eyes when it stopped and Keith calmly extracted himself from the crumpled wreck that seconds before had been a very quick motor car. That sequence became part of the *Grandstand* opening titles for a very long time and Keith must have done very well out of the resultant publicity for his thriving car parts business.

* * *

Rallycross may have seemed to be a bit of a circus but it demanded very real skill from the drivers. It was a gung-ho mixture of loose-surface rally driving and tarmac circuit accuracy with a dash of stock car antics. The cars had to be immensely strong to resist the rough ground, which they covered at nearly 100mph on some tracks with acceleration at astounding velocity to get into the first corner first. The view ahead was obscured by dust in the summer and mud in the winter and if you were slow off the mark you could be driving virtually blind. But even if you weren't you could still get it wrong, as Dutchman Piet Dam discovered.

Piet drove a BMW and was doing well at Lydden as he approached the finish line in the lead on the last lap. 'Dam's advantage,' I said, with the sonorous authority gained from years of hard-won experience, 'is that he got away first and has stayed in the lead. So with a clean windscreen he can see exactly where he is going.' Prophetic words again for he immediately lost control, left the track and planted his pristine BMW into the bank directly underneath the BBC camera.

Then on another occasion as Malcolm Wilson (now Ford's Rally Team boss) left the line to hurtle downhill at a Rally-sprint in Wales, I said, 'Now for something *really* spectacular watch *THIS*.' Malcolm must have been listening closely, for the words were hardly out of my mouth before he fed in too much power, got into a series of violent tank-slappers and rolled his Escort on to its roof, with him and his first-time woman passenger, who had only gone along for the ride, hanging from their seat belts. Malcolm probably told her it was like that all the time.

Until 1975 anything went in rallycross, which accounted for the increasingly awesome specials, like VW Beetles with Porsche engines and V8 Minis, that made the racing so spectacular. Continental superstars Bjorn Waldegaard (Porsche), Stig Blomqvist and Per Ekland (Saab 96s) raced them at Lydden and in 1974 Austria's Franz Wurz (father of today's Formula 1 driver Alex Wurz) electrified everyone at the Kent circuit and went on to win the European Championship in his brutal VW-Porsche. But then the FIA, the governing body of motor sport, decided that enough was enough and 'normalized' the Sport with regulations that outlawed the hybrids. Lydden's golden days were over, although rallycross itself went from strength to strength, especially on the Continent, where specialized and permanent circuits with excellent facilities contrasted dramatically with the run-down and tatty place that Lydden had sadly become. It was, in fact, the same old story we had seen in motocross. Big-time rallycross in the UK withered, as did Lydden (now owned by McLaren), but then Brands Hatch, where it had all begun in 1963, came to the rescue with the creation of a fine circuit that exploited much of its former Formula 1 Grand Prix circuit and facilities. The BBC's coverage at Lydden ceased but *Grandstand* was at the newly created British Rallycross Grand Prix at Brands, the first of its kind in the world, in 1982 and stayed with it until 1994, as did I. A new generation of drivers in even more exciting cars resulted and although it was now only a once-a-year occasion for BBC TV it was a very special one. Immensely powerful Porsches, Audi Quattros, Ford Escort Xtracs, turbocharged Metro 6R4s, Ford RS 200s, a beautiful Lancia Stratos and even a very special Citroen ZX vied for supremacy, driven by the likes of Martin Schanche, Olle Arnesson, Seppo Nittymaki, Will Gollop (twice a winner), Andy Bentza, Matti Alamaki and Kenneth Hansen. The location was excellent, the atmosphere great and the spectacle brilliant but, sadly, it is seen no more.

National TV coverage of motocross and rallycross may, sadly, be a thing of the past in Britain but I owe them an enormous debt of gratitude because they developed my commentary style and generated a lot of the foot-in-mouth 'Murrayisms' for which I became known. To my mind they are by far the most exciting two- and four-wheel motor sports and they demanded commentary to match. I loved them and still do. I reacted excitedly and enthusiastically to their drama, speed and aggression and when I moved full time to the more sophisticated tarmac-racing I took my whoops, expletives, shouts of amazement and malapropisms with me. No regrets at all!

CHAPTER NINE

You Name It, I Did It

Motocross had been big on television in the 1960s, and the rallycross that followed had been just as big, if not bigger, but when BBC TV's interest in the two sports dwindled to covering just their annual British Grands Prix I certainly didn't find time hanging heavily on my hands. From the early 1980s right up to 1992 there were regular transmissions on *Grandstand* of Formula Ford and Formula 3 races from all the main circuits and I got to know many of today's Formula 1 stars there in their early careers. There were powerboats too, plus, for a short while, the new craze of truck racing, which attracted enormous crowds and made for mind-boggling television. Two of my old mates, world-famous motor-cycle racer Barry Sheene and irrepressible prankster Steve Parrish, took to the massive juggernauts like ducks to water and gave us all a lot of laughs.

By now, to my great delight and satisfaction, I had become

the BBC's automatic choice as commentator whenever anything with an engine was involved. Powerboats were something new to me and they were terrific fun. It all began in 1975 when Robert Glen – a jovial, enterprising and energetic giant and top man at EP Barrus, the concessionaires for Johnson powerboat engines – sold BBC TV on the idea of a 'Formula Johnson' series – the powerboat equivalent of motor racing's Formula 3 for up-and-coming drivers. The first race was at Fairford in Gloucestershire, of Concorde test flight fame, and it was a great success, with an audience of some 4.5 million viewers. Robert and his wife Pep got everything going and it wasn't long before the BBC's coverage was upgraded to take in the Embassy Grand Prix at Bristol Docks.

In Peter Dyke, Embassy had the ultimate sponsorship manager. He thought big, acted big, owned a Rolls Royce, threw great parties and spent money with abandon. As a result, and because it is a great sport, powerboat racing was a blast. I've seen some spectacular stuff in my time but there's little to compare with the start of a major event at the daunting and very dangerous Bristol Docks. The boats lined up, rear end on to a floating jetty between the high solid walls of the docks which were thick with spectators, and on the signal to go leapt forward with a shattering blast of noise and great showers of spray. Their prows rode high as they skimmed along at colossal speed with just a few inches at the rear of the hull kissing the water. Too fast on the straights and you flipped over backwards; too fast on the corners and you did the same sideways. The sound was like tearing corrugated iron and the sensory impact was enormous.

Not nearly as great as actually being in one though: I was lucky enough to be driven by French ace Francois Salabert at racing speeds in his glorious Mercury-powered Formula 1 two-seater and the experience was incredible. I sat immediately behind him just inches above the water and we were doing over 100mph virtually riding on the propeller. 'Don't be tempted to put your hand in the water,' I was told. 'At that speed it's as hard as iron.'

That was impressive enough but the high points of my powerboat experience were the two events I covered in 1984 and 85 for South African TV at Loch Vaal, near Johannesburg. I stayed at the home of a wealthy local enthusiast on a curve of the Vaal River known as Millionaire's Bend, went on powered-raft barbecues, drove to the event in a speedboat that seemed fast enough to compete in the races and revelled in great weather and great company.

Sadly there weren't many powerboat years for me because, like motocross, rallycross and truck racing, the television attraction faded. But it was terrific while it lasted and it introduced me to many interesting people. These included Ted Toleman, the car-delivery tycoon who founded the Toleman Formula 1 team (later Benetton); the ebullient Welsh music shop owner and Powerboat Formula 1 World Champion Roger Jenkins; Dutch aces Arthur Mostert and Cees van der Velden; American and World Champion Billy Seebold, and British Champions Tom Percival, Bob Spalding, John Nicholson and the charming multiple Formula 3 World Champion John Hill, later sadly killed during an event at Abu Dhabi.

* * *

In 1988 came touring car racing, BBC TV's new blockbuster which, along with its coverage of Formula 1, would give the British public two enthralling motor-sport spectacles for years to come. I had been doing the odd touring car race for the BBC for years, but now they were to cover the whole of the RAC British Championship. Since it was then dominated by the awesome 500hp, flame-spurting and turbo wastegate-chattering Ford Sierra Cosworth RS 500s, spectacular entertainment was guaranteed. It meant a whole new world for me though: up to now all my race commentaries had been live and continuous from the circuit, but the British Touring Car Championship coverage was to break new ground.

Historically the BBC had always covered sporting events entirely with its own people and its own facilities – cameras, equipment, production, technical and engineering personnel. It had always done an excellent job but the Government was determined to break its monopoly and decreed that it must now subcontract a percentage of its output to outside production companies. For the new touring car programmes BBC TV therefore appointed BHP, owned and masterminded by my old friend Barrie Hinchcliffe. He had made a name for himself and his company by producing motor-sport films and I had already done a lot of work for him on rallying, Formula Ford and Formula 3. BHP's brief from BBC TV was to deliver finished 30-minute programmes on videotape that had only to be checked and loaded into *Grandstand*'s transmitters. It was an inspired decision and it worked wonderfully.

Because of my Formula 1 commitments I was able to attend very few of the actual BTCC events but BHP filmed everything that moved, fitted on-car and in-car cameras, did the interviews, filmed the prize giving and then returned to London with miles of tape. This, with a lot of hard work, was edited down to the necessary half-hour, notably by the ever-cheerful Steve Saint, now BHP's Managing Director. I contend that there is no such thing as a dull motor race because if you know where to look there is always something interesting and exciting going on, but even I have to admit that some can be processional and seemingly uneventful. Not the way BHP did it though – with far more footage than they could possibly use they were able to select the really exciting stuff and link it together to make half an hour of non-stop action, drama and excitement. Heart-pounding race starts, thrilling passing manoeuvres, massive collisions, stirring in-car pictures, angry confrontations, explanatory graphics – it was all there and it was fabulous stuff. I would go to the actual events whenever possible, and sometimes I would gloomily think, *Heaven knows what BHP will be able to do with that lot – nothing happened*. But when I got to Fitzroy Square the following Thursday to add the commentary I would be so fired up by what I saw that I could hardly wait to get at it and add my words.

But when I did so it was exceedingly hard work. With a normal commentary you talk continuously about the pictures you see on your monitor, which are identical to those the viewer sees at home. Your words do not have to coincide exactly with every vision change because the coverage is continuous, which enables you to overlap sequences while you interpret the pictures and add verbal colour. The BTCC situation was very different though: in order to feature 30 minutes of continuous exciting action, the pictures were far from continuous. They would leap from a fight between three cars at the front to four others battling for 10th place, miss laps where nothing had happened and then suddenly show a huge collision as three cars not previously shown took each other off, followed by in-car replays of how it all happened. In short the whole thing was dramatically edited highlights rather than whole-race coverage. Every picture sequence was there for a reason that had to be explained in commentary, but every one of them also had to appear to flow out of the one before and into the one that followed although in truth they may have been separated by several laps.

I therefore had to sit at an editing machine and methodically go through every inch of the tape studying how it had been put together to tell the race story before I could even think about what the words were to be. It used to take me seven hours for a half-hour programme, but I like to think the effort was worth it and the viewing figures seemed to show that it was. I could have laboriously written a script but I felt that if I did the result would sound like reportage rather than the spontaneous live commentary the dramatic vision cried out for. So I used to go through the whole thing meticulously, making a shot list with brief notes on what was coming up next, then go into the sound booth and commentate on the tape pictures that were pumped into a monitor in front of me. I knew what was coming, of course, because I had practically learnt the vision by heart and also had my notes to remind me but, because I was making the words up as I went along instead of reading from a carefully crafted script, the effect was that the race was live and continuous rather than recorded and edited. It was long-winded and labour-intensive, but it worked well.

The fact that the BTCC events were recorded could cause a bit of confusion. In the early days of the BBC Grand Prix coverage I had to do commentary on some of the long-haul events – like Brazil and South Africa – live on Sunday from a London TV Centre studio rather than the actual venue, and do everything I could to give the impression I was at the track without actually saying so. (For instance, 'I can't see the pits from my commentary position' – perfectly true because I was thousands of miles away, but the words gave the impression that it was because they were just out of my sight; or 'It's bright and sunny in Rio with a temperature of over 95 degrees. That's hot!', implying that you were baking in Brazil when in fact you were at Shepherd's Bush.) Well one year, having done the Brazilian Grand Prix from the Centre the previous night, I went to the Easter Monday BTCC meeting at Thruxton. A puzzled chap came up to me and said, 'How on earth did you manage to get back from Rio so quickly?'

'I came by Concorde,' I assured him. In fact, Concorde didn't fly to Brazil.

'My god, does the BBC pay for you to fly on Concorde?'

'No. As a licence holder you do and I really appreciate it. Thanks very much.' Later that day he passed me again, shaking his head, but I never did tell him.

In the early days I used to go to Silverstone and Brands Hatch to watch Mike Hawthorn and Tommy Sopwith driving the wheels off 3.8 litre Mk II Jaguars against Jack Sears and Jeff

Uren in, believe it or not, an Austin Westminster and a Ford Zephyr. There was a time when Grand Prix drivers also used to compete in Formula 2, touring cars and even rallies, and I've seen the great Jim Clark working miracles in a Lotus Ford Cortina. All sorts of unlikely cars won the British Championship, from an Austin A40 to a Ford Galaxie and a Hillman Avenger to a Sunbeam Imp, but in my opinion it came of age for the TV public with the stirring turbocharged Ford Sierra RS 500 battles between the great Andy Rouse, Steve Soper, Tim Harvey, Laurence Bristow, Rob Gravett and Jerry Mahony. To me it was a travesty of justice that, because of the scoring system, Andy won the Championship four times before 1986 but never did so again: over the years he was the most successful British Touring Car driver of all, winning 60 races as well as the Championships (for four different constructors), as well as nine class Championships and a record nine wins in one season. But the top honour was denied him after his last Championship victory with Ford in 1985. He was an inspired engineer, a superb driver and always more than helpful and considerate whenever I needed to talk to him, which was often.

Quite apart from the actual commentating aspects the BTCC was a difficult series for me because of its structure, which may have been fair but was also extremely confusing. There were four different classes with escalating engine capacities, and the top placings in each of them qualified for the same number of Championship points. This meant that while the fastest cars were the spectacular Sierra Cosworth turbos there were three other categories that all had to be featured, as a driver from any of them could win the overall championship. If their cars weren't shown, the manufacturers that missed out but who were contributing to BHP's production fund would understandably get stroppy.

After three years the BTCC lost its impact because of the domination of the Fords up front and the complications of the overall championship. Frank Sytner won it in a Class B 2 litre BMW in 1988 and John Cleland in a Class B Vauxhall Astra in 1989, for instance, in spite of the fact that the Class A Sierras were ahead of them on the track. The races were terrific but the whole thing was too messy to grasp. It was time for a change. So it was both a relief to me and a real shot in the arm for the series when Australia's Alan Gow arrived like a knight in shining armour to transform the BTCC, making it the great television spectacle it became and giving a lead that virtually every other national touring car race series in the world would follow.

Alan was, and is, a clear thinking, no-nonsense Australian entrepreneur who knew the motor-racing business backwards having cut his teeth down under with the great Peter Brock, Australia's Champion of Champions, in a country where touring car racing is an obsession. Seeing a great business opportunity he set up a commercial company, named it TOCA, took over the Championship from the RAC and, with great professionalism, completely reorganized it. There was a new name, Super Touring; a single 2 litre engine capacity; a great deal with BBC TV to cover the Championship; a skilled and experienced permanent staff to cover all the needs from organization and administration to scrutineeering and medical services; and aggressive promotion to attract the crowds. There were also sophisticated hospitality facilities for VIP guests; proper briefings for the media; top drivers readily accessible to the spectators for autographs; its own radio station and, of course, the best circuits.

The manufacturers loved it and took part with gusto; the racing was tremendous and its success was absolute. Crowds of over 30,000 regularly turned up at 12 meetings a year at Britain's main circuits, and the BBC audiences were well over 3.5 million. Soon France, Italy, Sweden, Germany, Spain, Portugal, South Africa, Australia and even America followed in TOCA's pioneering footsteps and Alan was involved with it all. It was a great achievement which dramatically affected me for now I was the voice of motor-sport's two top disciplines, Formula 1 and touring cars, with enormous worldwide viewing figures. To my amazement I was particularly big in Sweden.

There were many reasons why the BTCC was so popular. If you build a better mousetrap the world will beat a path to your door, and that is exactly what the perceptive and determined Alan Gow and his colleagues did: a better show for everyone, well packaged and presented. Above all, the decision to record and edit the races rather than give them live TV coverage was a master stroke that created fast moving, exciting coverage and made it such a hit on the box. But it also enabled drivers' personalities to be established and race incidents that could well have been missed on live coverage to be spotted and featured during the editing.

For me the man of the decade that I worked on the series

was undoubtedly Scotland's John Cleland. It wasn't just that he won the Championship twice for Vauxhall in two very different cars (an Astra in 1989 and a Cavalier in 1995), it was his endearingly cocky personality and the way he did it. John was a top-class driver with a rapier wit and an iron determination to fight his corner to the very end. His on-track persona was electric. The most memorable and contentious incident of my time was the colossal barging match he had with Steve Soper's BMW at Silverstone's Luffield Bend, which decided the 1992 Championship. John was in no doubt about who caused it. After unsuccessfully trying to get at Steve in his stationary car to explain his point of view he furiously told the BHP camera, 'The man's an animal!' and stomped off.

The viewers loved it, of course, as they did when Grand Prix driver and my ex-BBC colleague Jonathan Palmer took off Swedish woman driver Nettan Lindgren. As Jonathan sat in his BMW, its in-car camera showed burly Nettan angrily bearing down on him to give him a Swedish mouthful. 'Uh-oh,' I cried. 'Hell hath no fury like a woman nerfed!' I wouldn't have liked to have been at the receiving end of what Jonathan got.

One of the many good things about the BTCC was that it attracted manufacturers who wouldn't normally have raced in the UK. The TWR Volvos, for instance, which created a sensation by making their 1994 debut with massive-looking estate cars rather than saloons and which were wryly paraded with a dummy sheepdog on the roof. They were actually very effective, especially in the capable hands of quiet Swede Rickard Rydell, who later went on to race the modern-shape

S40 with great success and become a Swedish national hero. Maybe that's why I went down so well there. Audi got superb publicity for the four-wheel drive Quattro, which dominated the series in 1997 and enabled the charming Frank Biela to win the drivers' crown, and in 1994 Alfa-Romeo showed the way thanks to clever exploitation of the aerodynamic regulations. Ex-Grand Prix driver Gabriele Tarquini was the champion that year and heaven knows how many flights to and from Italy he made during the course of the season.

The BTCC was so clearly the best of all the Championships that they all wanted to drive in it, not least 'Smoking Jo' Winkelhock, the BMW works driver from Germany who took the Championship in 1993. (In fact BMW was the star marque during my time, with four Championship victories.) 'Smoking Jo', so called because he was never seen without a cigarette in his mouth, took me for some hairy laps at Donington in his 300hp BMW. I sat beside him in rapture as he hurtled round at what, for him, would have been about 80% effort but for me was absolutely electrifying. His line was perfect, the speed was massive and the noise in the bare cabin colossal, but the outstanding impression was the braking. He was so close to the apex of all the bends before he braked that I could easily see why it was so hard to pass in the races. And all the time he was chattily telling me what he was doing. Superb.

The best driver, I think, was Switzerland's Alain Menu. Among so many stars it is very difficult to make a fair comparison but Alain was always outstanding and his 1997 Championship win in the Williams-designed-and-built Renault

Laguna was well deserved. A surprise though was the failure of Grand Prix driver Derek Warwick. After a wonderful 11-year career in Formula 1 he switched to touring cars in 1995 by joining the all-conquering Alfa-Romeo team, which had swept all before it the year before. But he found it very tough going indeed. The whole technique of touring car racing is vastly different to that of Formula 1 and Derek also had to develop a much-revised version of the previous year's car. It didn't work and he retired mentally hurt, but has since more than made up for it by founding and developing with Roland Dane the Triple Eight Vauxhall works team, which dominated both the 2001 Championships.

I enjoyed my time with the BTCC immensely. In 1996, when it was announced that ITV would be taking over the Formula 1 contract from the BBC the following season, I expected to be given the boot, for I knew of nobody who worked for both channels on the sports side. However when Jonathan Martin suggested I carry on with the BTCC commentaries for the BBC if ITV were agreeable – and they were – I was delighted to do so. It went extremely well and I had no difficulty in switching from one organization to the other, doing Formula 1 for ITV one weekend and touring cars for the BBC the next for the whole season. I was given a co-commentator, Charlie Cox, and we got on extremely well. With his cheery Australian personality, deep knowledge of the sport, ability as a driver and natural eloquence those tensions that always exist when two people work together on race commentary were minimized. Not so good from my point of view, though, was that the BBC, stung by their loss of F1, decided to double the time for BTCC programmes from 30 minutes to a full hour, and also to do some of the meetings live.

BBC presenter Steve Rider, friend and motor-racing fan, had been pushing for live coverage for some time and this was about the only thing on which we ever disagreed – I thought it was wrong then and I still do. Of course I know all the arguments about the immediacy and prestige of live programming, but I don't think the 1997 BTCC live coverage was nearly as exciting, entertaining and impactful as the recorded and edited output. I was particularly disappointed with its inability to exploit the in-car camera pictures that had been such a dramatic feature of the edited programmes. The thing that finally got to me though was the one-hour slot. For each programme I had to make a three-hour journey to and from home, spend two seven-hour days at BHP slogging away at an editing machine and have an overnight stay in London. I wasn't enjoying it and felt it was too much on top of everything else I had to do, with my 17-race Formula 1 programme and all the travelling that involved. So I very reluctantly decided that enough was enough and told the BBC I did not want to renew my contract for 1998. They were charming about it and said they fully understood but the sad fact for me was that this was the end of my time with the greatest broadcasting organization in the world. I had enjoyed it all and was very proud of what I had been able to achieve with them, but there was no doubt in my mind that it was time to go.

I'd had a lot of great overseas experiences on the way though. For instance, South Africa is potty about Formula 1 and took the BBC's coverage with my commentary, which, with my many visits, had made me well known there. Car manufacturers like BMW, Mercedes-Benz and Toyota had factories in the country and in 1990 I was invited to go to Johannesburg to speak at the industry's prestigious Car of the Year Awards Dinner. When the time came I got up and made the speech, a light-hearted one on the theme of, '*A funny thing happened to me at the racetrack . . .*' and it got a good reception. But I still anxiously asked my host if it had been alright. 'Absolutely spot on, Murray, because we're here to relax and have a bit of fun. Last year it was a chap from Mercedes-Benz who talked to us for 45 minutes about automatic gearbox design!' The next day I was on the fabled Blue Train from Johannesburg to Cape Town and what an experience that was. Superb modern rolling stock, a 1000-mile, 24-hour journey in extreme luxury with my own bedroom, lounge and bathroom and impressive cuisine whilst the train rolled through the Transvaal, the Orange Free State, thc gold and uranium mining area of Klerksdorp, the Kimberley diamond minefields and the Drakenstein Mountains to the breathtaking beauty of the Cape Peninsula and the splendour of Table Mountain. The trip was all too brief but I was back again in 1994 at the invitation of my good friends Denis Joubert and Adrian Pfeiffer for 'An Evening with Murray Walker' at the Western Province Motor Club's Killarney circuit clubhouse.

Killarney is an excellent racetrack and during my visit there was a round of the South African Touring Car Championship, at which Shaun van der Linde (BMW) and Mike Briggs (Opel) were the top men. The weather was wonderful, there was a really great atmosphere, the racing was of a very high standard and, under Denis Joubert's control, the circuit, organization and administration were excellent. It is a great pity that, because of the distance, South Africa's drivers cannot compete in Europe, for they would certainly give us a run for our money if they did. But for something very different the motor sport highlight of my trip was an evening at the Cape Hell Drivers meeting at the Goodwood Oval, where powerful stock cars put on a fabulously exciting and brightly lit night display of controlled mayhem. We'd originally intended to stay the night and I was slightly taken aback when one of the officials solicitously asked me if I'd be wanting a woman. 'That's very considerate of you,' I said, 'but I've got one of my own at home thank you and I think I can manage until I get back.'

But with no disrespect to South Africa which is great, my favourite country in the world is Australia. I love everything about it: the people, their laid-back attitude to life, their cities and countryside, the food, the wines and the climate. People rightly point out that I have only been there when the weather is at its best and as a visitor who got a huge welcome. Australia loves Formula 1 and I was their link with it via the box. I certainly got special treatment whenever I was there but unsurprisingly that just made me like the place even more.

I first went there for the Grand Prix at Adelaide in 1985 where I worked for Channel 9 on touring cars as well as the BBC on Grands Prix and it didn't take me long to realize that they are practically a religion to the Aussies. These are very different touring cars to the ones in Europe though: not high-revving and comparatively delicate four-cylinder, 2 litre saloons but big, brutal, rumbling and enormously spectacular 5 litre V8s. There's no multi-manufacturer mix either: just Ford and Holden, full stop. Peter Brock, Jim Richards, Dick Johnson, Allan Moffat, Craig Lowndes, Larry Perkins and Mark Scaife are their heroes and for them the greatest race in the world is the Bathurst 1000. It's 1000 kilometres long, via 161 laps of the historic and spectacular Mount Panorama circuit, a sensational location about 130 miles west of Sydney. The 3.9-mile circuit is roughly quadrangular with two of its sides grossly deformed by a series of twisting and turning bends that climb and plunge to form a uniquely daunting challenge. The drivers love it. First held in 1963, the race lasts for some seven hours, the crowds are massive and only the brave and adventurous go to The Hill where nearly everyone is rough, tough and plastered and the atmosphere is ruggedly Australian. Some say it is peopled by a violent and mindless bunch of obscene and drunken louts, but since I've never seen them I couldn't comment. Australia calls the Bathurst 1000 'The Great Race' and I had always wanted to see it, but never thought I would – being held during the Grand Prix season on the other side of the world in early October it seemed unattainable. And until 1997 it was.

The Great Race was in a mess. Political disputes about its future, and particularly Channel 7's mammoth television coverage, had created endless and very highly charged altercations about who was going to do what, with whom and when. Then fearlessly into the maelstrom strode the redoubtable Alan Gow, Australia's own but of BTCC fame, and before you could say Ned Kelly the decision had been made to run the Bathurst 1000, icon of Aussie V8 racing, with cars to European specification. It was a sensational and controversial masterstroke to say the least. There was uproar but the die was cast and suddenly, thanks to producer Noel Brady, I was invited to join the Channel 7 commentary team. Fortunately for me the race was the weekend between the Luxembourg and Japanese Grands Prix so I was on the British Airways flight to Sydney and out to Channel 7's HQ as fast as I could get there. On 1 October I was motoring with Noel over the Blue Mountains to Bathurst. It was all I had imagined and with my BTCC friends already there to race against the cream of Australia's best there was the exciting prospect of a unique and action-packed international clash.

I arrived intending to take my usual walk round the circuit to discover what it was all about but, heavy with jetlag, I didn't need too much persuasion to ride round instead. The climb to the highest point at Skyline is long and steep. Allan Moffat, four-time winner at Bathurst and someone I knew well from my days at Channel 9, took me round with my jaw hanging slack as I took it all in. When I got back Noel Brady said, 'Peter Brock's going to take you round after lunch, Murray.' *Peter Brock!* Brockie is God in Australia, with nine Bathurst 1000 wins to his name plus heaven knows how many other major successes. This was bound to be very special indeed – we'd met many times before, but never like this.

'Hi Peter, great to see you again. And it's good of you to take me out. What are we going in?'

'The A30, Murray.'

An Austin A30? I thought. *My god, does he think I'm totally past it?*

But to Peter I said, 'That'll be nice, my mother had one of those.'

'Not like this one, Murray. It's got a race-tuned, 3 litre Holden engine in it.'

I might have known. With cameras all round the track and all over the A30, with Peter and I wired for sound, I had a fabulous three-lap blast round Mount Panorama that the whole of Australia would have given its eye teeth for. I have it on tape and sometimes play it to remind myself of a great occasion.

'How fast are we going, Peter?' I shout as we hurtle down the awesome Conrod Straight.

'140mph, Murray,' Peter grins back at me. In an A30. Incredible.

Later the same day I was taken out by Brad Jones, the reigning Australian Touring Car Champion in his Audi Quattro, the same as the one Germany's Frank Biela had used to win the British Championship that year, and it was equally inspiring. Two extremely nice people in two superb cars around a legendary circuit. What a day.

So would the innovative and daring 2 litre experiment succeed at the traditional home of the charging V8s? They told me it was a very different crowd to the usual one at Bathurst. 'What do you think of it?' I asked one of the regulars.

'They're a bunch of Chardonnay-drinking poofters, Murray.'

With so much at stake it was Channel 7's job to win the

Australian TV public over and they did everything possible to ensure it was a success. The telecast was to last an incredible 10 hours from 8am to 6pm and there were to be seven of us facing the cameras, including long-time Bathurst anchorman Gary Wilkinson, Allan Moffat, Richard Hay and myself doing the commentary, and studio, helicopter and pit-lane presenters. This seemed an amazing amount of time to spend on one event but Bathurst is mega in Australia and commands huge viewing figures.

Nothing moving or stationary escaped the cameras. They were beside the track, in helicopters, in the cars, under the cars, in the garages, on poles to be stuck into unlikely places during pit stops, on gantries and even in an airship. But sadly only about 20,000 people turned up to watch the race at the track – a great pity, for the event was full of non-stop incident in superb weather. Just one second covered the top six on the starting grid and the result was in doubt right to the closing moments after nearly seven hours of actual racing. The 'Sprint' Williams Renault Laguna driven by British Champion Alain Menu and Jason Plato dominated the proceedings until it expired after 114 of the 161 laps and one of the Australian 'Endurance' BMWs won in the hands of home-grown Aussies Geoff and David Brabham, to father Jack's delight. The broadcast went without a hitch, with the whole team working well together. But the jury was out.

The race simply could not have been a more impressive debut for the new-style Bathurst 1000 but how was Australia going to stomach the loss of its beloved V8s? The crowd was well down on the normal Bathurst attendance. A lot of them had turned up or tuned in for the novelty value and to see whether their hero Brock could get his 10th win at The Mountain, but he didn't. It wasn't so much a case of would they be back as would more of them come next year?

Alan Gow had done a five-year deal, so in 1998 I was lucky enough to make my 18th visit to the Australia I love so much for the second Super Tourer Bathurst 1000. The race was even better than it had been the previous year, with a wheel-to-wheel battle between the Volvo driven by new British Champion Rickard Rydell and his partner, the great veteran Aussie champion Jim Richards, and the Nissan Primera of lanky Englishman Matt Neal and Jim Richards' son Steven. After nearly seven hours of racing during which, including all their pit stops, the two cars were hardly ever more than five seconds apart, the Volvo pairing won by a mere 1.9 seconds to give Jim his sixth win on The Mountain. The Great Race had truly lived up to its name but it wasn't enough. The second time round Australia gave the Super Tourers at Bathurst the thumbs down. With a reduced number of top-class entries, no works BMWs and the need to create an unimpressive special class to swell the number of entrants, only 16,000 spectators attended the race and the vital TV ratings suffered. It was not helped by the fact that the spectacular motor cycle Grand Prix at Phillip Island was being televised the same day. I flew home and the V8s prepared for a triumphant return to The Mountain in 1999.

A very brave but predictably hazardous attempt had failed, but it had given me two wonderful experiences at one of motor sport's truly great events, taken me to Australia and enabled me to enjoy a bit more of a great country and its likeable citizens. I was only sorry that I was unlikely to be returning to Mount Panorama.

Australia is enormous but Macau is just a tiny area of the Chinese mainland (about four miles square) some 40 miles across the water from Hong Kong. But that's where I went each year between 1982 and 1993 to revel in a very different racing scene. It started when I got a phone call in my office at Masius from a chap I didn't know called Brian Langley. 'Hi Murray,' he said, 'I'm with TVB in Hong Kong where I'm their Steve Rider, and we'd like you to do the commentary on the Macau Grand Prix.'

I knew about Macau but not much, so I didn't need asking twice. It was the first time I'd ever been to the Far East and I remember stepping off the plane into the balmy warmth of Hong Kong's Kai Tak airport and telling Brian, 'This is fabulous. I never thought I'd get here.' It was to get even better, though, as we took the jetfoil for the one-hour trip to Macau, checked in at the very impressive Lisboa Hotel right beside the track and had a look at the superb Guia circuit.

Macau was then the Portuguese equivalent of Hong Kong and at the beginning of an economic upsurge. The Grand Prix had begun in 1954 as a low-key event for local clubmen but had blossomed over the years into something much bigger, with its main race for Formula Atlantic single-seaters. Its expansion was hardly surprising for the 3.8-mile Guia circuit is mindblowing. A cross between Hockenheim and Monaco, it has three long flat-out stretches along the seafront which lead to a demanding sequence of bends that wriggle through the outskirts of the town up a steep hill and then thread their way along a narrow walled road with a seemingly vertical drop that overlooks the harbour. Picturesque and unique, it is a race driver's dream and a race engineer's nightmare because, for the single-seaters, it is critical to get the aero balance right between maximum downforce for the twisty bits and minimum drag on the straights.

When I first went there the Macau GP was for Formula Atlantic single-seaters but there was also a major touring car event, the Guia Trophy, as well as motor-cycle races for international and local riders and other touring car events for local heroes and what were described as 'Gentlemen Racers.' They were the very wealthy, of whom there seemed to be plenty, with Ferraris, Porsches and other exotica to race. I was to commentate, unaided, on all of them.

The whole area on the land side of the main straight was a congested shanty town of tightly packed dwellings made of plywood, corrugated iron and sacking and my commentary position was a wooden platform floating in the South China Sea where the magnificent Mandarin Oriental Hotel now stands. The TV production unit was inside a crumbling single-decker bus that had no wheels or engine and was normally occupied by chickens. It was rather basic compared with the BBC! The producer was Chinese and his English was difficult to follow. He would cue me by shouting 'Talk, Walker!' into my headphones. It was all a bit rough and ready, but more than made up for by the great atmosphere. The weather was superb, the racing was tremendously competitive, and unlike

Formula 1 everyone lived together in the nearby hotels, talked to each other and partied together in the evenings.

At the centre of it all was the charming and enormously wealthy Teddy Yip, a motor-sport fanatic who had had his own Formula 1 team, Theodore Racing, and who was literally the social driving force of the meeting. On the first evening there was a cocktail party at his home on the hill where his race cars were prepared; the second night featured a 20-course banquet at the Lisboa Hotel; the next a full-on Japanese dinner, and on our final night a sumptuous buffet dinner back at the Lisboa. It was all what race organizer Phil Taylor rightly described as Fiesta Time. The ever-charming Roberto Moreno, who calls me Dad because I look so like his father, won the Grand Prix and did the victory lap wearing a rubber chicken's head. You don't see Michael Schumacher doing that at Monaco!

Over the years the Macau Grand Prix got better and better to become the unofficial Formula 3 World Championship. As Formula 1 wannabes beat a path to its door, Macau itself went through a colossal boom, with high-rise buildings sprouting everywhere to become a mini Hong Kong. The circuit infrastructure improved beyond recognition almost to match the best of Formula 1, with over HK$50 million being spent in 1993 on a superb new control tower, pit-lane and garages complex. All the years were special, but in my time there were three in particular. In 1983 Ayrton Senna, in his first-ever street race, dominated both 15-lap legs of the Grand Prix. It was something else that got my attention in 1987 though: Typhoon Nina, which raged furiously the whole weekend. I'd never seen anything like it and there was no question of being able to run the race until the very last minute, when the lashing wind and rain died down enough for just one leg to be run, with Martin Donnelly the winner. 1990 was a sign of things to come when German Formula 3 Champion Michael Schumacher met British Champion Mika Hakkinen. Hakkinen won the first leg and although Schumacher led the second Mika had only to follow him home to win on aggregate. But his determination to win both races was his downfall when he pulled out to pass Schumacher, hit the Reynard and spun out. Schumacher was hurt and Hakkinen, mercifully unscathed, flung his gloves into the ground in angry frustration. I sat next to him at dinner that night when he was understandably still downcast. 'I know you'll find this hard to believe in your present state, Mika,' I remember saying, 'but you'll get over it. You've the makings of a great driver and I'm sure your time will come.' Clever Murray!

For me the international races with drivers I knew were fine but the ones with Asian drivers were a nightmare. There were drivers from Macau, Indonesia, Japan, Thailand, Hong Kong, Malaysia and the Philippines and for a Westerner most of their names were either very strange or impossible tongue-twisters. The Chinese, for instance, put their given names after their surnames and it took me some time to realize that a chap whose name was, say, Wong Bong Kei should be called Wong Bong rather than Kei. And where would you put the emphasis on Japanese driver Morio Fukui's surname? And what about 'Here comes Ng Cheong . . .'? The Thai names were really tough to rattle off in excited commentary – try Somchai Chareonkinapa and Kajohnsak Saksirivejkul – but the

Indonesian ones were just impossible and I had to hope that none of them would do well enough to be mentioned. Fortunately for me, few did.

Standards at Macau weren't always what I had been used to either. One year there was what I used to think of as a Local Heroes race for 1600cc Nissans, which was won by a chap I shall call Fu Chan Wing (I've changed the names to protect the innocent – including me!). When his car was scrutineered, however, it turned out to have a 2 litre engine so he was wheeled out with some appropriately harsh words. Ping Sui Kwan, who had been second, was also given the boot on account of an illegality, so that left Choi Kin Seng as the happy legal winner. That evening, after giving a speech, I left the sponsors' hotel at about midnight to return to my own and saw a convivial Fu Chan Wing drinking in the bar with some of his mates. When he later left he was confronted by a couple of chaps in bike helmets who blew him away with Uzis. This seemed a bit extreme but apparently a lot of betting money had gone down the drain as a result of his exclusion and someone hadn't been too happy about it.

The Chinese look at life through different eyes. One year during a Local Heroes 350cc Yamaha motor-cycle race a rider lay unconscious in the middle of the track after falling heavily. As I watched with mounting concern the race continued, with his rivals miraculously dodging the inert body in their path, while the corner marshals held an animated conversation about what they were going to do. Agreement reached, four of them darted forward, seized a limb each and swung him over the armco barrier like a sack of spuds. *Blimey*, I thought, as he thudded to the ground, *if he wasn't dead before, he sure is now.* But no. With no one taking any notice of him he eventually came to, got up and sheepishly staggered off. They make 'em tough out there.

I discovered another difference in attitudes at my second visit in 1983. One of the visiting drivers, fun-loving Irishman Gary Gibson, phoned me at my Hong Kong hotel the day after the race. 'A friend of mine is the manager of the Mandarin Hotel, Murray, and he's letting me use their motorized junk. We're going round the island. Why don't you come along?' The junk was incredible, with two big diesel engines and fitted out as luxuriously as the very well-heeled guests of the superb Mandarin Hotel would expect. Arch practical joker Gerhard Berger and excitable Irishman Tommy Byrne were two of the party, and after a while they started throwing people overboard. At one point they were bearing down on me when Gary shouted, 'No! He's old.' – a backhanded compliment but one I was glad of at the time. I had to get off at the floating village of Aberdeen but after I had done so things got a bit wild and ended up with the Captain being chucked over the side. Luckily I was on the plane home by then.

Macau was magic. Enormous fun, close racing on a superb circuit in wonderful surroundings and the knowledge that the people I was getting to know so well would be the Grand Prix stars of tomorrow. René Arnoux, Ayrton Senna, Gerhard Berger, Martin Brundle, Jean Alesi, Damon Hill, Johnny Herbert, Michael Schumacher, Mika Hakkinen, Eddie Irvine, Heinz-Harald Frentzen, David Coulthard, Jacques

Villeneuve and Giancarlo Fisichella were all there in my time and they all went on to make their names in Formula 1, the pinnacle of motor sport. When I could, I used to go back to Hong Kong after the race and stay on to do the International Kart Grand Prix at Causeway Bay's Victoria Park the following weekend. That too was very special and for a change I actually stayed somewhere long enough to get to know it. As a result there isn't much of Hong Kong I haven't seen, although I haven't been for some time. I missed the event in 1985 when I was doing the RAC Rally for the BBC and again in 1992 when I had a hip replaced. Two years later I had to have the other one done and then the Grand Prix season and its aftermath got too busy for me to do the trip again – to my great regret. I wouldn't have missed Macau for all the tea in China.

CHAPTER TEN

A View from the Commentary Box

In 1978 BBC TV made the major decision to feature the entire Formula 1 season in its sports line-up. Before then there had only been limited coverage of the championship, confined to 'glamour' events such as the Monaco, British and Italian races commentated by the authoritative Raymond Baxter, so this was a new and exciting development. However, from the BBC's point of view there was a problem – on-car advertising. In 1968 Lotus boss Colin Chapman had achieved a major coup by getting substantial sponsorship from Imperial Tobacco, as a result of which his previously green and yellow cars were completely re-liveried in red, gold and white and the team renamed 'Gold Leaf Team Lotus'. This opened the flood-gates and most of the major teams began securing tobacco-firm backing, notably McLaren with Marlboro, Ligier with Gitanes and Lotus again, later, with John Player's JPS brand. The BBC, which was worried about *any* form of advertising on its channels, reluctantly agreed to stomach tobacco's association with Formula 1 because it regarded the sport as a special case. But the idea of sponsorship by condom firms was something else, and in 1976 when the Surtees team appeared with the word 'Durex' boldly displayed on its bodywork there was a crisis. In those days 'french letters', as condoms were then known, were certainly not a subject for everyday conversation and as far as the BBC was concerned a visible Durex logo was totally unacceptable for family viewing.

I arrived at Brands Hatch for the non-championship Formula 1 'Race of Champions' to be greeted by producer Ricky Tilling with the words, 'Hi Murray, we'll know by 11am whether we're going to be on or not.'

'What are you talking about Ricky?'

'Durex. We're not going to transmit the race unless Surtees agree to take it off their cars.'

Surtees refused so the BBC packed up and went home. By 1978, however, Durex had largely disappeared from the scene and now, with public interest fired by James Hunt's dramatic and successful battle with Niki Lauda for the 1976 World Championship, the sport was about to take off on the box. The good-looking and immensely charismatic James was the nation's new sporting hero and with the growth of TV the time was right to exploit Formula 1's enormous potential.

For me the timing was perfect. There was a massive gap waiting to be filled, for Raymond Baxter was now heavily involved with *Tomorrow's World* and other current affairs programmes and that, plus his new job as Public Relations Director for the British Motor Corporation, meant that he was not available. I was in pole position to replace him and well qualified to do so for I was an experienced broadcaster, had been an enthusiastic follower of Grand Prix racing since my childhood and had already commentated on some F1 races for the Corporation. I'd been behind the microphone at the awe-inspiring old Nurburgring for the 1969 and 1974 German Grands Prix, as well as the 1976 and 1977 British Grands Prix; I had also worked at Monaco for the BBC and had been on duty at Television Centre at 4am in 1976 when James Hunt clinched third place at Fuji in Japan to become World Champion.

So I was sent for by Jonathan Martin, then one of BBC TV's top sports producers and later to become Head of Sport. Over lunch at the Gun Room restaurant in Shepherd's Bush, Jonathan outlined the situation to me.

'After the first four long-haul events in Argentina, Brazil, South Africa and America, we're going to do recorded highlights of the European races, starting with Monaco. I want you to do the commentary, Murray. The drill will be for you to go to the event on the Thursday of race week, soak yourself in it until after qualifying on Saturday and then come back to the UK. You'll watch the actual race on Eurovision at the TV Centre on Sunday and then we'll edit it down to half an hour of highlights, on to which you'll dub the commentary for transmission later that evening.'

Of course I would rather have been able to commentate on all the races live from the circuit but that wasn't on offer and I was only too pleased to accept what was. It was a major step forward both for Formula 1 coverage and for me and

I subsequently signed a three-year contract. The BBC were never the best of payers, but given that I'd got the job of a lifetime I wasn't too concerned about the money, and it was only three years after all. Little did I know that 24 years of travelling the world to talk about my consuming interest stretched before me. Those years covered some 39 circuits, some 20 countries – most of them every year – and from 1980 to 1985 I was to be commentating on motor-cycle road racing, motocross, rallycross, Formula Ford, Formula 3, powerboats *and* Formula 1.

So then to the delights of international travel – the bag packing and unpacking, frantic drives on traffic-clogged roads to crowded airports, rushed schedules, hire cars, good and not-so-good hotels, lost sleep and the unremitting pressure of knowing that with a Grand Prix every two weeks I'd be getting ready for the next almost as soon as I returned from the last. All this in addition to my 'proper job'. I had no complaints though; it was a whole new life for me, the very few disadvantages of which were more than compensated for by the camaraderie of Formula 1, the non-stop buzz, and visiting and enjoying so many new places that I would never have seen otherwise. It was magic being an integral part of the Grand Prix scene, being able to talk to anyone and everyone, having access to the teams, their drivers and their garages and generally being in the thick of it all.

Lotus dominated the Championship in 1978 with their superb ground-effects Lotus 79 driven by America's Mario Andretti and the laid-back Ronnie Peterson from Sweden. I usually travelled alone to be the BBC's sole representative at the meetings but I found Formula 1 to be welcoming and it didn't take me long to settle in. Patrick Depailler won for Tyrrell at Monaco, the weather in Madrid was scorching for the Spanish GP, Niki Lauda won in Sweden driving the innovative Brabham fan car (which was immediately outlawed) and then Lotus really got into their commanding stride. The immensely likeable Andretti wrapped up the Championship in Italy with two races still to go but it wasn't an occasion to celebrate for him or anyone else.

After the Saturday qualifying session at Monza I returned to London and recorded my commentary on the race which started with an horrific multiple collision in which Ronnie Peterson's Lotus caught fire with him trapped in it. He was bravely rescued by Clay Regazzoni and James Hunt, with whose McLaren he had collided, but died in hospital from the effects of an embolism. It was a terrible accident that affected us all, but sadly there was more tragedy to come before the end of the season. Ronnie's Swedish countryman, the ebullient Gunnar Nilsson, who had driven and won for Lotus, used to join us in the London studio to watch the races. In 1977 he had sadly contracted cancer, and after the last Grand Prix of the 1978 season (in Montreal, where Gilles Villeneuve had scored an emotional home victory), he said to me in his ever-cheerful way, 'Goodbye, Murray. I won't be seeing you again.'

'Of course you will, Gunnar. We'll be back next year.'

I knew all too well what he meant but, in the awkward way you do, was trying not to show it. He died shortly after our meeting and Sweden had lost its second top racing driver in less than six weeks, a dreadful ending to an eventful year.

At the end of the season, BBC TV's *Grand Prix* was judged a great success and soon outgrew its original format to go live. But those early highlights programmes were very demanding. When I got back on the Saturday night I used to go to the Kensington Hilton Hotel at Shepherd's Bush and then, on Sunday, to the Television Centre for the race. Under great pressure and working against the clock, two teams of producers and videotape editors would reduce the coverage to half an hour and while they did so I would make notes of what was going into the programme. Then it was headphones on to record commentary on the condensed event as though I was watching it live, while Jonathan Martin bellowed into my headphones about what was coming up next. (If you want to know what it was like, try standing in your living room excitedly describing what you can see out of the window while your wife gives you a furious earful about coming home drunk with a pair of knickers in your pocket.) It was certainly hectic but videotape gave us the enormous luxury of being able to stop and do something again if we had to.

Sometimes when the editing couldn't be finished in time to record the words before the programme went on the air, I had to do the commentary live on transmission – and very occasionally without even having seen the pictures. This wasn't easy with highlights and it was certainly not the time to get into a flap. We weren't helped by the inferior coverage of the foreign host broadcasters whose standards were, to put it mildly, well below those of the BBC. In Spain, for instance, some 50 minutes of the 100-minute race showed nothing but Mario Andretti going round by himself! But whenever that wonderfully evocative *Grand Prix* theme music began – *The Chain* by Fleetwood Mac – I knew that when it stopped I would be starting. *BOOM! diddy BOOM! diddy diddy BOOM! BOOM!* . . . the butterflies in my stomach would settle and it would be down to me to capture the excitement, the drama, the colour, the noise and the danger that is Formula 1. And it was a fabulous feeling.

The Chain was so right for the programme and in 1988, a decade after it had begun, producer Charles Balchin said to me, 'Fleetwood Mac are in the UK for the first time for 10 years. I'd like you to go to Wembley and do your 30-second introduction for next weekend with them gathered round you. It's fixed with their manager.'

When I got there the manager said, 'They'll be coming out of that door and going on to the stage up those stairs, so you can do your piece while they're on the way.'

My God, that'll only take them about 30 seconds so if I get my words wrong I'm dead.

While I was pacing the floor worrying about my lines, a strangely dressed bloke with a beard appeared. 'You're Murray Walker, aren't you? I'm a big fan of yours. I always watch your show when I can. What are you doing here?'

Not knowing him from a bar of soap I explained my problem.

'Maybe I can help you then. I'm Mick Fleetwood.'

He got the rest of the band out of their dressing room about

10 minutes early, we had a great chat and my piece went off like a dream.

I travelled alone again in 1979 but now I knew the ropes and it was easier and a lot less stressful. Jody Scheckter, later to become my co-commentator, won the World Championship at Monza and I had my pocket picked as I literally fought my way through thousands of emotional *tifosi* to interview him. It was to be 21 years before another Ferrari driver, Michael Schumacher, won the Championship for the famous team of the Prancing Horse. In France Jean-Pierre Jabouille had the first ever Formula 1 win in a turbocharged car when he was victorious for Renault. It was one of the most exciting races I have ever seen with a titanic battle for second place between Gilles Villeneuve in his Ferrari and Renault's René Arnoux. At Silverstone Clay Regazzoni became the first Williams driver to win a Grand Prix, but what made 1979 so significant for me was that at Monaco James Hunt lost his appetite for racing and sensationally retired. Before long I was having another audience with the redoubtable Jonathan Martin.

'The *Grand Prix* programme is taking off, Murray. Next year we're going to do all the European races live and we're going to have two commentators. You're one and James Hunt will be the other.'

I didn't like it. I'm a human being with human feelings. I'd been doing the Formula 1 commentaries for two years alone and my way. There had been no complaints and a lot of compliments and now I was being faced with what seemed to be a vote of only qualified confidence. *They're easing me out*, was my first thought. *The next thing that'll happen is that they'll be saying, 'Thanks for all you've done, Murray but we want a younger man who has actually done it.' But JAMES HUNT! What does he know about commentating? He's a racing driver, and what's more I don't respect him. As a driver he's very good, no doubt about it, but as a person he's arrogant, rude, overbearing, drinks too much and is certainly not my idea of someone with whom I want to share the microphone.*

I was certainly startled at our first joint commentary, on the International Trophy race at Silverstone, won by Chile's Eliseo Salazar and definitely not one of the most exciting races I've ever seen. I summed it up as brightly as I could and turned to James – who was literally lying on the floor of the commentary box with his leg in a plaster cast as a result of trying to do a backflip on a snowboard while he was under the influence.

'And what did you think of it, James?'

'What a load of rubbish!' he replied.

Direct and blunt, but he was absolutely right. It had been a procession with little to endear it and James said it like he saw it. It was my first experience of that complete honesty and outspokenness which was to endear him so much to the viewers . . . but there were plenty more to come.

At Monaco 1980, the sixth Grand Prix of the season, there began the Murray and James Formula 1 commentary partnership that was to last for 13 years, 16 times a year for four days at a time. It started cautiously at arm's length and eventually developed into mutual respect and liking, but it went through some trying times on the way. Two people could hardly have been more different in terms of age, temperament, background and attitude. James was a free spirit, with a highly volatile and forcefully opinionated personality and a fearsome temper, who did not think or act like other people. For years he had been lionized and harried ceaselessly by his countless fans and given no peace by the media. He hated being so public and when he retired was worn out by the pressure and what had been a very turbulent lifestyle. He had lost his wife to Richard Burton, had just terminated a career that had seen him become World Champion of a sport where you literally put your life at risk, he drank to excess, smoked to excess, womanized to super-excess and was now literally yesterday's man. And how about me? At 57 I was more than old enough to be his father and unhappy about being paired off with someone I thought was lazy and unprofessional and whose private life I did not admire. We were a seemingly ill-matched couple with a potentially disastrous future.

At that first Grand Prix together our Monaco commentary position was a patch of pavement opposite the pit-lane. We sat on folding park chairs just behind the armco barrier, on the other side of which the cars blasted past at some 170mph. Between us was a solitary television monitor and over us a token piece of canvas in case it rained. The noise was deafening and to make it worse I wore an earpiece into which Jonathan Martin gave me the time of day in his imperious tones. Just minutes before the race James arrived: unkempt, unshaven, barefoot and half-sloshed, wearing a T-shirt and a frayed pair of cut-down jeans and carrying a bottle of wine. He sat down, plonked his plaster cast into my lap, the race started and off we went. I can look at the situation with wry humour now but I wasn't amused at the time, especially when a second bottle arrived for him as he finished the first.

It would be totally untrue to say that James and I disliked each other but we certainly had very little in common. I worked like mad to get information; James spent most of his time in the Marlboro motorhome and let it come to him. I stood up during the race going berserk with excitement; James sat down and was calmly authoritative in that wonderful public school voice of his. I did not regard it as my right to criticize the drivers; James was fiercely condemnatory whenever he got the chance. With his knowledge and experience of what it was actually like to race a Formula 1 car he had every right to do so, although he was often vindictively unfair in my opinion. 'The trouble with Jarier is that he's a French wally: always has been and always will be,' was a typical James remark. I knew that if things weren't very entertaining I only had to say something complimentary about Riccardo Patrese for James to fiercely gesture for the microphone that we shared. He never ceased to blame Riccardo for the collision at Monza that had caused Ronnie Peterson's death, and never forgave him even though it was subsequently established that the amiable Italian had been entirely innocent. I would give the mike to James who would then spew vitriol and bile over Patrese. He did the same, to a lesser extent, to Nigel Mansell and Ken Tyrrell. He regarded Mansell as a whinger undeserving of respect and had it in for Ken for having, according to James, once sent Jody Scheckter out on what James believed to be dangerous tyres. James's dislikes were often ill-founded at best and this was one of them, for I cannot imagine anyone less likely to have done such a thing than the experienced and honourable Ken Tyrrell.

The public loved James's tirades of course, and Jonathan Martin had been right to put us together. We may not have had the greatest respect for each other at the start, but our skills complemented each other perfectly, the viewers liked our partnership and as time went by we rubbed the corners off each other, grew together and worked even better. In the early days, though, I must have been as much of a pain to him as he had been to me. He later told me, for instance, that in the commentary box I used to shield my hard-won information notes with my hand like a schoolboy at an exam to prevent him seeing them. True enough, but I did so because I didn't see why someone I regarded as being too idle and unprofessional to find out for himself should benefit from my efforts. I must also have irritated James immensely by my attitude in the box. I was immensely fired up, totally focussed, literally on the balls of my feet, oozing adrenalin and all the time *I* wanted to be the one pouring out words about what was happening. I thought James slowed things down and he thought I talked too much. He may well have been right but I was never reluctant to ask his opinion on something about which he knew more than I. Jonathan Martin's insistence that we share the same microphone – to stop us talking over each other – was perceptive and correct but it caused more than a little friction because we had to pass it back and forth and whoever had it didn't want to give it up. I admit with some embarrassment that when James was talking and I felt I had something more important to say (which was often) I would get extremely agitated with him, waving my hand in front of his face and generally making it very plain that I thought he should shut up and return the microphone to me. We never actually came to blows but at Silverstone one year we came mighty close.

I was, as ever, standing up and in full flow, giving it plenty when James, sitting beside me, decided it was his turn. Instead of languidly waving his hand for the microphone he grabbed its wire and gave a sharp tug. It flew out of my hand into his and while he calmly got on with whatever it was he wanted to say I was seething with rage at being cut off in my prime. I regard myself as someone who is hard to anger but I actually had my fist back when I saw producer Mark Wilkin wagging a reproving finger at me and silently mouthing the words, '*NO,* Murray!' I backed off and it is just as well I did for that would have been the end of a great partnership.

It was a relief when we stopped doing highlights and stayed over on the Sunday to do live commentaries on the whole race from the circuits. It was not really an enviable job to stand in a vast empty studio in London at 5am with just a monitor in front of you, trying to give the impression you were in Japan and then keeping on top of a 90-minute race thousands of miles away. More to the point, it was all too easy to get something wrong – and if you did you could expect no mercy from the viewers, because as far as they were concerned you were there. We always had experienced people like journalists Joe Saward or Mike Doodson in constant electronic touch with us from the track and they would feed us information while the race was on. By and large it worked well but it wasn't the same as being there. 'It's starting to rain, Mark,' Mike Doodson would say to Mark Wilkin, who would write me a note while I was talking. 'And now it's starting to rain!' I'd say excitedly. 'This is *really* going to change things!'

One year we were doing our delusion act of seeming to be in South Africa when we were actually in London when James, who had very strong views on apartheid, suddenly launched into a withering attack on the evils of the system and the South African government. Quite apart from the fact that this didn't seem to be very relevant to the South African Grand Prix, it was politically provocative stuff for the BBC to be putting out in a sports programme and Mark rapidly passed him a note which read, 'TALK ABOUT *THE RACE*!' James finished his sentence and then said, 'Anyway, thank God we're not there!' Things didn't get much better the next year, when we actually did the race from South Africa. Someone from SABC TV came up to me and said, 'Do you have any objection to us using your BBC commentary here tomorrow, Murray, although I'm afraid we don't pay very much?'

'How much is not very much?'

'20 Rand.' [the equivalent of £40 in those days]

'You're right, that isn't very much, but I might as well have it as someone else, so OK.'

'That's great, would you fix it with James as well then?'

'Oh no. *You* fix it with James!'

Our contracts stipulated that if our commentary was used by another broadcaster we were entitled to negotiate an extra fee for ourselves. 'Yes, that'll be OK for the usual thousand pounds,' said James. So it didn't happen. When we arrived for the race on Sunday morning our commentary box had been changed from one with a superb view of the circuit to one with a single small window past which the cars flashed at some 200mph. When I started commentating there was a distinct delay before I heard what I'd said through my headphones and by then I was saying something else. I've never known anything so unsettling and I defy anyone to keep talking in those circumstances. James stormed out of the box and I took the headphones off altogether and did the best I could. It turned out that a connection had been made incorrectly by the BBC engineer: the words were transmitted all the way from Kyalami to London and back again before I heard them! But was our location switched deliberately in retribution? Well, it certainly seemed one hell of a coincidence and I greatly resented being penalized for something that had nothing to do with me, especially after I had agreed to help them out.

Life with James was always unpredictable. I actually used to see very little of him before the qualifying session on Saturday because there was no need, but on Sunday there was always the worry of whether or not he was going to turn up. He would stroll into the commentary box about five minutes before the race began and when it finished it was as though the chequered flag was connected to a spring on his arse. As the flag swept down James shot up and out of the box. That wasn't really a problem, but at Spa in 1989 he never arrived at all. While I did the job alone, producer Roger Moody was frantically phoning round to find him and sending our engineer to ask anyone who retired to come up to the box and be interviewed by me. The Belgian Ardennes region is notorious for its changeable weather and that year was no exception. I had a succession of rain-soaked drivers arriving in the box, among them Martin Brundle and Johnny Herbert, and I remember asking Johnny how close you had to be to the car in front to see its bright red rear light through the gloom. 'With your helmet touching it, Murray!' he said. And James? When he was finally located after the race he said he was very sorry but he'd been ill in bed. I was uncharitable enough to think he hadn't been alone and wasn't impressed.

My most dramatic experience with James occurred during our first time in Australia in 1985. Channel 9 were making a maximum effort to impress their countrymen with Formula 1 down under and were doing a great job. For the qualifying session we were joined by David Hill, their top man, who was brilliant at his job and not slow to make his feelings known. There had been an instant lack of rapport between the very English James and the very Australian David but everything went well until I handed the microphone to James who shrugged his shoulders, put it down and said, 'I've got nothing to say.'

David leant across and said, 'Pick the f***ing thing up and say something!'

Somewhat startled, James did so, and when the session finished he haughtily said to David, 'I'd like a word with you. I've never been spoken to like that by anyone in the whole of my life and I don't like it.'

'I don't give a f**k what you like,' said David. 'As far as

I'm concerned you're a hired hand and if you don't like it you can f**k off!'

James stayed but unsurprisingly there was a somewhat tense atmosphere between the two of them until the problem was eventually solved by David becoming Sky TV's Head of Sport in the UK and then one of Rupert Murdoch's top TV executives in America.

If I've given the impression that working with James was non-stop purgatory, it wasn't. Challenging, yes; tense, definitely, and often irritating, but 13 years is a long time and if there hadn't been basic mutual respect and an unforced ability to work together we wouldn't have lasted as long as we did. James almost invariably stayed at a different hotel to the rest of the BBC team and we were never the greatest mates out of the box because we were so different, but as the years rolled by he changed, very much for the better as far as I was concerned, and I must have too. We both mellowed. His second marriage had failed but it had produced two sons, Tom and Freddie, to whom he was a loving and very caring father. He used to bring them to Portugal for a holiday at Grand Prix time and stayed with the rest of us at the Estalagem Muchaxo at Guincho up the coast from Cascais. It was a very unusual place at the end of a superb bay at the extreme western edge of Europe and I was always immensely impressed with a side of James, as a warm-hearted dad, that I had never seen before. Over the years the decent and cheerful chap that had always been inside him took over and our relationship was transformed. Things were going really well in fact, but sadly they weren't to continue.

The one long-haul race that we had yet to do live from the circuit was Canada, because although CBC used our commentaries throughout the rest of the season they never did so for their own race at Montreal. However, in 1993 James said 'We'll be there next year, Murray. I've been working on it and things are looking good.' We were still to do that year's race from London though, at a time when things were bad for James. His many investments had gone belly-up, his divorce was turning out to be extremely messy and expensive, his Mercedes-Benz SL500 was sitting on bricks in front of his home without its wheels and he was so strapped financially that he could only afford to drive a very old Austin A30 van on crossply tyres. So, to save money and keep fit, he cycled almost everywhere. On the Sunday morning of the race he rode all the way from his home in Wimbledon to the Television Centre at Shepherd's Bush and when he arrived, looking pretty scruffy, I jokingly said, 'I hope you're not going to talk to your public dressed like that!' 'No I'm not, Murray,' he said and changed into a fresh set of clothes he'd brought with him in a basket on his handlebars. We did the broadcast with no problems (the fourth of Alain Prost's seven wins for Williams that year) and after he had done his *Daily Telegraph* column with journalist Gerry Donaldson he cycled back to Wimbledon. Two days later I was doing a job when my wife phoned me.

'Brace yourself, dear,' she said, 'I've got some very bad news.'

My first thought was my mother, for she was then 95.

'Is it Mother?'

'No, it's James. He's died.'

Human reaction can be quite illogical and mine was then. 'It can't be James, I was with him on Sunday.'

Sadly, he had succumbed to a massive heart attack and to my very genuine regret our long association was over. At times it had been stormy but it had worked extremely well, had given a lot of people a lot of pleasure and I was deluged with the most wonderful letters about it. James's brother Peter asked me to deliver the address at the celebration of James's life at the appropriately named Church of St James's, Piccadilly, and I was honoured to do so. The great and the good of motor sport were all there and it was a truly moving, warm and cheerful occasion, which is certainly what James would have wanted. In fact he left money in his will for his friends to have a party afterwards.

Like all of us James was a mixture but at heart he was an endearing, good and honest man. My address concluded with the words, 'We can only console ourselves with the knowledge that 45 years of James's life contained at least as much as 90 of anybody else's. His loved ones, motor racing, his countless friends and all those who admired him from afar are infinitely the poorer for his passing.' And I was right.

Who was to replace him then? Answer: No one. For James was irreplaceable at what he did and the way he did it. And that is no insult to Jonathan Palmer, who joined me in the commentary box for the next race, the French Grand Prix at Magny Cours. Jonathan had been an extremely competent and successful racing driver, having won the British Formula 3 and European Formula 2 Championships and driven for four Formula 1 teams. So he really knew what he was talking about and was very capable of doing so. He was and is a brilliant business man and had been BBC TV's Grand Prix pit-lane reporter for some years, but even so his sudden transfer to the commentary box was a real in-at-the-deep-end challenge. He coped extremely well and we were together until the end of 1996 but with the greatest of respect for an extremely hard-working, eloquent and knowledgeable chap I have to say that the two of us weren't a patch on James and I. How much of it was down to Jonathan and how much to me I don't know but the chemistry, that magic ingredient that makes it work, just wasn't right. There was no animosity and no clash of temperaments, although I have no doubt that I was my usual over-whelming self in the box that had irritated James so much. That can't have helped but where James had been loved by the public as a charismatic Formula 1 World Champion and a glamorous, roistering hell-raiser who was seldom out of the news, Jonathan was virtually unknown; where James had been outspoken, provocative and opinionated, Jonathan, new to the job and feeling it, went about his role very differently. His serious, almost academic, long-winded explanations about the minutiae of pit stops, fuel loads and tyres were certainly accurate and authoritative but they were too detailed for many of the viewers. Between the two of us we never got it together as a team as well as we might have done. Maybe time would have improved things, but there wasn't to be enough of it for 1997 was to see a sensational and totally unpredictable upset. After 19 years of Formula 1, BBC TV was out.

At the end of 1995 BBC TV Head of Sport and F1 aficionado Jonathan Martin had every reason to feel pleased with himself. *Grand Prix* had been running for 18 years and was doing very well. The public loved it, the audience ratings were impressive and he was negotiating with Bernie Ecclestone, the Czar of Formula 1, for another five years of the same with no reason not to expect it to happen. BBC TV was the unchallenged leader as far as sports coverage was concerned: they had pioneered, developed and perfected Formula 1 on the box and they hadn't put a foot wrong. Little did Jonathan know, though, that ITV were sick of being cut to ribbons by *Grand Prix* on Sunday afternoons and had decided that if they couldn't beat it they'd buy it. In went a mammoth offer of some £60 million, with the promise greatly to improve the show with more good people, much more air-time, much better facilities and a lot more than just the race itself. On 13 December Jonathan was sitting in his office when the phone rang.

'It's Bernie, Jonathan.'

'Hi Bernie, how are you?'

'Fine, thanks. I just rang to tell you that you've lost the contract and that we're making the announcement in half an hour's time.'

When the shell-shocked Jonathan picked himself off the floor he said, 'Bernie, you might have given us a chance to make a counter bid.' To which Bernie replied, 'Unless you've been cheating me all these years there's no way you can pay what they're paying so there was no point in asking.'

Terse and tough but true. The end of an era. Bernie

subsequently said to me, 'I didn't do it just for the money. ITV are going to make a much better job of it.'

I had been making an after-lunch speech that day at the National Motor Museum in Beaulieu, and knew nothing about the ITV coup until I turned on the car radio. To say that I was flabbergasted would be a massive understatement. *That's it then,* I thought. *It'll be the new broom policy with ITV. Sweep out the old lot. Start again with a new team and do it their way. So you've had it.*

The new contract didn't start until 1997, though, so the BBC still had 1996 to cover – in my swansong year I'd have plenty to do coping with what looked like being a great season. But to my genuine surprise and delight I got a phone call from ITV's Mike Southgate early in the New Year, saying he'd like to come and talk to me. When he arrived with Andrew Chowns, ITV's legal eagle, he got straight to the point.

'We want you to carry on with us, Murray. You'll be No. 1 commentator and this is what we'll pay you.'

It was a hell of a lot more than I was already getting and in a situation where it meant continuing what I loved or stopping altogether the only question was how ITV were going to tackle Formula 1. The answers were exciting but worrying – in a nutshell they were to appoint a specialist company to do the production as, unlike the BBC, ITV do not make their own programmes. Who it was would be decided by competitive presentations. ITV would have its own studio on site at all the races with its own presentation personnel, there would be two people in the pit lane, two commentators and the vastly experienced BBC would be doing the engineering as a specialist supplier. The personnel would thus be a mixture of the production company, ITV, freelancers and the BBC. I thought, *If ever I saw a recipe for politics, manoeuvring in the corridors, back-stabbing, deviousness, power struggles and double-dealing, this is it. But I've got nothing to lose. I'll go for it.* Not for one single second did I ever regret that decision.

I was sworn to secrecy and had to profess ignorance about my future for the whole of 1996 as the media speculated about what would be happening to me. I had the most incredible support from nearly all the papers, including *The Times*, *Sunday Times* and *Sunday Express* and wonderful pieces by Kate Battersby in the *Evening Standard* and Jeremy Clarkson in the *Sun*. But the most amazing of all was the *Daily Mirror*'s 'SAVE OUR MURRAY!' campaign, featuring two consecutive days of double-page spreads. 'If you think Murray should go to ITV, phone this number. If you don't, phone this one.' I was overjoyed when 1455 readers said I should join ITV and only 180 said I shouldn't. It may have been irrelevant in a situation where I had already signed to do so but they weren't to know that and it was really heartwarming for me.

After a fabulous last season with BBC TV, which saw my most emotional commentary of all when my friend Damon Hill won the World Championship in Japan, ITV announced that Chrysalis, led by the brilliant Neil Duncanson, would take charge of the production; Jim Rosenthal was to lead the presentation team with Tony Jardine and Simon Taylor, working in a superb £1 million mobile facility that would be transported to all the European circuits; Martin Brundle and I would be the commentators and the two pit-lane presenters would be James Allen and Louise Goodman – a very well-deserved first for a woman in British televised Formula 1. It had taken a lot of very good people a lot of very hard work to put it all together and it turned out to be an absolutely wonderful team that I had the greatest joy in working with for the next five years.

How did Martin Brundle get into the act? Quite simply because he was the best man for the job. In 1995 when he drove for the French Ligier team in Formula 1 he had to split the races with Aguri Suzuki to satisfy the team's Japanese Mugen engine supplier. When he wasn't driving he used to join Jonathan and I in the commentary box as a second expert. It was producer Mark Wilkin's inspired idea and Martin turned out to be a broadcasting natural. He is one of those very rare individuals, someone who is supremely good at his sport (eight Formula 1 teams, every place in the points except first, World Sports Car Champion and winner at Le Mans) and who can, unusually, talk eloquently, authoritatively and entertainingly about what he does so well. He is also a team player with an incisive manner and a very well-developed sense of humour. His grid walks before the races were to become one of the audience's favourite features of ITV's coverage and his throwaway one-liners in the box were a delight that made our partnership sound exactly like it was – fun.

We took to each other from the very start and, once we'd settled who was going to do what, we got on very well. I've worked with some very impressive ex-drivers, notably Graham Hill, Jackie Stewart, Alan Jones and Jody Scheckter as well as James and Jonathan, but I can say without a moment's hesitation that Martin is by far the best. We worked together better than any other pairing I have been a part of – chemistry again, I suppose but, whatever it was, it worked. It was the first time in all those years that I felt totally at ease with my partner in the box. We made a genuine team and it is no wonder he won the Royal Television Society's prestigious award for Sports Pundit of the Year two years in succession.

No disrespect to the BBC, for whom I worked very happily for 48 years, but ITV were true to their word to Bernie Ecclestone and made a much better job of their Formula 1 coverage. They had dabbled with it in the 1970s but had pulled out and left it to the BBC who, to their eternal credit, developed it and made it into a top TV sport. But the Corporation either couldn't or wouldn't go the last mile to make the most of it, and suffered when ITV decided they had to have it to boost their ratings. At their best, from 1994 onwards with their own facilities at the circuits, the BBC did the Saturday qualifying and the race – but little else. There were two commentators and a pit-lane reporter but the on-site backup was modest. ITV not only had a much bigger team of excellent people in front of and behind the cameras but gave Formula 1 much more air time, presented it from their own sophisticated studio at the circuits and did special pre- and post-season programmes, as well as the popular *Murray and Martin* half-hour features. For up to an hour before the races began and at least half an hour after they finished there were background stories and interviews, with Jim Rosenthal doing a brilliant job of holding it all together.

Initially there was an outcry about the coverage being

interrupted by commercials but ITV did everything possible to reduce the undeniable inconvenience to a minimum and to replay immediately anything important that had happened during the breaks. Nobody liked the interruptions but the money had to come from somewhere and they were more than justified by the superior content and presentation of the overall programming. The grumbling soon died down and the advertisers were delighted with the high-quality ABC viewers they got for their money. Coping with the commercial breaks was no problem for me – I had learned how to do it with years of experience at the Formula 3 races in Macau and working for Channel 9 on the Australian Grand Prix. Doing it the ITV way was easy: there were five two-minute breaks during the race (and if you think that is excessive you can thank your lucky stars that you don't watch German TV, where the breaks last six minutes!) and when the producer decided it was time for one he would tell me over my headphones and count me down for the last ten seconds before the start of the commercials. I had to stop talking immediately before they began and then, once they had, start again for the other countries that were taking our commentary (Australia, Canada, New Zealand, South Africa, Malaysia, etc) and who didn't have them. At the end of the break, as the UK rejoined us, I paused for a few seconds and then started again and if anything important had been missed during the commercials it would immediately be replayed. It all worked very well and I can only remember two really bad omissions. The first was during the 1997 Luxembourg Grand Prix at the Nurburgring when, in the same two-minute break, race leader Mika

Hakkinen retired with a blown engine as did his McLaren team-mate, new race leader David Coulthard, on the very next lap. When the viewers left us for the break Hakkinen was leading with Coulthard second and when it finished a mere two minutes later they were both missing with Jacques Villeneuve now the leader. That took a bit of embarrassed explanation but the 1997 Hungarian GP was even worse. World Champion Damon Hill, who had been dropped by Williams and was now with the second echelon Arrows team, unbelievably caught and passed Michael Schumacher in his Ferrari while the viewers were watching commercials. It was an incredible and inspired move and those watching in Britain were not at all happy to have missed it live, even if they did see it immediately afterwards. But by and large it all went well. It was as much of a pleasure to work with the ITV team as it had been with the BBC. Everyone got on extremely well, no one tried to do the other chap's job, and the atmosphere was terrific.

In simplistic terms, the art of sports commentating, if I can call it that, is to have the knowledge to be able to interpret what you see and the ability to communicate it with enthusiasm. In my case most of what I said came out of my head but to help me on my way I had three vital visual aids to hand in the commentary box. These were a map of the course with all the gear changes, engine revs, car speeds and advertising hoardings marked on it; a handwritten aide memoire containing potted information on the drivers' and race records that I painstakingly prepared before every race; and another which detailed the top six race positions and the championship placings for that year's events. Before I left home I made sure to look at the video and read the race report of the previous year's event and to check my 'commentator's kit bag', which contained everything I was likely to need – from my vital electronic pass and a penknife to throat sweets, rolls of sellotape, a waterproof, and notebook and pens.

Formula 1 is a great big family. It's a bit like a circus going from place to place – everyone knows everyone else and the routine is exactly the same wherever you are, just the place and the race are different. Thursday was a day to get settled in and was the most relaxed of the four-day event. I used to walk the course to check any changes and mark the advertising bridges on a map, which I taped underneath my monitor in the box. It was invaluable for locating where the cars were on the track when the producer went from one shot to another. Thursday was also for chatting and socializing with the teams, and throughout the weekend, if you were lucky enough to be doing the job that I was, you could breakfast with one of them in their motorhome, have lunch with another and dinner with a third. The food and wines were of the highest quality and so was the company. As a Formula 1 fan I was in my seventh heaven.

Friday saw two one-hour sessions of practice and I used to watch them from the commentary box to get the feel of what it was going to be like on race day. Saturday would start with more of the same and then build up to the one hour qualifying session. Martin and I used to dread the all too frequent situation where all the teams would wait in their garages for someone else to go out and clean up the track. The drivers were limited to 12 laps in the hour and only needed about 16 minutes to do them, so they would wait and wait until the conditions were right before they emerged. Sometimes it would be 25 minutes before a car appeared and we had to keep talking with nothing happening. It was obviously puzzling, irritating and frustrating for the viewers and hard work for us to keep the interest going but at least Martin and I no longer had the problem of having to cope with totally inadequate commentary boxes. It used to amaze me that, for so many years, the people who were expected to be on top of everything, informing the world about every last detail of what was happening, were provided with appalling working conditions. In the early days, Monaco was outrageous; in Belgium there were three of us, plus all the very substantial electronic equipment, in a box literally no bigger than a telephone kiosk; Monza defied description, and as soon as the race began in Portugal the grandstand crowd stood up and completely blocked our view of the track. Thankfully those days are long since over.

In the box I had two monitors to look at. One gave me the host broadcaster's pictures (ITV at Silverstone, Channel 9 in Australia, Globo in Brazil and so on) and the other gave me the telemetry information, which was as important as the race pictures. All the cars were equipped with electronic transmitters and when they crossed a cable buried in the track by the start line a signal was sent to a central computer which transmitted a non-stop flood of information to key screens in the control tower, the team positions on the pit wall, the hospitality suites and, of course, the commentary boxes. By constantly punching buttons while I talked I could see the race order, the lap times, the three individual lap sector times, the gaps between cars, who was gaining and who was dropping back, what the fastest lap was, who had retired, what incidents there had been, what lap everyone was on . . . and a lot more besides. The advent, in the 1980s, of all this instant knowledge literally transformed commentary. Where before I'd had to rely on a handwritten lap chart, converting race numbers into drivers' names in my head and juggling with a stopwatch while I was talking, I now had it all there in front of me, accurate to 1000th of a second. It meant I was constantly having to read two screens, the race pictures and the telemetry figures, and correlate them but it made the whole thing so much more informative and entertaining if I used it intelligently.

Sunday was what it was all about though: race day. With the crowds pouring in, the flags and banners, the high-rolling sponsors filling the unbelievably expensive Paddock Club to drink champagne, eat superb meals and be addressed by the drivers, plus the build-up to the start, it made for a wonderful atmosphere. Some places had more buzz than others – Monza was always terrific, with its historical setting and the fanaticism of the Ferrari-loving *tifosi*; Indianapolis, with its incredible scale and the enthusiasm of over 200,000 spectators – but they were all special in their different ways. After the final half-hour of practice in the morning there was a seemingly endless four-hour wait to let the teams finalize their cars, while the tension before the race slowly increased. Jim Rosenthal, Tony Jardine, often a guest personality like Stirling Moss or Eddie

Jordan, and pit-lane reporters James Allen and Louise Goodman would spend nearly an hour setting the scene with background stories and interviews and Martin would do his grid walk. Then, after my energetic limbering-up exercises in the commentary box to get the adrenalin flowing, I'd be poised like an athlete on the start line waiting for those five red lights to come on, one at a time, above the twin lines of multicoloured projectiles with their engines screaming at some 18,000 revs. Lights out and the race was on. *Go! Go! Go!* Now it was down to the two of us in the commentary box to tell the race story as it developed for the next 90 minutes and more.

The start was always the most exciting part of the race. When those five lights went out some 18,000 horsepower was going to be fed to the rear wheels of the 22 cars and they were all going to arrive at the first corner closer to each other than at any other stage of the race. The spectacle was fantastic, the noise unbelievable, and the likelihood of there being a multiple collision was considerable. So there was massive tension in the commentary box and an explosion of emotion as the cars leaped forward. There were no fixed rules between Martin and I on the commentary – I would deal with most of the build-up to the race and the actual start, but Martin was free to jump in whenever he wanted; for instance, when he spotted that someone had stalled on the grid – so we just had to work it out as we went along. Martin always handled the replays because he had the luxury of being able to analyse what had caused them while I was talking. Unlike my days with James Hunt, we each had our own microphone – and it worked well once I'd learned to accept that there was someone with me who had as much right to talk as I had!

In the commentary box we had difficulties that the viewer never appreciated, most of these to do with driver identification. With eleven teams of two identically liveried cars and numbers that were almost invisible, even if you knew where to look for them, the only way to tell the drivers apart was from the design of their helmets. Those helmets were not only appearing lower and lower in the cars because of the modern emphasis on driver safety but often had a confusingly similar appearance. After following, say, Montoya in a Williams, suddenly the producer would cut to a rear shot of a McLaren spinning off the circuit. Was it Coulthard or Raikonnnen, both of whom have predominantly blue and white helmets? Rather than wait for positive identification, all too often I took an instant flyer at it in my excitement and was frequently wrong. No excuses. I would rather have been wrong and have to correct myself than lose the impetus and drama of the commentary.

If it was difficult for me what must it have been like for the spectators at the track and the television viewers? The problem is, of course, that the sponsors, who pay massive money for the privilege of having their names and logos on the cars, do not want them adulterated by big race numbers or the drivers' names. Fortunately, some of the teams appreciated the difficulties of identification and used slightly different liveries on their two cars. So one of the Renaults had a red tip on its nose-cone, the Saubers had different coloured driver mirrors, and when Nigel Mansell was driving for Williams he had a red No. 5 on his nose-cone in contrast to his team-mate's white No. 6. Indeed I claim the credit for that after I asked the technical boss of the Williams team, Patrick Head, if he could do something to differentiate his two cars. 'Here comes Red Five!!' I would gleefully cry.

You're living on your nerves and reflexes all the time in the box. Formula 1 isn't like football, athletics, boxing or cricket, where the spectators in the grandstand can see all the action. With no specific point of reference like a ball you have to follow 22 competitors racing round a 2.5-mile circuit at speeds of up to 200mph. They get strung out, sometimes collide, make pit stops, lose position, rejoin the race, use different strategies, lap each other, crash, go off, retire and form an ever-changing pattern which the viewer has no way of interpreting for himself. The commentator has to do it for him. I loved doing it, building up the drama and excitement, but it wasn't as easy as a lot of people seem to think and with a dangerous sport like motor racing there is an ever-present threat of disaster.

The hardest thing I ever had to deal with was the most publicized and visible accident in the history of motor sport – the death of Ayrton Senna, which happened live on television in the homes of countless viewers all over the world. The 1994 San Marino Grand Prix meeting at Imola had already had grim happenings and at the start of the race on Sunday there was a collision that sent a wheel into the crowd and brought the safety car out to lead the drivers round at greatly reduced speed until the debris could be cleared. On lap seven the race resumed, with Senna's Williams just ahead of Michael

Schumacher's Benetton, but as Ayrton took the Tamburello curve flat out he lost control. Even though a lot of speed was scrubbed off he slammed into the concrete wall at some 135mph. In previous years I had seen Michele Alboreto, Nelson Piquet and Gerhard Berger do the same thing at the same place and come to little harm – in Berger's case, despite his being unconscious while his car caught fire – so my immediate reaction to Senna's crash was one of excitement rather than horror. *Wow, that's a big one!* was my first thought but it was immediately obvious that it was a lot more than that. The race was stopped as the medical staff, under the direction of Professor Sid Watkins, tried to save the stricken Senna's life. The cameras of RAI, the Italian host broadcaster, stayed with the scene and I was getting some very disturbing pictures on my monitor, but fortunately, for the very first time at a foreign Grand Prix, the BBC had its own camera unit and direction, so producer Mark Wilkin was able to show the British viewers something else. As the coverage continued I saw his pictures but was also still getting those from RAI. The greatest racing driver in the world was lying immobile and gravely injured beside the track. I had no way of knowing how serious his condition was although I was by now fearing the worst. What to do? I obviously had no justification for making reassuring statements like, 'Don't worry, I know it looks bad but I've seen things like this before at this very place where the drivers were OK – today's cars are very strong and I'm sure Senna will be all right'; nor could I say, 'This is terrible. I fear from the body language of the medics around Senna that this is a potentially fatal accident' because I didn't know that it was and, anyway, it would have been unacceptably alarmist to say so.

For what seemed like hours the horrible scenes continued until a helicopter took the mortally wounded Brazilian to the hospital, where he died. A truly great man had met his maker and I honestly do not know how I found the right words to cope with it. It is not an experience I would like to repeat.

When I reported to the BBC at Silverstone for my first broadcast in 1949, Formula 1 did not yet exist and Grand Prix racing was still struggling to recover fully after an exhausting war. Alfa-Romeo and Maserati ruled the circuits, Ferrari had yet to win, there were only five major races and British cars and drivers were of no consequence. The cars had their engines in the front and the drivers wore thin cotton trousers, short-sleeved T-shirts and linen helmets. They had no safety belts and their cars were flimsy death traps; there were no barriers between them and the thousands of spectators lining the track and no gravel traps to slow them if they went off. The medical facilities were minimal.

In those days, so soon after a world war that had taken literally millions of lives in appalling circumstances, attitudes towards death were very different. 'Motor racing is dangerous. If they don't like it they don't have to do it. The throttle works both ways and if they can't stand the heat they should get out of the kitchen,' was the general view in the sport and several drivers were killed each season, with no great reaction except regret. In the mid-1960s, however, Jackie Stewart courageously championed a much-vilified crusade for greater safety which, together with changing public attitudes, gradually led to major improvements. Thanks mainly to the untiring efforts of Bernie Ecclestone, FIA President Max Mosley and FIA Chief Medical Officer Professor Sid Watkins, it's all very different now, with safer circuits, safer cars, infinitely better medical facilities, fireproof clothing and greatly improved marshalling.

Ayrton Senna's tragic death was the catalyst for even greater efforts to make Formula 1 safer with major changes to car construction and the regulations. I am sure they would have come anyway but the worldwide impact of the great Brazilian's untimely demise undoubtedly hastened their introduction in a vigorous effort to avoid anti-motor-racing legislation. Ironically, Senna was a close personal friend of Sid Watkins who, as an individual, has undoubtedly done more than anyone else to make Formula 1 safer. The drivers do not dwell on the fact that their job could take their life. 'It may happen to others but it won't happen to me,' is the usual, if unrealistic, attitude. They never talk about it and, to be honest, I never raised the subject during interviews. It was just something one did not do. Everyone knew it *could* happen; everyone hoped it *wouldn't*. Of course none of them would race if they thought they were going to be killed but the fact is that they could be and retirement from racing is often caused by the belief that the risks are no longer acceptable. That was certainly the case with James Hunt and I believe it was with Damon Hill, too.

No one was more conscious of the hazards of the sport than Senna but he adopted a fatalistic attitude and just got on with it. Nevertheless, his concern for his fellow drivers in what is an extremely selfish and self-centred profession was unusual. During that fateful weekend at Imola, Ayrton visited his countryman Rubens Barrichello in hospital after his high-speed crash on the Friday and the following day, very much against the rules, commandeered a course car to get to the scene of Austrian driver Roland Ratzenberger's fatal crash. He then unsuccessfully tried to get into the trackside Medical Centre at Imola – something he had succeeded in doing at Jerez in Spain in 1990 where Lotus driver Martin Donnelly had an appalling accident from which he miraculously recovered. Senna may have appreciated the dangers of racing but at Imola on the Saturday he, like most of the people who were there, received a forceful reminder that its consequences could be fatal. There had not been a death at a Grand Prix since 12 years earlier when Osella driver Riccardo Paletti was killed at the start of the 1982 Canadian Grand Prix, and Ratzenberger's death was a wake-up call for everyone. Sid Watkins seriously suggested to the badly shaken Senna that he should withdraw from the next day's race but Ayrton felt it was his destiny to continue and did so – with tragic results.

Motor racing can never be entirely safe and nor do I think it should be. Of course it should always be the objective to have safer cars and circuits, better medical facilities and protective clothing, and highly trained marshals with efficient warning systems, but not to the extent that it encourages dangerous driving. Knowing how safe today's racing conditions are, the modern Grand Prix driver already takes risks that would have been regarded as suicidal in the 1950s. Would Stirling Moss have taken the 150mph risk to pass Fangio that Senna, enraged by what he felt to be an injustice, took in attempting to overtake Prost in Japan in 1990? Definitely not. Neither Senna nor Prost was even scratched by their collision that took them both out, but in the flimsy cars of Stirling's time death would almost certainly have been the penalty. And if motor racing was sanitized to the extent that it posed no risks, where would the line be drawn in other hazardous sports? No more mountain climbing? No more parachuting? No more fishing? (You'd be amazed at how many deaths that causes.)

Senna was right. I strongly believe that the individual should be left to make his own mind up about whether the risks are acceptable, provided spectators are given the maximum protection. In the old days no one gave a second thought to their safety but now there are most demanding requirements to protect them. And rightly so.

Above: Italy's Ferrari-loving *tifosi* worshipped 'Big John' Surtees, who uniquely won eight car and motor-cycle World Championships.

For years my father and I made *Sound Stories*, long-playing records of the TT races. Great fun to do and full of evocative drama.

Above: Go! I had always wanted to see Australia's fabled Bathurst 1000 touring car race and in 1997 and 1998 I made it by joining the Channel 7 commentary team for two unforgettable experiences of 'The Great Race'.

Left: At Bathurst 1997, Australian Touring Car Champion Brad Jones took me round in his Audi Quattro at racing speeds whilst I commentated. Fun? You bet!

Below: The British Touring Car Championship made for superb television and I worked on it for ten wonderful years. Here are the turbo wastegate-chattering Ford Sierras of 1994 led by top-man Andy Rouse.

CHAPTER ELEVEN

My Wonderful World of Formula 1

So what's it like to drive a Formula 1 car? I'd often wondered and in 1983 I got the chance to find out. After five grim years since James Hunt had won the World Drivers' Championship, Ron Dennis' McLaren team had fought back to finish second to Ferrari in the 1982 Championship with the brilliant MP4, designed by John Barnard and with Niki Lauda and John Watson at the wheel. However, with normally-aspirated Ford DFV engines against the turbocharged Ferraris, Renaults and Brabham–BMWs, a full return to their former glory days had yet to come.

One day I was leaving a lunch function when Ron asked me if I had ever driven a Formula 1 car. My response was no. When he then asked if I wanted to, my answer was an unequivocal 'yes' He said he would be in touch. I thought, *Sure, it'll be like the couple who say 'Come and spend a weekend with us in our place in Nice' and that's the last you hear about it.* I should have known better, for Ron Dennis is a man of his word and not long afterwards the phone rang. 'Get to Silverstone on Thursday, Murray, you're on.'

Full of eager anticipation I rode up on my BMW R100RS motor cycle and Ron gave me a duffel bag, telling me, 'Get into this lot – you'll be going out in the lunch hour.' 'This lot' was a set of Niki Lauda's overalls, fireproof Nomex long johns and vest, racing boots and a pair of racing gloves to accompany my own helmet. To my surprised delight I got into Niki's gear without a struggle and then took stock of things. It was a Goodyear tyre test day and all the teams were there.

'We're looking forward to the lunch hour, Murray,' one of my mates said, and it suddenly struck me that I was going out on my own for the first time in a Formula 1 car watched by people I'd been talking frankly about for years who'd be waiting with relish for me to get it very wrong. BBC TV were also there to record a feature on my epic drive so, with my co-commentator World Champion James Hunt as my guide and mentor, my pride was very much at stake.

James' advice was this: 'Just remember two things, Murray. Don't stall it and make sure you stop at the right garage when you come in. If you don't the mechanics will have to push you. You won't be very popular and you'll lose a lot of face.'

So, in my Unipart-sponsored MP4 carrying John Watson's No. 7, I gave it a bootful and shot out of the pit-lane like a cork out of a bottle, nearly running over a cameraman's foot as I did so. Other than that though there were no worries, and at the end of the lap I came in for the usual check. It was on leaving the second time that I stalled the car to produce the embarrassing, head-nodding shot that has been shown on television countless times but, loving every second of it, I stayed out for lap after lap, grimly concentrating on getting the line right for Copse Corner – and totally failing to see the 'come in' arrow that McLaren had been showing me as I passed the pits. When I finally spotted it I expertly drew up to the McLaren garage and stopped, only to see, with horror, that Ken Tyrrell was standing beside me.

Oh my God, I've stopped at the Tyrrell garage by mistake.

'Don't move,' said Ken as I went to get out. 'Next time come in when you're told to. Three times you stayed out. Right?'

'Yes, Ken. Sorry.'

And off he went, chuckling. Always out for a bit of fun, he'd seen what was going on and taken the opportunity to give me a ribbing.

I found it wasn't difficult to drive the McLaren. With a superb manual gearbox, a light clutch and 'only' 500hp, about which Lauda was very disparaging, it was like an incredibly high-powered motor bike. Terrific power, superbly responsive, sensational acceleration and unbelievable brakes. After getting the feel of it I did the best I could but was very careful. The trick was to stay within your limits and not go off. I certainly wasn't going to risk that. ('Sorry Ron, it's in the armco at Abbey.' 'Not a problem Murray, we'll get another one out for you.')

'Well done, Murray,' said James when I got out of the car. 'You've done something that any Grand Prix driver would give his eye teeth for.'

'Have I? What's that?'

'You've improved your lap time by half a minute!'

This fabulous experience was made fantasy when we did a dummy podium ceremony for the cameras, with me on the top step spraying the champagne, Niki Lauda on the second step and John Watson on the third.

'Don't get any of the champagne on my overalls,' said Niki. 'It stinks and takes days to wash out.'

When I was floating around on Cloud Nine afterwards, John asked what speed I was doing down Hangar Straight.

'I don't know, John, they don't have speedometers – I thought you knew that.'

'Ha, ha. Very funny. How many revs were you pulling then?'

'I just saw a flash of 9000.'

'What gear were you in?'

'In top, of course.'

'Murray, that's 150mph!'

Amazing. I certainly wouldn't have been doing that if I'd realized how fast it was, but in a thoroughbred like a McLaren MP4 it's very easy to get there before you know where you are. I was immensely indebted to Ron Dennis that day, but 15 years later I was to become even more so.

In 1998 McLaren had the inspired idea of producing a Formula 1 'tandem' two-seater to give a very few incredibly privileged people the ultimate thrill of experiencing race-speed Formula 1 performance with a star driver instead of tremulously bumbling around by themselves as I had. With their brilliant designer Gordon Murray in charge, the team made a full-spec F1 car powered by a state-of-the-art 10-cylinder Mercedes-Benz engine identical to those in the 1998 team cars. Thanks to a much smaller fuel tank, which compensated for the passenger's weight, its performance was little inferior to the single-seaters that Mika Hakkinen and David Coulthard drove to win that year's World Drivers' and Constructors' Championships.

I was to be one of only three passengers on its press launch day but first, to satisfy McLaren's meticulous standards, I had to have a very tough medical at the Royal Brompton Hospital. Chest and spine X-rays, heart monitoring on the treadmill, a long one-to-one with a specialist – the lot. To my smug delight I came through with flying colours while one of the Formula 1 journalists from a leading national newspaper failed, despite being half my age. Next it was down to the McLaren factory at Woking for a seat fitting – a fascinating process that requires you to sit in the car on a bag of plastic granules which are chemically heated while they form your shape, from which your very own carbon-fibre seat is made. Then it was up to Silverstone for the big day. I had nothing to worry about: I was to be driven by my commentary box colleague Martin Brundle, who had beaten Ayrton Senna time after time in the 1983 British Formula 3 Championship, had finished in the Grand Prix points nearly 40 times and who had given his Benetton team-mate Michael Schumacher a challenging run for his money in 1992.

The car looked and felt superb as I snuggled down into the minimal space behind Martin. I had to splay my legs as wide as I could until they were immovably compressed between the inside of the tub and the outside of Martin's seat. The six-point harness over my thighs, shoulders and waist was tightened until I couldn't move a muscle and then a massive carbon-fibre bar was pinned tight up against my chest to support the back of Martin's seat. I'm not claustrophobic, but I could sympathize with several of his subsequent passengers who chickened out at the last moment. I had the choice of resting my hands on my knees under the bar or having them immovably trapped between it and my chest. I chose the latter, in the naive belief that if anything happened I could, with one mighty bound, spring free. On with the Nomex balaclava, a neck brace to steady my head against the G-forces, my helmet and the thick padded plastic collar that ran round the cockpit rim to absorb helmet impact if we hit something. I had a panic button with a big red light to alert Martin if things got too much for me, but there was no way I was going to use it.

'What happens if we go off into the armco backwards and the car catches fire?' I asked Martin. 'You'll be out like a jackrabbit but I'll be trapped by all this gubbins.'

'That won't happen, Murray.'

'Why not?'

'Well, it won't – and there's not much petrol in it anyway.'

And with that comforting knowledge we shot out of the pit lane.

Three laps in the wet and then in. McLaren had said that no one, but no one, was ever going to do more than three laps but when we stopped Martin expressed the opinion that it hadn't been very exciting, and suggested that if it dried out in the lunch hour we'd have another go. I thought it was bloody exciting but relished another ride.

Sure enough the track dried and Martin said, 'Do you think you can stand five laps this time? If you can we can do an out lap, three quick ones and then in.'

'Martin, I'll stand five laps if it kills me. I'm never going to be able to do this again.'

What an experience! 'You'll think I've forgotten my braking points,' said Martin, 'but I won't have.' It's a good thing he told me, for we took Copse at 140mph, hurtled through the daunting Maggots–Becketts–Chapel complex at what seemed suicidal speed, hit 190mph down the Hangar Straight, got up to 165mph on the way from Club Corner to Abbey and held it until, with no change in the wailing cry of the 800hp Mercedes-Benz engine just behind me, I could see the Abbey apex approaching at undiminished speed. *This is what he said it was going to be like*, I thought, *so I suppose it's all right*. But I also told myself that after 75 years of happiness life didn't really owe me anything. Then those fantastic brakes took over and in literally just a few yards we slowed to 50mph, powered through the tight left/right and rocketed up to the unforgettable sensation of taking Bridge Corner without even a lift.

I reckon I'm pretty fit but as we entered the fifth lap I'd had enough. Even though you're so tightly constrained in the cockpit that you can't move a millimetre you still accelerate and decelerate with the car and experience those enormous braking and cornering G-forces. Your guts go on when your body brakes with the car and if you fail to brace your head it ricochets between the driver's headrest in front of you and your own behind you. If Martin had said 'Another lap?' on the intercom (through which his exultant cries of 'Yee-haw!' were ringing in my ears) my pride would probably have made me agree but I wouldn't really have wanted to – I was exhausted.

In still slightly slippery conditions we had gone round only eight seconds slower than a really good lap in a top race car and my already enormous respect for the skill, fitness and stamina of the Grand Prix driver multiplied 10 times over that memorable day. Before our run I had written some spoof notes on a scrap of paper and I pretended I had coolly made them while we were circulating. 'You crossed the white line leaving the pits, Martin,' I said. 'You were a bit late changing up to sixth on the Hangar Straight, you missed the apex at Stowe and you hit the brakes too early for Woodcote.'

'No way, Murray. We were flat out through Woodcote actually!'

Magic. At the end of 2000 the McLaren two-seater programme ended after only about 130 people worldwide had been lucky enough to participate in the incredible experience. If, like my mother, I live to be 100 I'll never forget it.

For someone as keen on motor sport as I am, I had a dream job. I was representing the BBC or ITV in front of enormous worldwide audiences and no door was closed to me in the Formula 1 paddock. With my electronic pass I could swipe my way in, go anywhere, talk to anyone – in the team's motorhomes, their garages, the vital tyre suppliers' areas, the pit-lane and the media centre. In the commentary box I had the finest view you could get plus the specialized telemetry that told me, at a glance, what was happening on the track. Away from the circuits I had the sort of access opportunities my fellow enthusiasts would die for, especially to the drivers who, these days, are like unapproachable gods. Such is the pressure on them that when they are not actually on the track they spend hours with their engineers poring over telemetry traces to find that critical extra tenth of a second. 'Where am I losing time? Where is my team-mate faster than I am? Can I brake later anywhere? Should we change the car's setup? If so how? Are the tyres working as hard as they should?' and so on. Formula 1 is now so scientific and technology-led that drivers have to do infinitely more than just get in the car and drive the wheels off it. To reach the top you have to be multi-talented.

I'm forever being asked who was the greatest Champion, and I always say that it's impossible to compare directly drivers from different eras in different cars on different circuits and with different rules, regulations, politics and competition. Was Jim Clark 'better' than Michael Schumacher? Was Jackie Stewart 'better' than Alain Prost? Was Niki Lauda 'better' than Ayrton Senna? Some would say yes in all those cases, and I could give you subjective answers, but I certainly couldn't prove that I was right. For what it is worth the greatest racing driver of them all in my opinion was Italy's immortal Tazio Nuvolari, who raced mostly before the war and who I was lucky enough to see winning the 1938 Donington Grand Prix for Auto Union. He was a charismatic genius and I could go on for a very long time about his personality, his driving and his amazing record.

But as far as Formula 1 is concerned, which began in 1950, there is one man who, for me, stands out above all the rest, regardless of era – Juan Manuel Fangio, Formula 1's five-time World Champion, who uniquely took the supreme honour in 1951 and then four years in succession, 1954–57, with four different constructors: Alfa-Romeo, Mercedes-Benz, Ferrari and Maserati. It is true that he only drove in 51 World Championship races (there were only seven or eight a year in his day) and that he always had the best car, but he won 24 of those races – over 40% – and had the best car because he was the best driver and therefore had the constructors beating a path to his door. Fangio was a quiet and humble Argentinian with a winning smile and gentlemanly charm who, like Nuvolari before him and Senna after him, had charisma oozing from the roots of his hair. He was one of those very rare people who create a buzz of respectful excitement the moment they enter a room. He didn't even start racing in Formula 1 until he was 39, an age by which most Grand Prix drivers have retired these days, and he was 46 when he brilliantly won one of the greatest races of all time, the 1957 German Grand Prix at the fabled Nurburgring, to take his fifth Championship before retiring as a living legend to his beloved birthplace of Balcarce in Argentina.

One of Fangio's greatest admirers was the very wealthy Italian Count Volpi, who had run his own team in the 1950s. In 1984, as a mark of his respect, he commissioned the great producer Hugh Hudson, of *Chariots of Fire* fame, to produce a film on Fangio's life. The result was superb. Monaco was closed out of season to film the great man driving the Maserati

250F in which he had been victorious 27 years before, thrilling sequences from his epic long-distance Chevrolet race wins in South America were recreated and Fangio drove his 1955 Championship-winning Mercedes-Benz W196 again for the cameras. But oddly the finished film story climaxed at the beginning with brilliantly edited footage of his historic 1957 Nurburgring win. Hugh Hudson asked me to do the commentary, which I did, but about a year later, when the film had still not appeared, I had a call from him.

'Count Volpi isn't happy, Murray. He wants the German race to be at the end instead of the beginning and that makes a nonsense of your words so I'd like you to do them again. It'll mean a trip to Rome though, I'm afraid.'

I wasn't complaining. I flew first class to Rome, where I was collected by a chauffeur-driven, Mercedes-Benz 500 stretch limousine and taken to a suite in the magnificent Excelsior Hotel. The next day, after I'd killed time by taking a tour of the city and the Vatican, I reported to the studios.

'We have to wait for Count Volpi,' said the American editor. Now in my mind's eye the Count was a short, fat, bald and dark Italian in a blue serge suit, but when he arrived he was tall, languid, immaculately dressed in a Harris tweed sports coat and flannels, spoke superb English and had with him one of the most stunning women I have ever seen, positively dripping with jewellery and breeding.

The editor indicated he was ready and off I went, twenty to the dozen. At the end I was well pleased with what I had done for my simulated live commentary, particularly for the final laps of the race when Fangio, pushing his Maserati way beyond the limit, caught and passed the Ferraris of Peter Collins and Mike Hawthorn after what had seemed like a disastrously long pit stop.

'Was that OK, Count Volpi?' asked the editor.

'Yes, very good indeed but halfway through Murray said "AND then Fangio . . . I think it would have been better if he had said BUT then Fangio . . ."

'Count Volpi,' I said, 'I'll gladly do the whole thing again [I was being paid an obscene amount of money] but you have to realize that it was all coming out of my head, not a script. Next time I might not say and *or* but!'

Anyway I did it again and this time the Count was happy and so was I. But for me the best of Fangio was still to come. In 1987 Pirelli, whose tyres Fangio had used, organized a magnificent lunch in his honour at the Porter Tun Room of Whitbread's London brewery and Tom Northey, their publicity chief, asked me to host it. As part of the deal I had to do a film interview with the great man at his suite at the Hyde Park Hotel and I spent a whole morning with the maestro. I'd always thought of him as a bit uncommunicative but rapidly discovered that this was because, like me, he only spoke his own language. Spanish isn't much use in England but, with the help of Pirelli's gifted linguist Robert Newman, we got on very well indeed and I was charmed by my hero. At the age of 76 he had just arrived off a flight from Brazil where, at 125mph, the steering wheel had come off the Formula 1 Mercedes-Benz he had been demonstrating, but he could still tell me what gears he had been in and what revs he had been pulling in the Maserati all around the tortuous 14-mile

Nurburgring during his inspired laps in the 1957 German Grand Prix.

'Things are so much better now,' he said. 'Alberto Ascari and my friend Stirling Moss who drove with me for Mercedes in 1955 were my greatest rivals. You have to be calm and collected as a race driver and they both were, but in my 10 years of racing in Europe I saw 30 of my friends and competitors killed. They were hard times. But it is not so much courage you need as absolute faith in yourself – and you also need luck. Fortunately I had both.'

The next day I could hardly believe my eyes as past me in the traffic down London's busy Chilwell Street came a gleaming W196 Mercedes-Benz single-seater driven by the helmetless, silver-haired legend. As I ran after him he passed an impassive mounted policeman, stopped in the courtyard of the brewery, looked up and said 'Hello, Murray.' *Fangio remembered me!*

'Next time you are in Argentina,' he said, 'come to Balcarce and I will show you my museum.'

At Buenos Aires I was later to drive the very Mercedes-Benz in which he had finished second in the legendary Mille Miglia but by then Fangio had sadly died. I had, though, the honour of having been with my hero, who personalized for me a superb print of himself in his Grand Prix Mercedes. It hangs on my study wall to this day. I used to wonder what people get out of autographs but not any more. Fangio gave me some of his life.

Almost a year later to the day I achieved another of my ambitions – to be in the same room as Enzo Ferrari. It would have been enough to be there – he didn't have to speak to or acknowledge me – just be in the same room, this man who, to me, was the greatest in the history of motor racing. So you can imagine my joy when, in March 1988, the BBC said they'd arranged for me to go to Maranello to interview him.

When I got there I was introduced to Franco Gozzi, a long-time colleague of the Commendatore, who said to me, 'Three historical questions. Mr Ferrari likes historical questions.'

Not on your life, I thought. *I haven't come all this way to ask him three historical questions.*

Signor Ferrari greeted me in his office, where he sat facing a portrait of his beloved son Dino who, years before, had tragically died of kidney failure following a long battle with muscular dystrophy. On his desk was a black glass prancing horse that had been given to him by Paul Newman. As ever, he was wearing dark glasses. Sitting nervously before him, I thought, *He's 88, he's been interviewed hundreds of times in his own language. He's been asked every question I'm likely to think of countless times already and here am I, an English foreigner, to ask them again. Somehow I've got to get his attention or I'll be out before I realize I've arrived.*

'Signor Ferrari,' I said. 'You don't know me but you knew my father. When you ran a motor-cycle racing team in the 1930s you used Rudge-Whitworth bikes and you bought them from my father, who was the Rudge Sales Director and who raced them very successfully, including here at Monza where you met him and my mother.'

Now, not many people know that Ferrari had a motor-cycle team in his early days and I thought I saw a flicker of interest behind the dark glasses. Maybe I'd struck gold.

'What was your father's name?'

'It was Graham Walker.'

'And what is your name?'

'Murray Walker, Sir.'

'Yes, I bought them from Signor Borrani who was the Rudge distributor in Milan.'

I'd broken the ice. I have to be honest and admit that it wasn't the best interview I'd ever done because having to do it through an interpreter, let alone one whose instructions had been ignored, wasn't easy. But I'd got him to talk, including his view that Nuvolari was the greatest of them all and that, heartwarmingly, two of the drivers who had impressed him most in his long and illustrious career were Englishmen Peter Collins and Stirling Moss.

Enzo Ferrari famously always used purple ink when he was writing and I was later sent a copy of his very limited edition autobiography *Le Mie Gioie Terribli* (*My Terrible Joys*). Written inside it in purple ink is 'To Murray Walker. Enzo Ferrari.' It isn't quite in a glass case but it certainly occupies pride of place on my bookshelves as a cherished reminder of a very special day.

Just a few months after our meeting Enzo Ferrari died, shortly before his cars finished first and second in the 1988 Italian Grand Prix at Monza, thus preventing the seemingly invincible McLaren team from winning every race of the season. The *tifosi* went mad and so did I. The Old Man at the racetrack in the sky must have been very happy too.

Fangio and Ferrari: two truly great men of motor racing. But right up there with them must be Sir Jackie Stewart and it has been my very great pleasure and privilege to know him, commentate on his racing prowess and work with him at the racetracks since the late 1960s. No one, but no one, has done more for motor sport than he. His achievements are awe-inspiring: three times a World Champion, the catalyst for Ken Tyrrell's success, the safety crusader whose courageous insistence on higher standards transformed Formula 1, a brilliant businessman, one of only two F1 drivers to found an eponymous Grand Prix-winning team (the other was Jack Brabham), President of the British Racing Drivers' Club and honoured by his country. But behind the scenes Jackie has also benefited Formula 1 enormously by his tireless fundraising for the Grand Prix Mechanics Trust – and has given me and many others some truly wonderful times in the process.

Among his many achievements Jackie is a brilliant shot and was only prevented from representing Great Britain in the Olympic Games by illness. His enthusiasm for clay pigeon shooting is shared by a lot of Formula 1 people, among them Roly Vincini, once chief mechanic to Bernie Ecclestone's Brabham team. Big Roly is an outgoing chap and one day at Silverstone he said to Jackie, who was forever masterminding competitions for the likes of the Princess Royal, Sean Connery and other top people, 'When are you going to do something for us mechanics, Jackie?'

Jackie promised he would, and so began the Grand Prix Mechanics' Challenge, one of Formula 1's most enjoyable and sought-after social occasions, the magnitude and success of which is typical Jackie Stewart. He takes over the fabulous Gleneagles Hotel in Scotland, where he has his shooting school, and organizes a magnificent two-day clay pigeon competition between the Grand Prix teams, their sponsors and the media. I've had the wonderful experience of being on four of them, including one as captain of the media team, and they were hugely enjoyable. You fly to Edinburgh, get bussed to Gleneagles where you are fitted out with a complete set of Barbour clothing, and then spend a whole day practising and the next competing. There is a superb gala dinner where everyone gets a prize, including a gold Rolex watch for the individual winner, and where the haggis is played in by Regimental Highland pipers in full regalia. You are made to feel like royalty the whole time and it costs nothing, for Jackie not only personally raises sponsorship to cover everything but also manages to realize at least £100,000 for the Trust every time he does it.

A lot of mechanics have benefited from the Trust as a result of Jackie's fundraising. He really is an amazing chap and is equally impressive as a television presenter and commentator having, amongst other things, masterfully fronted Australia's Channel 9 coverage, the best in the world, for years and made an enormous contribution to Formula 1 on television with his wit, wisdom and humour. One year the BBC made the mistake of putting both Jackie and James Hunt in the commentary box with me at Brands Hatch for the British Grand Prix and there was a tense rivalry between the two World Champions. During the race Jackie said, 'I can tell from the shape of his right rear tyre that Lauda has a puncture. He won't realize it himself yet but he'll know soon from the curvature change he'll see in his mirror.'

'That shows how long it is since you've driven a race car, Jackie,' said James, witheringly, 'because you can't see the rear tyres in the mirrors of the modern cars.'

'Oh, can't you, James? Well, I did three laps in a Tyrrell yesterday and I could see them very clearly.'

Ouch!

Another of my abiding memories of Jackie in the commentary box is from the 1978 USA-East at Watkins Glen (there were two Grands Prix in America every year in those days, the other being at Long Beach). It was in October and I had driven there from New York, marvelling at the glorious turning colours of the maple trees in Upper New York State. Jackie, who had been working at Silverstone the previous day, flew in by Concorde and helicopter and arrived clutching the magnum of Möet & Chandon champagne for presentation to the winner. The race, dominated by Carlos Reutemann's Ferrari, was processional and we struggled desperately to find something exciting to say. It being America, the commentary box lacked for nothing, including a well-stocked fridge and, towards the end of a lacklustre event under threatening skies, BBC producer Jonathan Martin reached into the fridge, took out of can of Coca-Cola and pulled the ring tab. A spray of Coke shot between us and landed on the inside of the window. 'Aha!' said Jackie. 'This could change everything – I see a few spots of rain!'

Sadly Watkins Glen, an excellent circuit with a terrific atmosphere, fell off the Grand Prix calendar after 1980 but it literally went out with a bang. There was an area on the infield known as 'The Bog', because that's what it was, and a tradition grew up of pushing wrecked cars into it. Over the years things got wilder and wilder and they climaxed in 1980 with a very roughneck element totally out of control. They shoved in a coach that had brought a party of Canadians to the race, complete with their luggage, and then rushed around chucking sticks of dynamite about the place. The previous night I'd watched, goggle-eyed, while a gang of men and women linked hands and danced round a campfire chanting at a couple who were having sex in front of it. Not at all like our own dear Silverstone.

Nineteen-ninety six was my last British Grand Prix for BBC TV but because I was sworn to secrecy about my imminent transfer to ITV I had to go along with all the speculation about what would be happening to me and the belief that this was to be my final Formula 1 commentary from Silverstone. Bernie Ecclestone knew the score of course but, master publicist that he is, he wanted to exploit the situation and, bless him, pay me a very real compliment. On the Saturday afternoon after the qualifying hour which, to Britain's delight, had seen Damon Hill take pole position in his Williams–Renault, Bernie said to me, 'I want you to go round in Damon's car tomorrow.'

'I'm very flattered, Bernie, but I don't think it's a very good idea.'

'Why not?'

'Well, I have driven a Formula 1 car but it was a long time ago and I don't fancy going round in a Williams for the first time in front of 90,000 people.'

'No, no. I mean the *parade* car. Be at the drivers' briefing tomorrow. It's immediately after that.'

So when the time came I went and stood on the red carpet that led to the line of immaculate vintage Rolls-Royces. To my very great surprise, instead of going to the cars when they came out of the briefing the drivers formed a circle round me, through which Michael Schumacher emerged holding a magnum of champagne, saying, 'We know this is your last one here for the BBC, Murray, so we've all signed this for you.'

To say that I was touched would be a huge understatement, but I didn't have any illusions that the drivers had thought of it – it was Bernie. I still have the champagne and it will never be drunk. What was an enormously emotional experience was then made even more so by my slow lap as I sat between Williams team-mates Damon Hill and Jacques Villeneuve waving an enormous bunch of flowers at the massive crowd. The cheers were for Damon but I heard them too and was very moved. All the time I was having to hold on to Jacques to stop him falling on to the track. He proceeded to win the race, with Damon failing to score, so maybe I helped prolong the outcome of that thrilling Championship, which went right down to the last race in Japan before Damon clinched it.

With Damon fired from Williams, Jacques Villeneuve became World Champion in 1997, my first year with ITV and the start of its excellent new in-depth coverage of Formula 1. But then it was the years of McLaren versus Ferrari and Mika Hakkinen versus Michael Schumacher. There's no friendlier and more helpful a team in the whole pit lane than McLaren when you get to know them, but their boss Ron Dennis' reserved personality and management style rubs off on them to give them an undeserved image of grim and soulless efficiency, typified by the team's calm and dignified colour scheme of black and grey with flashes of red. In contrast, Ferrari are steeped in emotional imagery: the Mille Miglia, Targa Florio, Maranello and Monza; Enzo Ferrari himself; Nuvolari, Ascari, Fangio, Gilles Villeneuve and Lauda; soul and passion, scarlet and yellow; the prancing horse and the fanatical support of seemingly the whole of Italy, not to mention most of the rest of the world.

Behind the microphone I always tried hard to be objective and not to favour one team or the other, although I never attempted to hide the fact that, as a Briton, I was happiest when a British driver was winning. 'Here comes the President of the Nigel Mansell fan club,' they'd say in Australia and I'd just grin and walk on. I'll freely admit that sometimes my 'trousers on fire' commentary style resulted in my emotions showing but I was a bit dismayed when I was accused of heading the Schumacher/Ferrari Adoration Society. It wasn't intentional but my respect and admiration for the Maranello team, their history and the great comeback they'd made since Michael joined them in 1996 was obviously working its way through into my commentaries. Even placid and tolerant Mika Hakkinen had a good-natured go at me, and since he doesn't hear too much of what I'm saying during the races it must have got to him via his team-mates. Then I received a letter from Martin Whitmarsh, McLaren's Managing Director, the gist of which was this: 'Dear Murray, Here at McLaren we all very much enjoy your exciting and informative commentaries and share your admiration of Ferrari[!] but we feel we have failed to communicate to you our own love of the sport, our enthusiasm and our successes. So I'm inviting you to visit us here at Woking and spend the day with us meeting all your old friends and having an open look at all our facilities. Please let me know if you would like to come so that I can make the necessary arrangements. Kind regards, Martin.'

I had been to the McLaren HQ before, but not recently and certainly not with as generous an invitation as this. So I pitched up on the appointed day to be met by three old chums waiting for me in the reception area: Jo Ramirez, McLaren's logistics and administration manager and one of the nicest people in Formula 1; George Langhorn, the team's ex-tyre man and now the boss of their paint shop, and Chris Robson, whom I had known since he looked after the Brabham team tyres.

'Hello, Murray! Glad you could make it. Let's have a coffee while we tell you what's happening.' And then I got a detailed department-by-department tour of the whole factory. All my old friends were there: Martin Whitmarsh himself, team manager Dave Ryan, Neil Trundle (the 'del' of Rondel racing, of which Ron Dennis had been the 'Ron' before they did a reverse takeover of Teddy Mayer's McLaren team), designer Neil Oatley, Tyler Alexander ('been-there-since-Bruce McLaren') and many more. Every time I entered a new department someone I knew appeared as if by magic with words like 'Hello, Murray. What are you doing here? Nice to see you. Let me show you round my patch.'

About halfway through it all I said, 'I know why I'm here, you know.'

'Oh yes, Murray. Why's that then?'

'To be brainwashed.'

'Yes, you're dead right!'

Back in the canteen George Langhorn produced a stunning memento of a great day – a McLaren carbon-fibre rear wing endplate, complete with sponsors' logos, mounted on a polished metal plinth with a dated plaque inscribed, 'To Murray from all his friends at McLaren.' To remind me who they were, an amazing 196 of the workforce had signed it in white paint. I was truly impressed by this display of turning the other cheek. Instead of saying, 'Why the hell don't you stop banging on about Ferrari, you so-and-so?' as a lot of people would (and did), McLaren decided to give me the VIP treatment and more – and believe me it worked!

In my time with the BBC it had a virtual broadcasting sports monopoly on radio and TV and a veritable Hall of Fame of commentators who were legends in their own lifetimes: David Coleman on athletics, Henry Longhurst and Peter Alliss on golf, Peter O'Sullevan on horse racing, the superb John Arlott and his successor Brian Johnston on cricket, Harry Carpenter on boxing, Dan Maskell on tennis, Kenneth Wolstenholme and John Motson on football, and my favourite Bill McLaren on rugby. They were masters of their craft with distinctive voices and styles and an ability to enthuse viewers who were not necessarily interested in their sports.

I am neither knowledgeable about nor a great follower of rugby but if there was an international where Bill McLaren was going to be commentating I would be glued to the box.

His personality and knowledge of the game, allied to his Scottish accent, fiery passion and forceful delivery, made it live for me. I really did watch the games as much to hear what Bill said about them as for the play itself. It was a characteristic that those past masters shared but sadly, with the notable exceptions of Peter Alliss and John Motson, they are no longer with us or are now retired, and I think it is going to be very difficult for others to take their places. Not because they are irreplaceable – no one in this world is – but because they worked in a monopoly situation.

Until comparatively recently anyone good enough to become the BBC's voice of his sport would command the majority audience and would continue to do so until it was time for him to go. Sometimes he did so because he decided it was time to hang up his microphone and sometimes because the grim reaper did it for him but very seldom was he supplanted by a BBC colleague. If you were the BBC's man it was your voice that the public heard and if you continued to do the job to the BBC bosses' satisfaction it was your voice they continued to hear. I was lucky enough both to be in that position until the BBC lost the Formula 1 rights and then to be kept on when ITV acquired them but it is much harder, if not impossible, for any commentator on any sport to become dominant now because there are so many channels and so much competition.

When you are under pressure in the commentary box it is often very difficult to be totally objective. You are a human being and like everyone else you have your likes, dislikes and preferences. You are operating in a highly charged, extremely emotional, split-second and hair-trigger atmosphere where there is never time calmly to deliberate about what is the best and fairest way to express yourself. 'Should I say *this* or *that?*' is not a luxury you have time to consider. The words pour out. Sometimes they aren't the right ones, sometimes they are in the wrong order and sometimes they can give offence. However, in an environment where swearing and advertising were off limits I think I can honestly say that I never used bad language or, with a few notable exceptions, let a tobacco or non-motoring brand name cross my lips. There seemed to be a filter in my head that stopped it happening but there were situations where it was unavoidable. Benetton knitwear very cleverly used the company name for the team and did very well indeed out of it; and whenever I talked about the 'Orange Arrows' to differentiate it from the 'Yellow Jordan' or the 'Scarlet Ferrari' I was automatically using the sponsor's name. There were, though, times in a technical sport where it was essential to talk about suppliers who were not the actual car constructors and I freely did so. Explaining how important the tyres were without mentioning the brand names – Dunlop, Pirelli, Goodyear, Bridgestone and Michelin for instance – would have been impossible but it was difficult to know where to draw the line. The fuel companies like Shell, Mobil, Elf, Texaco and Petronas and the electronics, brake, sparking plug and other suppliers all made a vital contribution to the cars' performance but, wrongly or rightly, they never got a shout from me because it was not so dramatic. I just tried to be fair and balanced and the fact that

I got very few complaints hopefully indicates that I got it about right. I've often had people ask if anyone ever tried to bribe me to give their company or product mentions in my commentaries and the answer is no, not ever – hopefully because they knew I wouldn't do it. I was very flattered too when, at my wonderful Indianapolis retirement party in 2001, Eddie Jordan said in his speech that, 'One of the things I've always liked about Murray is that he never says anything unpleasant about anybody.' Does that mean that I was too bland? I hope not for I always tried to speak as I found and to be non-partisan.

One time I do speak with a partisan voice is when those who knew the sport in earlier times criticize its modern-day status. 'It's regimented and soulless,' they cry. 'All the fun is gone out of it. Everything is controlled and organized to maximize the show and its income. You can't get your mates into the paddock any more. They can't get at the drivers and the cars. It costs a fortune for the punters to attend – how can Bernie Ecclestone justify the outrageous prices? It's no longer a sport – it's dominated by sponsors and political correctness. Even the circuits are more and more like each other.'

I couldn't agree less. Yes, Formula 1 has changed since 'the good old days' but the fun certainly hasn't gone out of it judging by the number of people following it in every country it goes to, and countless more that it does not. In my opinion, it is better than it has ever been. Old-timers may well speak in awe of Fangio, Moss and Clark but in years to come it will be Senna, Prost and Schumacher with equal reverence. How can

Bernie justify the high prices? Because people will pay them, that's why. Life is about supply and demand.

So where does the sport go from here? We live in a highly mobile society with an almost obsessive interest in automobiles and everything to do with them. Formula 1 is their most glamorous and exciting expression and I cannot see it becoming any less attractive especially now that car manufacturers are becoming so heavily involved with it. For those who can afford it, digital television coverage will inevitably increase its popularity, but I cannot see it ever capturing a majority of the audience unless its cost to the viewer drops dramatically. Bernie's digital TV coverage of Formula 1 is far superior to that of terrestrial analogue television, but you have to be a super-enthusiast to pay the premium and be prepared to juggle with its alternative channels. I've always felt that what most people want is to have a good picture and someone telling them what is going on. But then I would, wouldn't I?

CHAPTER TWELVE

This is *My* Life

Formula 1 may have massive appeal from Europe to South Africa and South America to Japan but there's a vital and enormous slice of the world that couldn't care less – the United States of America. It is baseball, basketball and American football that grip them by the throat. Even their own specialized series for single-seaters (Champcars and IRL) and saloons (NASCAR) create comparatively little nationwide interest; certainly nothing like as much as Formula 1 does in its domain. But both provide superb spectacles and so vast is the American population that even their minority sports attract enormous attendances, especially at Indianapolis, the self-styled 'World Capital of Auto Racing'. There's certainly nowhere else that comes near it in terms of size, spectacle, history, tradition and facilities.

In the past there was a lot of prejudice and misunderstanding between the respective aficionados of Champcars and Formula 1. 'Formula 1 is boring, boring, boring,' said the Champcar enthusiasts. 'There's no passing and the races are dreary processions. You can't get at the cars, the teams or the drivers who hide away in their exclusive paddock and the prices are ludicrous.'

'Wrong – it's the technical pinnacle of motor racing and a genuine sporting contest,' retorted the Formula 1 fans. 'Your racing's a manipulated promotion with yellow flags to stop the cars and close things up at the slightest excuse, the drivers aren't as good and it's nothing like as professional.'

Thanks to television both sides see things more objectively now, but I have to admit that I used to be pretty superior about Indy racing, dismissing it as a series for fat old chaps with funny names, and even a few women, who drove dinosaur cars in rigged conditions and which Americans flocked to because they had nothing better to compare it with. (Nothing intolerant or lacking in understanding there, then!) But over time five people woke me up and dramatically changed my attitude: Jack Brabham, Colin Chapman, Jim Clark, Nigel Mansell and Nick Goozée.

In 1961 double World Champion Jack Brabham shook the American establishment rigid by finishing ninth in the hallowed Indy 500 in his diminutive, rear-engined Cooper against their big and clumsy front-engined juggernauts. Two years later Jim Clark really put the wind up them by nearly winning in his beautifully engineered Colin Chapman Lotus. In 1965 he blew them all away by taking the trophy. The mould was broken. Indy racing was never the same again, especially after Graham Hill rubbed salt into the wound by finishing first in 1966. I watched that cracking race on a satellite link at the Finsbury Park Astoria cinema as part of a mixed audience of American servicemen and British enthusiasts. I found it enthralling but it wasn't until 1993, when Nigel Mansell left Formula 1 and went to the States, and especially after I met Nick Goozée, that I really started to appreciate Indy-style motor racing.

America's top team owner is Roger Penske, a phenomenally successful business tycoon and ex-driver. His cars are made in Britain (in Poole, Dorset) and Nick is his head man there, responsible for the design and manufacture of the Penske single-seaters that dominated their scene for so long. American-style racing on their specialized Super Speedways and Oval tracks has no more articulate a supporter than Nick, despite the fact that his roots are in Formula 1 as an ex-Brabham mechanic and colleague of McLaren's Ron Dennis. We met at a function and developed a friendship which generated a lot of good-natured argument about the pros and cons of Formula 1 versus Champcars. Then one day in 1993, when Nigel Mansell was sweeping all before him in his American rookie year, Nick said, 'It's about time you got to know what it's really all about instead of airing your groundless prejudices. You're coming to the Indy 500 with us.' What an educating and fantastic experience that turned out to be.

Indianapolis is the state capital of Indiana, a pleasant city about three hours drive south of Chicago, dominated by the quite incredible 2.5-mile Super Speedway on its outskirts. If I hadn't seen the IMS, the Indianapolis Motor Speedway with its famous winged-wheel symbol, I would never have believed it. It holds over 400,000 people and is always packed out for the race, the preliminaries for which took up the whole month of May. I got there in good time and wandered round with my jaw hanging slack, marvelling at its unrivalled facilities, the lavish hospitality rooms and enormous tiered grandstands, the wonderful Hall of Fame museum and the 18-hole championship golf course contained within the track – but most of all at the fabled Gasoline Alley, the team garages steeped in history at which I renewed my friendship with an amazing number of British ex-Formula 1 people, like Mo Nunn and Nigel Beresford, who were now happily working in the States. Excitement was at fever pitch after the closest ever finish in Indy history the year before, when Al Unser Junior beat Scott Goodyear by less than half a car's length after 500 miles of racing at well over 200mph. Could first-timer Nigel Mansell, partnering the great Mario Andretti in the Lola team owned by Carl Haas and movie star Paul Newman, beat the established aces?

I got a preliminary flavour of a magical occasion as Roger Penske's guest at the glitzy pre-race dinner at the Indiana Roof Ballroom hosted by Chevrolet boss Jim Perkins. I sat between the great Brazilian Penske driver Emerson Fittipaldi and his lovely wife Teresa. Double Formula 1 World Champion Emerson, who had won the Indy 500 in 1989, was starting from the third row of the grid but little did we know how well he was to do on race day. I went from the Westin Hotel to the track as part of the Penske entourage, complete with police outriders. When we arrived there wasn't a seat to be had and the notorious Snake Pit inside Turn One, Indy's equivalent of 'The Bog' at Watkins Glen, was full to bursting point with some very rowdy characters, already well tanked up. Seeing some 420,000 fired-up people in one huge lump was overwhelming, but it got more and more emotional as the tension rose with the uniformed massed bands, the National Anthem, the Invocation and the strains of *Back Home Again in Indiana* until, amid utter silence, there came that world-famous Indy tradition, the instruction from Mary Hulman of the circuit-owning Hulman family: 'Gentlemen, start your engines!' America sure knows how to put on a show and nowhere better than Indy. It was electrifying.

I had one of the best vantage points at the whole circuit, a front row seat in the Penske Penthouse Box high above the track on Turn One. There with me, as my guide and tutor for what was going to be a complicated race for a newcomer, was Karl Keinhoffer, who had been Roger Penske's engine man since Penske's days as a world-class driver. Off went the 33 starters, with the front row of Arie Luyendyk, Mario Andretti and Raul Boesel preceded by the Chevrolet pace car. When it swept off the track the rolling start race was on and the incredible sensation of speed, noise, colour, and aggression as they blasted away below me was something I'd never experienced before.

Mansell was driving a blinder and it wasn't long before, from eighth on the grid, he went into the lead. Just a few weeks earlier he had suffered an enormous crash at Phoenix and when I was with him in the Newman–Haas motorhome at Indy he asked if I'd like to see his back. When I asked why, he peeled off his overalls and from his neck to the base of his spine there was a long livid heavily stitched scar from his recent operation. It was typical of gutsy Nigel that he was competing so soon and now here he was leading his first Indy 500. As he hurtled below me I stood up, leant over the rail, shook my fist and inanely shouted, 'Go for it, Nigel!' only to feel a tug at my sleeve. It was Karl. 'Sit down, Murray. This is a long race. Two hundred laps. If Nigel's still there after the last yellow you can get up again but I'd leave it until then if I was you.'

Wherever Nigel is there's drama and just a few laps from the end he clipped the wall with his right rear wheel. Out came a yellow flag to bunch up the field and my heart sank. Amazingly he raced on to finish a brilliant third behind Indy-specialists Fittipaldi and Luyendyk, a mere five seconds down at an average speed of nearly 160mph over the 500 miles of his first ever race on a Super Speedway. Tough luck indeed but he had the consolation later of clinching the PPG Champcar Championship in his rookie year, a superb achievement.

They modestly call it 'The Greatest Race in the World' at Indianapolis. It was certainly one of the best I'd ever seen and undoubtedly *the* best from the point of view of overall spectacle and organization. The more you know about something the more you understand and appreciate it and Indy 1993 made me see Champcar racing through different eyes. Nick hadn't finished with me yet though. A year later he said, 'You've seen a Super Speedway but to get the full picture you need to see an Oval race. It'll blow your mind – so now come with us to Nazareth.' How lucky can you get!

Nazareth is a state-of-the-art one-mile oval track in the Pennsylvania Bible belt, home of the mobile churches and the great Mario Andretti. Nigel Mansell had won there the previous year at an average of nearly 160mph and at racing speed a lap takes about 22 seconds. So the 200-lap Bosch Spark Plug Grand Prix wasn't going to take long. I joined Nick and his other guest, ex-Penske Formula 1 winner John Watson and it was a fabulous experience, for not only was it living legend Mario Andretti's last oval race before he retired but all the other Champcar stars were present too: Nigel Mansell, the reigning champion; Emerson Fittipaldi; Michael Andretti back from his unsuccessful time in Formula 1 as Ayrton Senna's McLaren team-mate; Bobby Rahal; Al Unser Junior; Arie Luyendyk and Jacques Villeneuve. Mario, whom I'd known since first meeting him at the Nurburgring with Jackie Stewart in 1969, talked to me in his motorhome and signed his new book for me but, sadly, didn't win the race. It was a glorious 1-2-3 for Penske drivers Paul Tracey, Al Unser Junior and Emerson Fittipaldi and even more exciting than I'd expected it to be.

I was invited to join the ABC TV team for a brief spell in the commentary box but, as a Champcar novice and oval racing ignoramus, it was a taxing job. Keeping tabs on everyone when they come past you at some 220mph every 20 seconds or so and are continually dodging in and out of the pits for fuel and tyres, as well as trying to keep on top of the tactical changes caused by the yellow flag periods, is very much an acquired art. It is very different and, yes, the Americans are right, Champcar racing is not only massively entertaining but a lot more relaxed and informal than Formula 1. Even the ordinary punters can get into the paddock and chat with the drivers – though how the hell the teams cope with it is beyond my understanding. There is a great deal to be said for both the top single-seater disciplines, Formula 1 and Champcars, and now that they are both in each other's countries I hope they get the mutual recognition they deserve.

Those Indianapolis and Nazareth trips were colossal bonuses on top of a pretty unusual existence. Rushing round the world, appearing on the box, making personal appearances, giving after-dinner speeches and doing all the other things that get you known by the public is a very satisfying way of life. I suppose the truth is that I'm a bit of a ham: I like people, enjoy performing and making speeches and am always immensely flattered when I'm recognized. I've never had the slightest ambition to be an actor and could never learn the lines but I used to love the challenge and excitement of making presentations at Masius and got a terrific buzz out of commentating. Although I never thought about it when I picked up the microphone at a Grand Prix, I was subconsciously aware of the fact that I was about to talk to millions of people all over the world who would give everything to be where I was and who were relying on me to inform and entertain them. It was a big responsibility which got the adrenalin flowing, but although I knew I had an enormous audience out there from Britain to New Zealand and Canada to South Africa I hadn't got the faintest idea who they were.

Television is a tremendously powerful medium which takes you into people's homes and makes you their friend, so away from the commentary box I'm constantly recognized by people who are complete strangers to me. I was walking through Southampton with my mother once when a chap spotted me and cheerily said, 'Hello, Murray!'

'Hello there,' I replied.

'Who's your friend, dear?' asked Mother.

'I've never seen him in my life, Mother.'

'Well, he seems to know you and he used your Christian name.'

'Ah, that's because I've been in his home!' (On his television, of course.)

'Well, if you've been in his home you must know who he is!'

And I had no answer to that.

As a result of getting to be a bit famous I had some wonderful experiences, one of which I was well and truly set up for. In 1997 I did a very successful video called *Murray's Magic Moments* and when it was launched Ivor Schlosberg, the South African boss of production company Astrion, asked me to address the big trade buyers at the Sports Café in London's Lower Regent Street. I was in full flow about what was in it and how we'd made it when I became aware of a subtle change in the atmosphere and that the audience weren't looking at me. They were looking just to my left. I took a quick glance over my shoulder and there was Michael Aspel. It didn't immediately register and as everyone burst out laughing I said, 'What the hell are you doing here?'

'Murray Walker,' came the reply. 'You thought you'd come here to talk about your video but *This is your Life!*'

If you're like me you'd love to be the subject for what is one of the most watched and successful TV shows of all time and I was really delighted. I said something stupid – I can't for the life of me remember what – and then started to go on with what I'd been saying.

'Murray, we have to go,' said Michael. 'They're waiting for us.'

Now to the extent that I'd thought about it, I'd always assumed there was several weeks' delay between 'the hit', as they call it, and the actual show, but that isn't the case at all. You go straight to the Shepperton Studios, where the programme is recorded in front of a live audience.

'We've got a very special driver and limousine just up the road,' said Michael as we walked towards St James's Square, where I had worked for Masius. When we got to the car the uniformed chauffeur got out to open the door for me. It was Damon Hill! After more flabbergasted reaction from me to camera we drove to Shepperton, where I was shown to a dressing room and introduced to two of the female programme staff. As transmission time got near I decided I'd better spruce myself up a bit. 'I think I'd better have a shave,' I said.

'OK, Murray, we'll get you an electric razor.'

They showed no sign of leaving the room so I had my shave and then said, 'Better go to the loo. Where is it?'

'It's just there, Murray, and we're not leaving, you know. We're the Suicide Squad!'

'What do you mean?'

'Well, sometimes the subject panics and tries to do a bunk or phone their friends to tell them they're on the show. So we're here to see you don't!'

No fear of that though, I was really looking forward to it, and when it happened it was great. They must have done a fantastic amount of research and detective work to find the right people from my past and it was a really moving experience to have them appearing through those sliding doors to greet me. Elizabeth, who had done so much behind the scenes to make it happen, had been brought up from our Hampshire home; they'd somehow located Peter Johnson, my best wartime Army friend from the Royal Scots Greys, and spirited him down from Leeds with his wife; Jonathan Martin from the BBC was there with a lot of my chums from those happy days – including Max Robertson with whom I had done my very first broadcast in 1949; so were the ITV Formula 1 team and Eddie Jordan, Damon Hill, Johnny Herbert and Martin Brundle; my oldest friend Brian Emerton from Enfield; Peter Gwynn from my Masius years; and Stirling Moss, Nigel Mansell, Michael Schumacher, Chris Rea and Raymond Baxter had all recorded pieces. No less than four British Touring Car Champions came on to remind me about the great times I'd had with them, but the thing that very nearly broke me up was when my 99-year-old mother appeared on the screen to say that she was sorry she couldn't be with us but that I'd been a good son and to have a great evening. They'd been down to Beaulieu where she lived and interviewed her that very morning.

At the end of a memorable and emotional evening John Surtees, whom I'd competed against at Brands Hatch so long ago, rode in on the superb MV Four he had raced to victory at the Isle of Man TT to say some very nice things. Then we all went to the Green Room for a wonderful party that lasted a long time. It was certainly one of the very high points of my long TV career.

For a while *This is your Life* got to be a bit of a regular occasion for me. After taking part in Nigel Mansell's show I got a phone call at home from David Coulthard's mum, Joyce. 'Murray, it's my husband Duncan's 50th birthday on 18 August and I'm getting a lot of his friends together for a big party including a pretend *This is your Life.* I wondered if you'd come up to Scotland and do the "red book" for us?' Only too pleased to oblige, I met David at Glasgow airport and he drove me to Gatehouse of Fleet, near his Twynholm home, where the party was being held. Joyce had managed to kid Duncan that they were having a quiet family dinner but when they arrived at the hotel it was thronged with literally dozens of well-wishers. I marched in to do the traditional surprise introduction: 'Duncan Coulthard, you thought you'd come here to have a quiet dinner with Joyce but *This is your Life*!' Umpteen warm-hearted friends paid tribute and reminisced about their times with him, David made a touching speech about what a great dad he had been and then the party began. Duncan is a whiz on the electric guitar and formed an impromptu group with three of his talented chums who just happened to be there. All too soon it was time to return home to the South but I subsequently took part in others for

Raymond Baxter and Eddie Jordan as well as helping Michael Aspel do the hit for Damon Hill's tribute.

Like most people, I suspect, I've fantasized about the phone ringing and a voice saying 'I'm the producer of *Desert Island Discs,* Murray. Sue Lawley would like you to be her guest.' It has never happened but one day out of the blue I did receive a call from Radio London, which covers an enormous area.

'We've got a programme called *Morning Star* and we'd like you to be on it.'

'Great, I'd love to – what's it all about?'

'It's a one-hour show and you choose 10 records which we play and you talk about yourself. If you could have a think about what records you want and let us know we can fix a date.'

So I sat down and worked out which records I wanted (Benny Goodman, Tommy Dorsey, Artie Shaw, Woody Herman, Peggy Lee, Bob Crosby, Ella Fitzgerald and Frank Sinatra) and rolled up on the day. It was a 9am show and with about five minutes to go the producer said 'We'd better go into the studio now.'

'OK. Where's the other bloke?'

'What other bloke?'

'The chap who's going to ask the questions.'

'There isn't anyone else, Murray.'

'What? Do you mean to say that I've got to fill in all the gaps between the records in a 60-minute programme?'

'That's right and we're on the air in one minute.'

So off we went with me improvising away between the

discs and it actually went very well – so well in fact that about halfway through, just as I'd introduced the Tommy Dorsey Band playing *The Song of India*, the producer came in and said, 'This is fantastic. The switchboard is jammed solid!'

'Oh, is it?' I said, smugly preening myself, 'that's good.'

'Yes, you're appealing to all the old housewives!'

With my advertising background and commentary associations I was a natural for company presentations and really enjoyed doing them. Pirelli's Tom Northey phoned me one day and said, 'We've got a sales conference coming up on 7 October, Murray. Can you host it for us?'

'Yes, sure, Tom. Where is it?'

'The Mandarin Oriental Hotel, Singapore!'

It was for Pirelli's Asian distributors and I was to do the links, introduce the speakers and interview two of motor sport's greatest personalities – Stirling Moss and his Swedish brother-in-law, legendary rally driver Erik Carlsson – about their successes using Pirelli tyres. I got there early to get everything teed up and when Stirling arrived a couple of days later I said, 'You're a snappy dresser, Stirling. There's an excellent Chinese tailor near the hotel who I've ordered some stuff from. Do you want to see him?'

'Does he do shirts?'

'Yes, he does.'

'With hidden buttons?'

'Yes.'

'Double cuffs?'

'Oh yes.'

'Three-ply collars?'

'God, I don't know how many plies there are, Stirling, but I'm sure he'll do what you want.'

'What does he charge?'

'Twenty quid.'

'Did you haggle with him?'

'Well no, I didn't actually. I'm no good at it and anyway if he does hidden buttons, double cuffs and three-ply collars for twenty quid and makes a bob or two for himself he's welcome as far as I'm concerned.'

'Wrong attitude, old boy. They like you to haggle. It's part of their culture and if you don't you make things a lot harder for people like me who do. Anyway I've got an Indian chap in London who does them for fifteen quid. So thanks for asking but no.'

I thought, *Stirling's right. Why give it away if you don't have to?*

I was in the market for a new electric razor so, totally against my nature, I went round Singapore haggling away until I got the one I wanted for £52. When I got home and looked in the Argos catalogue it was £48 so I haven't bothered since.

On the day of the conference, incidentally, during a riveting interview with Stirling and Erik about their brilliant careers, I looked at the hundreds of Indian, Malaysian, Pakistani, Indonesian, Philippine and other passive Far Eastern faces gazing blankly at us and realized that none of them had got the slightest interest in what we were talking about. It was like having a discussion about the principles of nuclear fission in front of people who were expecting to see a strip show.

They were very courteous and attentive but I think I was the only one there who got anything out of it.

It was a very different and much more appreciative audience at the Wimbledon Speedway Stock Car meeting in October 1988 though, where James Hunt and I raced each other for charity. We started on opposite sides of the track with each of us trying to catch the other over a three-lap dash. James thought he'd work a crafty flanker on me and the moment the flag dropped he raced across the grass infield and got to within a few yards of my rear bumper. But in his determination finally to close the gap he overdid it, lost the plot and ended up stationary, with the nose of his car stuck in the fencing. *Aha!* I thought, as I came round the bend to start my last lap, *Two can play at that game.* So I drove smartly into the back of his Ford, rammed it right into the fencing, reversed out, finished the lap and won by a foul. It was the only way I was ever going to beat James and very satisfying it was too.

As was my epic drive at the Blakesley Soapbox Grand Prix later the same year. Blakesley is a village close to Silverstone and the course starts on a man-made ramp at the top of a hill and plunges past the friendly Bartholomew Arms, where I had been known to take a beer or two. I was there to do a piece for a BBC Radio Four programme called *Mad Dogs and Englishmen* about the potty things the English do. 'Have a go, Murray,' they said. 'We'll put you in "Bloodshed". It's a Formula 1 soapbox which holds the hill record and if you've got big enough balls you can't help doing well because if you take a deep breath it'll just go round all the corners without braking.'

The things I do for England. I frightened the life out of myself but they were right. I kept right off the stoppers and we fairly flew down the hill – 54.62 seconds compared with the winner, speed king Eddie Edwards' 52.79. Not bad, great fun and as I recorded commentary all the way down we got a cracking piece for the programme. An action photo of my sensational debut (and finale) was still hanging in the Bartholomew Arms the last time I was there.

Fame seems to generate its own ever-increasing momentum. The better known you become the more people want you to do things for them, to be at their functions and to appear on their shows. The more you do the more publicity you get and the more publicity you get the better known you become. And so on, *ad infinitum*. It's a sort of benevolent circle. From about 1983 that's how it increasingly was for me. As a result of becoming well known for commentating I was asked to do all sorts of other things and it grew and grew. It was just as well I'd retired from my proper job because if I hadn't I'd never have been able to fit it all in.

Apart from the weight-lifting, rowing, military tattoo and an aircraft programme the BBC had tried me on long ago in 1949, the first major non-motor-sport production I can remember being in was Noel Edmonds' *Late, Late Breakfast Show* at Chessington Zoo where, believe it or not, I commentated on a very dramatic and realistic Roman chariot race. Producer Mike Lego liked what I had done and that quickly led to another appearance, commentating on a weird event at night, under the walls of Wormwood Scrubs prison, involving

Honda Quads, a very large ball and the pop group Bananarama. Don't ask!

Not everyone approved though. Jim Reside, my *Grand Prix* producer, kept counselling me not to do Noel Edmonds' shows. 'They'll certainly get you well known, Murray, but it will be for the wrong reasons. You're a professional commentator not a clown. Being sent up and having to do silly things, which is what the Edmonds show is all about, will sully your image. You shouldn't mix stupid with serious.' Well, I enjoyed doing them and didn't take any notice but Jim may well have been right. It was undoubtedly Noel's shows that publicized and increased awareness of those undeniable and not infrequent gaffes that both irritated people and endeared me to them, so the jury is out on whether the shows were a good or bad thing for me.

I won the dubiously desirable Golden Egg Award for 'A Lifetime Devoted to the Glorious Cock-up' in 1985 and nearly ended up being drenched with gunge in 1992, but my most impactful of several appearances with Noel was at a time when he had the 'Whirly Wheel' feature. Every week viewers would volunteer to do something unusual on the next show without knowing what it was going to be. Noel would spin a big wheel and, when it stopped, the name opposite a pointer would pay the forfeit. For my particular week the victim had to go to Santa Pod Raceway, home of the spectacular drag racing events, and do the car long jump – race off a wooden ramp at high speed in a road car, fly through the air and try to clear 12 cars lined up side by side. Not something that the ordinary motorist gets too much practice at but, not to worry, there was a resident lunatic who did it for a living and he demonstrated how. 'They always land on the roof of the eighth car, Murray, because of the speed, the flight trajectory and the fact that the heaviest part of the car is at the front. So all you have to do is stand by the eighth car and when Fred lands there you'll be on the spot to interview him.'

Well, Fred was a brave man and when his time came he trundled off in the aged Hillman Hunter that was about to breathe its last, lined it up with the ramp and went for it, revving the motor hard to clear a misfire. He hit the ramp at about 70mph and when he passed me at the eighth car he was still climbing. As he finally came in to land he clipped the 12th car and careered on down the runway into the side of the brand new BBC Mercedes-Benz that had come to collect him. Needless to say the item was a riot with the viewers.

So was the 1989 BBC TV *Sports Review of the Year* special feature I took part in. The *Sports Review* is one of the Corporation's top programmes and always includes a fun piece. This time it was to be a role-reversal challenge for three of its commentators, who would each do another's sport. Golf's Peter Alliss would commentate on athletics, horse racing's Peter O'Sullevan on the Portuguese Grand Prix and I would do the Grand National. Commentating is just as competitive as anything else and I was determined not to be the duffer. I bought the *Sporting Life* and mugged up all the horses, jockeys, owners, trainers and Aintree itself, which I had been to for the British Grand Prix. I got a tape of the event and studied it and on the day it went beautifully, including my line about the jockey who had a riderless horse alongside him going over the jumps. 'He's absolutely determined to win – he's even brought a spare horse!' It should have gone well though because, like a Formula 1 Grand Prix, the Grand National is what I call a crash, bang, wallop event – lots of action, speed, colour and drama. So the commentary style is the same and if you get the facts right it should just be a case of stringing them together with passion and enthusiasm.

What I really wanted to do was snooker – my way, just as I do motor sport. 'And here's Steve Davis! He's got special chalk on the end of his carbon-fibre cue and he's wearing some absolutely unique shoes with a non-slip tread pattern. For Steve this is the Big One. He faces the balls – which one is he going to hit? – and SLAMS the white into the pocket. NO – HE'S MISSED! FANTASTIC!!' In Jeremy Clarkson's show 12 years later I was able to do just that and it got a great reception.

Over the years a lot of advertising agencies approached me to appear in commercials but they almost invariably wanted me to make an idiot of myself or do a hideous travesty of a race commentary. When they did I said no although I have to admit that appearing in some of the shows that I did won't have done my 'professional commentator' image much good either. However, there were times when I was able to look at a TV commercial script and think, 'Yes! This could be a winner.' Hopefully my years in the advertising business helped my judgment and I was able to take part in three very good, funny and memorable productions.

The first two were in 1988 for the Austin Metro with the

brilliant Eric Idle, of *Monty Python* fame, taking the part of a very flash, jazzy-suited and jewellery-laden car salesman trying to persuade Nigel Mansell and me to purchase a Metro. I have to say that the commercials were a great deal better than what was a worthy but very ordinary car, but even so they probably didn't do much for the sales of Metros. But the Pizza Hut epic was something different. The massive Pizza Hut chain wanted to boost sales of their new Stuffed Crust Pizza with Pepperoni and their excellent agency, Abbot, Mead, Vickers, produced a superb script which I loved the moment I saw it. The storyline featured Damon Hill and me entering a Pizza Hut restaurant and ordering Stuffed Crust Pizzas with Pepperoni, with me irritatingly yakking away non-stop in commentary style, to Damon's acute embarrassment. We did it at a reproduction Pizza Hut which had been built in the studio and it took us two days to make the 30-second commercial, including no less than 26 takes of the complicated first sequence before we got it right. Because there was so much pizza eating we had a bucket just out of camera into which we could spit the uneaten pizza slices at the end of each shot. The pizza itself was actually jolly good – I ate more in a day than I'd previously eaten in a year – and happily the commercial was a roaring success. I used to get people shouting at me in the street, 'Had any good pizzas recently, Murray?' I was told that the Pizza Hut group in Australia actually introduced the Stuffed Crust with Pepperoni version there just so they could run the commercial!

But in terms of achievements I reckon the Lords Taverners' Balloon Debate, held in the Long Room of the world-famous cricket ground, took a lot of beating. In case you don't know (and I didn't) a Balloon Debate is conducted between four people, each of whom has to talk about a person of their choice, who is put into an imaginary balloon basket and sent aloft with the other three unfortunates. The contestants each talk for 15 minutes, split into seven-, five- and three-minute segments and at the end of each segment, following an audience poll, one of the subjects is thrown out of the basket. The object, of course, is for your chap to be the one who is still there after the last vote and the trick is to pace yourself so that you don't fire off all your ammunition in the first two segments but leave yourself with enough for an emotional and life-saving three minutes for your hero at the end.

The Long Room at Lords is cricket's Holy of Holies, from which the greatest cricketers of all time, from W G Grace to Sir Don Bradman and Ian Botham, have emerged to make history, and there was an audience of over 500 people in dinner jackets and black ties for a gala dinner and what they hoped was going to be a great evening. In such an historic location and before such a prestigious audience I was unashamedly nervous, especially as the other three speakers came with very impressive credentials: former England cricketer Chris Cowdrey, the witty comedian and presenter Barry Took and horse-racing doyen Lord Oaksey. In assessing the opposition I thought, *Chris Cowdrey has to be the hot favourite. He's a famous cricketer, the son of an even more famous cricketer, he's talking at the home of cricket in front of a cricket-oriented audience and he's promoting the famous and much-loved cricketer Allan Lamb.* I didn't seem to have much chance of saving my man, James Hunt, from a sticky end. But I was wrong. To my surprise Lord Oaksey's nominee, top jockey Lester Piggott, got thrown out of the basket after the opening round of seven-minute speeches and Barry Took's typical sports fan got ejected after the three five-minute perorations. That just left Cowdrey for Lamb and Walker for Hunt, with three minutes each to make their final cases.

I was to speak last and was elated to hear Chris faltering. He had shot his bolt, failed to reach a climax and was floundering. If there is one person in my life that I can go on about for a long time it is James and I'd planned, and was able to deliver, a rousing finale which not only got me a terrific and very satisfying round of applause but also got Allan Lamb heaved out of the basket, leaving James there to continue his imaginary journey alone. For my efforts I got a superb cut-glass rose bowl, but the thing that surprised me most was how very unimpressed I was with cricket's most prestigious location. I'm sure that if you are a cricket buff with passionate enthusiasm for all the greats who have been there it must be like being in heaven to be in the Long Room at Lords, but to me, as a cricket novice, it was just a rather tired-looking long room.

With the very notable exception of my receipt of the OBE from Her Majesty the Queen at Buckingham Palace in 1996, of which more later, my most honoured experience has to be the State Banquet at Windsor Castle in early October 2001, to which Elizabeth and I were invited, on the occasion of the King and Queen of Jordan's State Visit to Britain. King Abdullah's father, the much-loved and truly great King Hussein, had been a passionate motor-racing enthusiast and I can only assume that it was because of this association with my sport that we were invited. Whatever the reason, it was a glittering and spell-binding occasion. In my childhood I had seen my father and mother getting ready for full-dress functions many times. Tails and white tie for the man were more usual then, but this was the first time I had worn a tail coat and all the accessories, including decorations, and it felt very grand.

We drove into the magnificently floodlit Windsor Castle and, after being received by Her Majesty, King Abdullah, Queen Rania and the Duke of Edinburgh, moved to the sumptuous St George's Hall, whose restoration had only recently been completed. Its atmosphere of history, tradition and splendour simply took my breath away. The decor was as it had been before the fire only better, immaculately and perfectly recreated by the country's finest craftsmen, with suits of armour and hundreds of coats of arms of the nobility as a backdrop for the single table that ran the length of the vast, high-ceilinged room and at which over 160 people were to be seated. The place settings had taken two and a half days to lay out with perfect to-the-millimetre precision and symmetry and the whole thing was awe-inspiring. Just about anyone who was anyone in the Establishment was there, from the two Royal Families and their retinues to the Archbishop of Canterbury, government ministers and members of the opposition. As a patriotic Englishman I felt immensely proud to be there as Her Majesty and King Abdullah made very significant speeches in the light of the appalling and recent tragedies of 11 September, and the final sight of the Pipers of the Scots Guards marching the length of that fabulous room, round the massive table in their full regalia with their bagpipes skirling, was one that will be with me forever.

CHAPTER THIRTEEN

Every One a Winner

For someone to whom motor sport means so much, I've been very fortunate to be around since Formula 1 began back in 1950. From the original daunting Nurburgring to state-of-the-art Indianapolis, I've marvelled at the skill of drivers from Ascari, Fangio and Farina to Button, Montoya and Raikonnen. In the 1930s, long before Formula 1, it was my privilege as a youth to watch pre-war legends Nuvolari, Caracciola, Rosemeyer, Von Brauchitsch and Lang in action but until 1978 it was primarily motor-cycle racing that occupied my attention. Until then the Formula 1 stars were almost as inaccessible to me as they were to anyone else.

People think I spent my commentating years constantly wining, dining and socializing with the drivers but that was certainly not the case. With the gigantic increase of worldwide interest in Formula 1 since the early 1970s and the exponential expansion in media coverage, they've become increasingly pressured, remote and unapproachable to the media except by appointment. When they're not racing they're testing and often go from a race in one country on Sunday directly to a three-day test in another country on the Monday. When they're not testing they're doing promotional work for their sponsors and when they're not doing that they're spending rare and treasured time at home. Even then they have to train rigorously for hours every day. The modern Grand Prix driver may be paid a lot of money but he works very hard for it, risking his life every time he is at the wheel. In my opinion he deserves every penny he gets.

The money comes from the sponsors who pay the teams many millions of pounds to have their logos on the cars and benefit from worldwide TV exposure – something the tobacco companies can get no other way. They also make sure they get their pound of flesh by having their drivers attend functions and talk to company guests in their Paddock Club suites on race day. Many of them, and especially the tobacco companies like Marlboro and West, use the out-of-season winter months to take their drivers on long and demanding promotional tours of places like Eastern Europe, South America and China. A small price to pay for such a pampered and high-earning lifestyle you may think but for the drivers it is an irritating and often exhausting distraction from their main purpose. Knowing well which side their bread is buttered, they generally do it all with good grace but some of them are strong enough and indispensable enough to be able to say no and get away with it. The very independent Jacques Villeneuve is well known for having a 'minimum promotional work' clause written into his multi-million pound contract and you don't see Michael Schumacher meeting with the locals in many Chinese villages. Schumacher is in so much demand that he can make his own conditions, to the extent of being virtually incommunicado at race meetings so that he can concentrate on his job – which is to drive and win. Villeneuve is good enough and independent enough to be able to say, 'You may be offering me millions of pounds but if I've got to do something I hate I just won't sign.' Few of the others have the ability or determination to do the same, but I have no doubt that most of them would dearly like to.

So usually the only time that I was able to talk to the stars was when they were professionally on parade and it's easier to develop friendships with some than with others. I never got at all close to three-time World Champion Nelson Piquet, for example – we just had nothing in common except motor racing and I always felt diffident about approaching him for any reason other than a professional interview, although I admired him as a wonderful racing driver. Eddie Irvine too was someone I was never particularly anxious to approach, not because he was unable or unwilling to talk – I've never known a driver more frank with his views, which were invariably well-founded and realistic – but simply because I was never sure whether he was going to be curt and dismissive or charming and communicative. Although there was never anything abrasive about our relationship, it wasn't helped by my writing an article, when he was driving for Jordan, accusing him of being more interested in making his first £20 million than succeeding in Formula 1. Eddie was understandably upset by this, but the problem was resolved when I accepted this wasn't right and apologised to him later. ('Don't ever apologise, Murray,' a top motor-racing journalist once said to me, but I always believed that if you got it wrong you should do so.)

Like many of us I am thin-skinned enough not to want to be rebuffed. Conversely, so many of the other drivers were, to me, a delight and especially the charming Jean Alesi, Rubens Barrichello, the courteous and clear-thinking David Coulthard, Alain Prost, the dry-humoured Keke Rosberg and Jackie Stewart, the ultimate professional. Mika Hakkinen was a lovely bloke but talking to the media was certainly not his forte: like John Surtees in his earliest days, Mika was expert at answering questions with as few words as possible – not the media man's dream interviewee.

But even though there were drivers over the years whom I particularly liked and respected, I'm not going to try to rank them – they were all superstars. Some were just *more* than that. Stirling Moss, for instance, one of the very greatest of them all, made an enormous impact on me and everyone else in 1948 when he burst on to the racing scene as an 18-year-old boy wonder. The war was only just over, the world was hungry for new sporting heroes and here was this fresh-faced public schoolboy blowing them all away in his 500cc Cooper-JAP. He became lionized by the media and adored by the public, like no one in motor racing before him, but it is difficult to convey the colossal stature of the man to today's enthusiasts, denied the pleasure of seeing him in Grand Prix action.

His legendary years were when I was primarily a motorcycle man but I saw many of his races and in my view Stirling is the best British racing driver of all time, even though he never won the World Championship. Racing against Mike Hawthorn, Jack Brabham, Phil Hill, Jim Clark, Tony Brooks and Dan Gurney, he finished second four times in succession but it was his misfortune that his career was also concurrent with that of the greatest of them all, Juan Manuel Fangio. That cost Stirling three Championships. He was a better sports car driver than the Argentine though and in my opinion his win for Mercedes-Benz at the 1955 Mille Miglia, where he averaged over 98mph for 1000 miles on everyday Italian roads, equals the fabled Nurburgring German Grand Prix victories of Nuvolari (1935) and Fangio (1957). Early in 2002 I had the gigantic thrill of riding as Stirling's passenger on semi-closed London roads in his Mille Miglia car with its famous race number 722. 'Try the brakes, Murray,' said Stirling, moving his leg across, 'there aren't any!' He gave the Mercedes a burst of power up the Kings Road and I did so. He was right.

Stirling was the sensation of the meeting at the second broadcast I ever did, the 1949 Manx Cup, where, as a 19-year-old newcomer, he electrified the experienced opposition by building a huge lead, only to retire two laps from the end. But it wasn't until after he had retired from racing, following his disastrous 1962 crash at Goodwood, that I got to know him well. After his recovery, he re-invented himself to make a very good living as 'Stirling Moss: personality and living legend', as a result of which we meet frequently. Now, 40 years on from the event that so very nearly took his life, I can proudly say that Stirling and his charming wife Susie are my friends. Not only that but I am often mistaken for him – we've the same-shaped head and are both balding.

In 2000 Stirling and I were doing a lecture tour on the P&O ship *Victoria*, and taking it in turns to do the talks. I was strolling round the deck one day, taking the sun, when a woman on a lounger grabbed my arm and said, 'I just wanted to say how very much I enjoyed your talk.'

'Oh, that's nice. Glad you liked it. Thank you.'

'Yes, I'm not actually interested in motor racing but you make it live. You really are *very* good.'

'Well, thank you again. I do my best and it's nice to know it's working.'

'It certainly is and I'll be at the next one. That commentator chap is good too but you're much better.'

As someone who would like to have been Stirling Moss if I hadn't been me I was flattered and pleased.

I've been driven by Stirling with a running commentary on how he does it, notably in the world-famous Ferrari 250 GTO; I've interviewed him many times; I've worked in the commentary box with him; I've spoken at functions with him; I've listened to his wonderful anecdotes and I've marvelled at how he still drives with such style and speed at Historic Racing events all over the world. He is a charismatic English gentleman whom I so admire and it has never been anything less than a pleasure to be associated with him. In recognition of his contribution to the sport, he was a worthy recipient of a knighthood in the millennium honours list and he richly deserved it both for his achievements and his years as a worthy ambassador for motor sport.

Motor racing's had a number of well-deserved British and Commonwealth Honours, amongst them Sir Frank Williams, Sir Stirling Moss and Sir Jackie Stewart, but three-times World Champion Sir Jack Brabham, Australia's most famous and successful racing son, was the first to have his achievements recognized with a knighthood. As with Stirling, I watched and admired Jack Brabham from the sidelines until his retirement in 1970. Yet I didn't know him well until two things brought us much closer together – Goodwood and Nick Goozée. Like Stirling, Jack is a racer and he can't keep away from it. Having built successful businesses in Australia and Britain, he became enthusiastically involved with the ever-growing development of Historic Formula 1 and Sports Car racing, the annual pinnacles of which are those wonderful events hosted by Lord March at his Goodwood Estate: the Festival of Speed and the Goodwood Revival. It would take wild horses to keep me away from them, and Jack feels the same. Every year he is there, well into his seventies, driving Coopers, Brabhams and anything else that takes his fancy, with passion and zeal to stir fond memories of a magnificent career. So thanks to Goodwood, and mutual friend and Penske boss Nick Goozée, who used to work with Jack at Brabham and who brings us all together at his glorious Dorset home whenever he can, I now enjoy a close friendship with Jack and his wife Margaret. Jack is enthralling to listen to and he spoke at my retirement party at the National Sporting Club at the end of 2001.

While Jack Brabham has a very special uniqueness – the only Formula 1 World Champion to win both the Drivers' and Constructors' titles in his own right – John Surtees has another which has never shown any sign of being challenged. In the entire history of motor sport he is the only person to have won both the motor-cycle World Championship and Formula 1 World Drivers' Championship. Nuvolari and Rosemeyer were motor-cycle racers of great ability and went on to become four-wheel superstars but there were no World Championships in their day; Alberto Ascari never achieved the success on two wheels that he did on four, and although Geoff Duke and Mike Hailwood were legendary motor-cycle champions neither made it right to the top in cars. John Surtees was a master of both disciplines though and I was commentating on BBC Radio when his brilliant career took off. In August 1951 at Thruxton, in lashing rain, I gingerly clambered on to the slippery roof of the double-decker bus that was to be my BBC commentary position, confident that Geoff Duke was going to win the 500c race for Norton. But, on a self-built and tuned Vincent Grey Flash, 17-year-old John Surtees sensationally gave him a close-fought run for his money and then led Geoff for over half the 1000cc event. He was young and inexperienced with the media then and hadn't got much to say for himself but went on to become cheerfully chatty to the point of verbosity. John has very firm views about things, does not suffer fools gladly and is quick to speak out forcefully if he feels that something is wrong – which he frequently does. He will doggedly argue the hind leg off a donkey and expects everyone associated with him to match his own very high standards, which does not always make him the easiest person in the world to work with.

After Thruxton 1951, Surtees was big news and went on to become one of the greatest short-circuit riders that Britain has ever seen. Weekend after weekend, for some five years I commentated on his non-stop successes across Britain. Then, after unparalleled success with his privately owned Nortons, John became a works rider for the Italian concern MV, who desperately needed someone with his riding, engineering and leadership qualities to help them defeat Gilera. It was the start of five years of almost total dominance. He won his first World Championship in 1956 and became virtually unbeatable, excelling at the toughest race in the world, the Isle of Man TT. I had the pleasure of commentating on no less than six consummate Surtees victories there, including the 1959 Senior event, which John won in the foulest imaginable conditions of rain, hail and bitter cold. I interviewed him immediately after he got off his bike and he was literally trembling with cold and fatigue It was an epic ride. In 1960 he took his seventh World Championship but then, having won everything several times over and needing a fresh challenge, he turned to cars.

John was an immediate success and went on to a turbulent 13-year career of ups and downs. After his first season in Formula 1 with Cooper he had the strength of mind to turn down a deal imperiously offered by Enzo Ferrari himself, but after several team changes in 1963 he joined the Maranello concern to make history. 1962 had been a terrible year for Ferrari and they needed John's unique blend of engineering and development skills, racing savvy, outspokenness and determination as much as MV had in similar circumstances in 1956. John transformed Ferrari's fortunes. He learned to speak Italian and endeared himself to the notorious *tifosi*, who called him Big John. He won his first race for Ferrari and then, in 1964, in one of the most exciting finishes ever to a season, clinched the Formula 1 World Drivers' Championship for himself and the Constructors' Championship for Ferrari. Surtees had done the double – bikes and cars. It was a superb and unique achievement.

Sadly, it was never to be as good again. In 1966, he had a bust-up with Ferrari and left but he was still to win one of the most exciting and dramatic Grands Prix of all time. While I was revelling in the titanic motor-cycle racing battles between MV's Giacomo Agostini and Honda's Mike Hailwood, John was masterminding Honda's second go at Formula 1 and won the legendary 1968 Italian Grand Prix at Monza, where he beat Jack Brabham to the line by a mere two-tenths of a second.

John could be obstinate and outspoken in sticking to his guns. Had he been listened to more he and his teams would have been even more successful. He was never anything other than helpful and considerate to me, and always enormously informative. I lost touch with him when he stopped racing bikes, so when I became a Formula 1 man it was good to meet him again regularly, at his Grand Prix demonstrations of the pre-war Mercedes-Benz 'Silver Arrows' and Auto-Unions and his appearances at Goodwood. There is no one else in the history of motor sport who has had such a varied and successful career.

* * *

I could only rank the stars of my time subjectively but there's absolutely no doubt about who gave me the greatest *entertainment* value: Nigel Mansell. Like him or loathe him, there was always drama and excitement when Nigel was around. He mortgaged his house to buy a Formula 3 drive and discharged himself from hospital with a damaged spine to test drive for Lotus. He sat in a pool of petrol for the whole of his first Grand Prix, angrily took Senna by the throat in Belgium and, in Barcelona, heart-stoppingly raced the great Brazilian, wheel-to-wheel, at over 200mph until he yielded. He won his first race for Ferrari in a car that no one, especially Ferrari, expected to last more than a few laps, made a fabulous passing move on Senna to win in Hungary, was black flagged in Portugal, excluded in Spain, collapsed in the searing heat of Dallas while pushing his Lotus home, lost the 1986 World Championship with a burst tyre in Australia and the 1987 Championship when he crashed in Japan during practice. He threw away the Canadian Grand Prix in his Championship year by going too slowly on his last lap, impossibly passed Gerhard Berger at the notorious Peraltada Corner in Mexico, had his wheel come off as he left the pit-lane in Portugal, daringly double-bluffed team-mate Nelson Piquet to win the 1987 British Grand Prix, was forever vociferously complaining about anything and everything and mischievously rejoiced in fouling up my interviews. 'Red Five', as I used to call him in commentary (after his car number), was magic.

Do you detect a note of affection? Indeed you do. Nigel was not everybody's cup of tea but he was mine. The man's determination and will to win was awe-inspiring, he was superb on the track and we always got on well – even after Brazil, where I did an excellent 20-minute interview with him in 40-degree heat only to find that I had failed to switch on the microphone. I shamefacedly asked him to do it again, which he did with good grace, but he never let me forget it. Every time I fronted up to him afterwards he'd say with a smirk, 'Have you turned the microphone on, Murray?' Before an interview got going we'd always have to go through an irritating ritual: just as I got into the first question Nigel would reach forward and tug the microphone wire, twist his baseball cap sideways or screw up his face to throw me. I'd grit my teeth knowing that if I said, 'Look Nigel, are we going to do this bloody interview or not?' he'd probably say, 'OK then, not' and stalk off. It always worked out all right in the end though.

In terms of Grand Prix victories and World Championship points Nigel is the most successful British driver of all time. He was a tiger in the car but, in the eyes of many people, a king-sized pain in the neck out of it. One of the top men with the Williams team once remarked that he wished Nigel was a human light bulb that he could plug into the car for the race and then put back on the shelf until the next one. He was only half joking. Thin-skinned and with a hair-trigger propensity to take offence, Nigel had to be handled with extreme care. 'He's actually got a very well-adjusted personality,' someone said to me once. 'He's got a chip on *both* shoulders.'

It took him 72 races to win his first Grand Prix and the Lotus team manager Peter Warr, certainly not Nigel's Number One Fan, made a famous comment he was later to rue: 'Nigel Mansell will never win a Grand Prix as long as he's got a hole

The legendary Juan Manuel Fangio winning one of the greatest races of all time, the 1957 German Grand Prix. I was later to meet The Master and commentate on his victory for the film on his life.

Three great World Champions on the podium for the 1966 German Grand Prix, two of whom I am proud to know as friends. John Surtees (left), Jack Brabham (centre) and Jochen Rindt who was sadly killed in 1970.

'I was on full opposite lock!' John Surtees tells an astonished Stirling Moss and me how he nearly lost the plot.

Michael Schumacher and I did a duet of one of my 'Murrayisms' at my 2001 Indianapolis paddock party. Who says he isn't a good sport? I thought he was tremendous.

Indy boss Tony George (fourth left) gave me one of the original 1911 Indianapolis bricks at my party with (left to right) Ross Brawn, Flavio Briatore, Bernie Ecclestone, Paul Stoddart and Eddie Jordan in attendance.

I was in good company when I received my 'Bernie' award – with Professor Sid Watkins, Jenson Button, Michael Schumacher and The Master himself.

It's all over. The commentary box at Indianapolis 2001, as I left it after 53 marvellous years.

in his arse.' He won 31, exceeded only by Michael Schumacher, Alain Prost and Ayrton Senna, was World Champion in 1992, and only Schumacher has won as many races (nine) as Mansell in a single season. Hard-to-please Lotus boss Colin Chapman, one of the greatest motor-racing leaders and personalities of all time, was his guide and mentor. Nigel certainly had more fans worldwide than any other British driver has ever had; the British fans adored him and in Italy the passionately enthusiastic and very knowledgeable *tifosi*, lovers of all things Ferrari, nicknamed him '*Il Leone*' for his courage and forceful driving. He was a man of the people, a real showman who instinctively knew how to work a crowd. There's no denying that he is difficult but he delivered excitement, drama and pleasure which outweighed many times whatever frustration, irritation and dislike he generated. I've stayed with Nigel and his charming wife Rosanne at his homes in Florida and the Isle of Man, flogged round a golf course with him in driving rain and winds to satisfy his passion for the game and been driven round my beloved Isle of Man TT course by him. He has always been a true friend to me.

I have no doubt that, had he stayed with Williams after 1992 instead of leaving in a huff (caused by a row over money and some very clever politicking by Ayrton Senna) he could have won two, and maybe three, more World Championships. Despite his success he was not the luckiest of drivers but he went on to win the American Champcar Championship in his rookie year in 1993 and to return triumphantly to Formula 1 in 1994 where he won his final Grand Prix before retiring from the sport. He gave me and all his countless fans an enormous amount of pleasure and I'll not forget him.

Unsurprisingly I've always had a soft spot for British drivers. No offence to the others, but it would be unnatural if your countrymen didn't enthuse you. Added to which I've been with most of them all the way from their earliest days. Take Damon Hill – I commentated on his famous double World Champion father, Graham, who was even my co-commentator once. After Graham was killed in a plane crash in 1975, life was really tough for the Hill family but his wife, Bette, did a fabulous job of bringing up the children and it was she who encouraged Damon to switch from motor cycles to cars. I followed and talked about him from the day that Brands Hatch owner John Webb launched his career into Formula Ford in 1984. I was there on the day and remember wondering whether Damon, who had done well at Brands in motorcycle racing, really wanted to race cars or whether he felt his heritage obliged him to. As time went by it was very clear that he was genuinely motivated. It was a long, hard struggle but he got there. On the way up he was good but initially showed no superstar promise in the way that Senna and Schumacher had: in Formula Ford, Formula 3 and Formula 3000 he won races but no Championships. But, like Nigel Mansell, he got his head down and grafted away until he got the job as Williams test driver.

If I had a fiver for every lap I talked about Damon I'd be a rich man but to be honest I never thought of him as a future World Champion. I'd failed to recognize the characteristics he shared with his father – talent, self-belief and unlimited determination. He did an excellent job as a test driver and badgered away at Frank Williams. When Mansell flounced off in 1993 Damon took his place, winning three times in his first season, and when Alain Prost retired he was joined by the great Ayrton Senna, but tragically not for long. After two races together Senna was killed and only just into his second season Damon had the awesome responsibility of leading his shocked and demoralized team against the might of Benetton, Ferrari and McLaren, an uncanny repetition of 1968 when his father had to do the same thing for Lotus after the death of Jim Clark.

Damon so nearly won the Championship in 1994. Two years later came that elusive prize but it was all downhill thereafter, with only two brief flashes of his old form with Arrows in 1997 and Jordan in 1998. His comparatively brief Formula 1 career – just 115 Grands Prix compared with Nigel Mansell's 187 and Riccardo Patrese's 256 – finished in 1999. But Damon had given me and the fans some truly outstanding memories – his pole position for the British Grand Prix in 1994 and his dramatic defeat of Schumacher's Benetton the next day; that inspired race at Suzuka in 1994 to keep his Championship hopes alive; 1997 in Hungary where he drove for Arrows and, beyond belief, caught and passed Michael Schumacher's Ferrari to lead the race, and, of course, Japan in 1996, when he drove to victory and the World Championship. As he crossed the line it all welled up inside me. 'And I've got to stop now,' I choked, 'because I've got a lump in my throat.' It was an honest sentiment that reflected the feelings of the whole of Britain, for not only was Damon loved for himself but he had created another Formula 1 record by becoming the first-ever World Champion son of a World Champion father.

He is a fine bloke – lively, quick-witted, and good company. He's also a caring father, with a lovely wife in Georgie, and four children. In 1996 he was moody, but who wouldn't have been with the Championship stress that he was suffering? I well remember that after six wins from the first nine races he had a massive lead over his Williams team-mate Jacques Villeneuve but things then started to go wrong. In Portugal with only two races to go the pressure on Damon was enormous as I sat opposite him in the Williams motorhome. He looked worried and stressed. At the time he was training for some six hours every day and I thought it was getting to him.

'You're not overdoing it, Damon, are you?' I asked, genuinely concerned. 'You're looking really gaunt and peaky.'

'What did you say that for?' he replied angrily, got up and stormed off.

My God, what did I say that was so wrong?

I went over to him and said, 'Look Damon, if I've said something to offend you I'm sorry but it was well meant. You know me well enough to realize that I'm not trying to wrong-foot you.'

'I'm sorry, Murray,' he said. 'I was a bit distressed. I'd just been interviewed by some foreign bloke who asked me, "What would you give to have your father back for just one hour?"'

It was no wonder that Damon was feeling sensitive. The pressure got even greater when Villeneuve won at Estoril and Damon scored no points but it all came good in Japan with that glorious victory that won him the Championship. With all the wisdom of hindsight I think he was wrong not to retire at the peak of his career as World Champion at the end of 1996. By the exalted standards of the Williams team Damon had had a bad year in 1995 (second in the Championship but 33 points behind his rival Michael Schumacher) and Frank Williams signed Germany's Heinz-Harald Frentzen for 1997. Ironically Damon then brilliantly won the World Championship in 1996 but the die was cast and he was out of Williams. He dragged on for another three seasons with Arrows and Jordan and even won at Spa in 1998 but the enthusiasm wasn't there. His last season was very sad to behold but it was his life and it is all too easy to make someone else's decisions for them when you aren't involved. It is difficult to see his unique 'World Champion Son of a World Champion Father' achievement ever being equalled and I am very proud to be able to call him a friend.

In their very different ways, Stirling Moss, Jack Brabham, John Surtees, Nigel Mansell and Damon Hill have all proved that there is life after Formula 1 which, for me, is a great relief. Tragically though it sometimes defeats even the best. Ayrton Senna paid its most extreme penalty and it gave one of its brightest stars, Alain Prost, a grindingly hard time after he had hung up his helmet.

Softly spoken (I was forever asking him to speak up at interviews), and intensely analytical, Alain was smooth and unspectacular behind the wheel. His nickname – 'The Professor' – sums him up perfectly and the result, after 13 years in

Formula 1 with McLaren, Renault, Ferrari and Williams, was a proud statistical record which remained unbeaten for years until, eventually, Michael Schumacher eclipsed it.

His Grand Prix career began a couple of years after mine. I first met him in 1980 at the Belgian Grand Prix at Zolder. It was the fifth race of the year but the first I had actually attended, since the first four had been long-haul events that the BBC had covered from London. I talked to Alain and found him to be impressively professional. Like Nigel Mansell, he generated drama. It was, for instance, at a very wet Monaco in 1982 that he was the subject of one of my classic prophesies that backfired.

'Here comes the gallant little Frenchman in his turbo-charged Renault, almost home for his sixth Grand Prix win. Nothing can stop him now.' As I said it he lost control, slammed into the barrier, lost a wheel and retired. (That was a truly incredible race, incidentally, with an amazing five different leaders on the last lap.) The Renault was fast but unreliable and Alain moaned about it for the whole of 1983 although he was up for the title right to the end. When he got to the last race in South Africa he retired again, Piquet took the title – and the balloon went up. I was at Kyalami and interviewed Prost, who was resigned but bitter. He spoke his mind and got fired for it so he rejoined McLaren and a year later I found myself in a replay situation in Portugal, where he had just lost what could have been his second successive Championship, by half a point, to team-mate Niki Lauda. When I interviewed them together in a tiny room crammed with about 60 media people Alain was downcast, to put it mildly.

He won it convincingly the following year, though, and in 1986 at Adelaide the boot was once again on the other foot. Last race of the year again: Nigel Mansell led the Championship by six points from Prost and only had to finish third to win it. But with what turned out to be a flash of inspiration I said, in vision, on the Channel 9 TV breakfast show that I thought Prost would win the race and the Championship. One of my oft-stated clichés is that, 'Anything can happen in Formula 1 and it usually does' and amazingly Mansell had his famous rear tyre blowout and Alain took a lucky win. Alain commented on it when I interviewed him. Modestly I said it was just a gut feeling, which it was but, of course, if I'd been wrong it would have been another of Murray Walker's classic gaffes!

Prost's rivalry with Ayrton Senna was one of the most bitter in the history of Formula 1. With McLaren in 1988 and 89 there were no team orders, they were as good as each other, both were determined to win and, since they had little effective opposition, the rivalry was extreme and there was a lot of mutual suspicion. In 1989 at Monaco, with Prost three points ahead of Ayrton, I waited for hours outside the Marlboro motorhome to interview Senna, whose debriefing sessions with his engineers were notoriously long. Eventually the door opened and a weary-looking Prost emerged.

'Alain,' I said. 'What in God's name do you talk about in there for four and a half hours?'

'Oh this and that, Murray, but I do not like to be the first to leave!'

The rivalry between them got more and more intense until,

in 1990 at the last race of the year, with Prost now driving for Ferrari, they collided in Japan for the second year in succession. It was a controversial coming together caused by Senna angrily feeling that he had been cheated out of the best side of the starting grid and having a cold, steely resolve to lead at the first corner even if it meant taking Prost off at some 150mph. After it had happened Senna vehemently denied that it was deliberate, but subsequently he admitted that it had been. As a man and a driver he had my greatest admiration and respect but I never forgave him for that.

At the end of 1991 Prost again suffered for his honesty and outspokenness when, after continually criticizing his car and the team in public, he was fired by Ferrari, as he had been by Renault. Too late to get a decent drive for 1992, he took a sabbatical, during which he worked in the next box to me as French TV's expert commentator and devoted himself to replacing Nigel Mansell at Williams in 1993. It was pistols at dawn again between him and Senna because Ayrton desperately wanted the drive too. Alain got it and cakewalked the Championship, the fourth and last of his career, but then, sadly for him, he decided to become a team owner.

Alain had had a magnificent racing career which made him one of the greatest of all time but Formula 1 kept its misery for him to the very end. The fact that you are a supremely good racing driver is no guarantee that you will also be a successful team owner. Only two top Grand Prix drivers have founded and run their own teams with any long-lasting success – Jack Brabham and Bruce McLaren – and of those only McLaren still exists. Year by year after Alain took up the reins I watched him age, his fingernails chewed down even more than usual and his face increasingly lined with the worries of trying to stay afloat, let alone beat his lavishly funded and experienced rivals. It was a depressing sight. Sadly, he didn't appear to have all the entrepreneurial skills needed to compete successfully with men of the calibre of Ron Dennis, Frank Williams and Eddie Jordan and in 2002 his team foundered. Formula 1 isn't called the Piranha Club for nothing.

Ever the gentleman, Alain came up to me in the paddock at Indianapolis in 2001, just before I went to the box to do my last Grand Prix commentary. 'Is this really the end, Murray? I can't believe it. It's a sad day after all these years. We are going to miss you.' From someone who had been so much a part of my Formula 1 life and whom I admired and liked so much they were very greatly appreciated words.

The Senna story is even more dramatic, with a heart-rendingly tragic ending. I'd really need a whole book to probe the enigma that was Ayrton Senna, but indicative of this extraordinary man is the fact that his real full name was Ayrton Senna da Silva. He dropped the 'da Silva' bit after his second season in Britain because it is a common name in Brazil and he wanted to establish himself as someone out of the ordinary. He certainly did so by becoming one of the greatest – millions of people all over the world would say *the* greatest. Three times a World Champion, 41 times a Grand Prix winner and a record 65 pole positions – a prodigiously talented racing driver but, above all, a deep-thinking God-fearing perfectionist who was obsessive about being the best at everything he did. He *had* to win. He was ruthless on the track but courteous off it, although very few people got through to the private man who lived inside the public figure.

I made a special journey to Brands Hatch on 29 September 1981 to see the Brazilian sensation who had won two Formula Ford Championships and 12 out of 17 races in his first year. He seemed quiet, pleasant, very mature and obviously a bit special. 'How can I get a video of today's race to take back to Brazil with me?' he asked. I said I'd send him one if he won the race. He was second but he made the fastest lap and I sent him one anyway. In 1982 he swept all before him in Formula Ford 2000 and, the following year, had a thrilling season-long tussle for the Formula 3 Championship with Martin Brundle. He won it with a stunning 12 victories and I was behind the BBC microphone to tell the world. At the end of the season he went to Macau for the Blue Riband event of Formula 3, its unofficial World Championship. I was there to do the commentary for the Hong Kong TVB channel and Ayrton won both heats, immediately phoning Bernie Ecclestone, then Brabham boss, in England to tell him he had won, having tested for him for F1 the previous week. With an eight-hour time difference Bernie was probably still in bed but Ayrton got his Formula 1 drive in 1984, with the Toleman team that later became Benetton. I was almost apoplectic with excitement at Monaco when, after sensationally driving through the field in appalling conditions from 13th on the grid, he was about to take the lead from Alain Prost, only for the race to be stopped. A star had been born and Ayrton was in immediate demand.

Towards the end of the season I was staying at the Bruckl Wirt Hotel at Niklasdorf with Ferrari and Toleman for the Austrian Grand Prix and, during dinner, went over to the Ferrari table to ask their designer, Mauro Forghieri, to sign a book for me (yes, I do it too). On the way back I joined Senna and Toleman boss Alex Hawkridge, to find a heated discussion going on about the fact that Ayrton was breaking his contract to join Lotus in 1985. Typically, Senna knew he was worthy of a better car and with his obsession to win was determined to go. The announcement was made and an angry Hawkridge suspended him from the Italian Grand Prix at Monza to teach him a lesson. Alex was one of the very few people who would have done that and a distraught Senna just couldn't believe it was happening.

But in 1985 he was with a team that could win and in his second race for Lotus he did so in Portugal. In a replay of the foul conditions he had overcome at Monaco with Toleman, he drove an inspired race to stay on the track when almost everyone else was spinning off, including Alain Prost, the man Ayrton felt had beaten him unfairly at Monaco. Senna had arrived with a vengeance. At Estoril my first of many post-race interviews with him as a winner was in even worse conditions than the one with Lauda and Prost the year before. With no control whatsoever over who had access to him, and with a vast throng crowding under the one bit of shelter from the driving rain, I had to get my elbows out, throw decency to the winds, and fight my way through to him. I got there first and it was as though he had been winning Grands Prix all his life – cool, calm and very collected. Yes, of course he was glad to have won his first Grand Prix, no, it hadn't been as easy as it looked because in fact he had gone off like everyone else but had been able to scrabble back. And he was very happy to have given the team its first win since 1982. For me it was one of those 'I was there' days, but there were lots more to come.

From ten starts at Monaco Senna won six times, to beat Graham Hill's previous record of five victories, and I can proudly say I commentated on every lap of every one of them. It was an incredible achievement by Senna at the circuit where, more than any other, driver skill and fortitude are paramount. He would have won in 1988 too, his first year with McLaren, had he not lost concentration as a result of leading his team-mate Alain Prost by an uncatchable 53 seconds. Into the barrier by the tunnel entry he went and, totally distraught, disappeared into his nearby apartment for hours – an indication of the intensity of his feelings, which I was to see again in times of extreme stress.

In order to keep on top of things I always went to the many Grand Prix weekend press conferences. A lot of them are dreary affairs with the drivers mouthing politically correct platitudes, eager to get it over with as soon as possible. The conferences may be boring and irritating for them but tough – they're a vital part of their highly paid lives. Senna wasn't like that though and some of his performances were electrifyingly dramatic, particularly if he felt he had been wronged, which was not altogether unknown. His mastery of English, his eloquence and clarity of thought were truly impressive and he could hold a vast roomful of media people enthralled when he was in full flow. On several occasions I sat overwhelmed by his passionate outpourings as he furiously denounced injustices he thought he had been done – one of them lasted an hour and a half. In 1990 I had to sit down in Australia and interview him for BBC TV about his collision with Prost at Suzuka, where he had quite clearly not only been in the wrong but could well have killed them both. I wasn't looking forward to it, to be honest, but was preceded by Jackie Stewart who was doing the same thing for Australia's Channel 9. In the most wonderful interview I have ever heard, using all his considerable debating and communication skills and his deep knowledge as a three-times World Champion, Jackie calmly and patiently took Senna apart until he lost his temper and was shouting angrily in an effort to justify himself. The interview ended acrimoniously and then I was on. I'd like to say I did as well as Jackie but the truth is that I didn't. 'I think he honestly believes what he's saying, but then so did Hitler,' said Jackie afterwards – and I agreed with him for Senna's total self-belief was not always justified.

But he continued to work his magic on me for the whole of his six-year career at McLaren, with spellbinding pole positions and race after race of complete mastery, the greatest of which was his drive in an inferior car to win the 1993 European Grand Prix at Donington in unspeakable conditions. I was sorry for my friend Tom Wheatcroft who owns Donington and who, at enormous personal expense, had achieved his ambition of holding a Grand Prix at his circuit only for the weather to be atrocious, but it was certainly a memorable race.

Then, seeing a better chance of winning, Senna left

McLaren in 1994, as he had left Toleman ten years earlier, and joined Williams. The car wasn't as good as he had hoped it would be and there was a bright new star for him to overcome – Michael Schumacher.

The first race of the year was the Brazilian Grand Prix at Sao Paulo, Senna's home city, and his press secretary, Betise Assumpcao (now Mrs Patrick Head), arranged for me to interview him at his magnificent personal skyscraper headquarters, from which he ran his various businesses. We toured the building, admired the view of the city from its rooftop helicopter pad and then joined the great man himself. By his side was a replica model of the 1985 Lotus 97T which had given him his first victory and in the adjoining office was his father, Milton, with his brother, Leonardo. Ayrton was relaxed, cheerful and friendly even though he was under pressure to leave for the circuit.

'I know you're a thorough chap, Ayrton, so tell me, do you get the videos out over the winter to relive the races and see if you can learn anything?'

'Yes, Murray, I do and always with your voice.'

It was one of the nicest compliments I have ever been paid.

'Well, thank you for that but what's left? You've won three Championships, you've won every race there is to be won. When are you going to stop and what is there to go for now?'

'Bigger numbers,' he said.

Tragically that was an ambition not to be achieved. Schumacher beat him in Brazil and did so again in Japan. Two weeks after that we were in Italy for the first European race of the year at Imola and on the Friday I was yet again facing Ayrton for our pre-race chat. During the winter I had been looking at some tapes of the 1983 Formula 3 season and realized that, since then, I had stopped pronouncing his Christian name properly as 'Eye-eer-ton' and was now calling him 'Airtun'. I thought I'd better put that right, and did so for the Brazil race but had so many critical comments about 'going all foreign and not calling him Airtun like the rest of us' that, for Japan, I reverted to the 'English' version. So there I was for race three with the Master.

'Airtun, two races down, no points and Schumacher well ahead. I guess you're not too happy?'

'What happened to Eye-eer-ton?' he asked.

I was flabbergasted. 'How on earth did you know about that? You don't even see the telecasts – you're in the car.'

'Oh, I keep in touch,' he said with a wide smile.

And that was the last time I spoke to him. Two days later he passed away at Maggiore Hospital following that heartbreaking accident. Ayrton Senna was one of the most outstanding personalities I have ever met, a genius the like of which there have been very few in the history of the sport.

I've said I'm not going to try to rank the top Formula 1 drivers I've seen, but nevertheless I've always said that, in my belief, the very best of them was Juan Manuel Fangio. I can't prove it, I just believe it – or at least I *did*, because now I'm not so sure. It could be Michael Schumacher. Put all the things you have to consider into the pot and it's a mighty close-run thing. Better than Senna? Better than Prost? Jim Clark and the rest of the superstars? Yes, I think so, but Michael's a long way from being everybody's Number One, especially in Britain.

'Tell me what that arrogant bastard Schumacher's *really* like,' someone once said to me.

'Hey, just a minute,' I replied, 'have you met him? Have you talked to him? Why do you say he's arrogant?'

'You've only got to look at him haven't you? And he's German.'

'Well hang on. Your prejudice is showing. I fought them during the war but just because you're German doesn't mean you're off limits. You're wrong. He's a really decent bloke, he's never been anything other than helpful and considerate to me and I've got a lot of time for him. He's as friendly as you can expect anybody in his position to be. In fact he's an amazingly normal bloke if you know him. Ask anyone who does. Loves his wife, children and football. All that sort of thing. All you see of him on the box is when he's under colossal pressure at the track with the whole of Italy and Ferrari depending on him and with every Tom, Dick and Harry wanting a piece of his life. "Can I have my photograph taken with you, Michael?" "Are you going to win, Michael?" "Can I interview you, Michael?" "Will you do something for my charity, Michael?" "Can I have your autograph, Michael?" "You have to meet the sponsor, Michael." Fair enough, he's their hero but he's there to do a job, which is to win races, and with the competition he's got he has to focus on that totally. Nobody's going to give him any medals, let alone the money he's paid, if he takes his eye off the ball for an instant.'

I don't think I convinced him, but that was what I felt and still do.

I first met Michael at the classic Formula 3 confrontation between himself and Mika Hakkinen at Macau in 1990, where the German triumphed following a mistake by the Finn. At the Mandarin Oriental Hotel I talked to a euphoric Schumacher, showing all the uninhibited joy that we later saw so often in Formula 1, and I was impressed. He went on to win at Fuji in Japan and hasn't looked back since. In 1991, when Mercedes-Benz sponsored Michael for a grand prix drive with Eddie Jordan's team in Belgium, it was obvious from the first practice session that he was special and I went and stood at the back of the Jordan garage to see what happened. It was as though Michael had been driving Formula 1 cars all his life. He had never been to Spa before, a drivers' circuit if ever there was one, and had only been round it on a bicycle but he was totally self-assured and incredibly quick. No one expected him to start seventh on the grid, with just Senna, Prost, Mansell, Berger, Alesi and Piquet ahead of him, but he did so, only to burn his clutch out at his first Formula 1 standing start. At the end of qualifying I remember thinking, *Blimey, if this bloke's like this first time out at Spa, he's going places. I must get an interview for the archives.* Schumacher was very matter of fact about what he had done. Benetton snatched him from under Eddie Jordan's nose and the rest is history.

So what *is* he really like? Well, he's similar to Ayrton Senna in some ways but totally different in others. He's not charismatic like the Brazilian but serious, matter of fact and straightforward – although just as thorough and businesslike.

Ask him a question and you get a carefully considered answer which is right on the button. Like Senna, he is the complete master of every aspect of his craft, physical and mental, from keeping super-fit and knowing everything there is to know about his car to building the whole team around him, to nurture and support him and do everything his way. It is always tough for his team-mate because, no matter what the contract says, Schumacher is absolute Number One. At Benetton no one got near him, except Martin Brundle, briefly. At Ferrari Irvine pragmatically accepted the situation whereas Barrichello appeared to try and fight it. But Michael was, and is, the Master. Like Senna he has a total command of English, and it always amazed me how well he coped with the idiomatic nuances of what to him was a foreign language.

Of course Michael Schumacher is not the perfect paragon of virtue, without faults. Like Senna he is ruthless on the track and, because of his determination to win, has been involved in more brutally controversial moves than most. Take Adelaide 1994, where he took out Damon Hill to win the World Championship (by trying to regain his racing line I believe, to general derision from my hardened and cynical media friends); Jerez 1997, where he rammed Jacques Villeneuve, this time to lose the Championship and be rightly excluded from its final classification as a penalty, and regularly chopping across the track from pole position at the start to block his rivals. 'Legal but unfair,' the experts say. 'Are we racing or playing children's games?' retorts Michael. Personally, I strongly disagree with it being allowed as I think it is both dangerous and unsportsmanlike, but rules are rules and what Schumacher consistently does is not against them.

Tough and ruthless he may be, but cold and heartless he most certainly is not. Witness his open love for his family, his unbridled leaps for joy on the podium, his tearful breakdown at Monza 2000 after he had matched Ayrton Senna's 41 Grand Prix wins, his abject misery at Monza 2001 just five days after the devastating terrorist attacks of September 11 and his ability to relax, let his hair down, be human and party all night with the best of them at Suzuka's end-of-season celebrations. But above all Michael is a racer with so many stunning victories to his name: Belgium 1995 where, from 16th on the grid, he brilliantly outdrove Damon Hill, using slick tyres on a rain-soaked track to win, albeit with some extremely robust wheel-banging tactics that earned him as much criticism as praise; Spain 1996, his first win for Ferrari, where he ran rings round everyone in the wet; Monaco 1997, where the same thing happened; Hungary 1998, where an inspired race strategy from technical director Ross Brawn required Schumacher to gain 19 seconds in 25 laps to permit a third race-winning pit stop and he did it (shades of Fangio at the Nurburgring 1957); Malaysia 1999, where, after a six-race lay off recovering from a broken leg, he pulverized the opposition and then selflessly moved over to let team-mate Eddie Irvine through to win; Japan 2000, where he became Ferrari's first World Champion since Jody Scheckter in 1979, and, for me, Indianapolis 2001. He didn't win there, but he showed that he was a warm and very generous human being.

Michael had already contributed to my *This is your Life*

programme with some kind words, he had led the drivers who gave me a signed magnum of champagne at Silverstone to commemorate my last British Grand Prix for the BBC, and we had sat together at the wonderful Grand Prix Ball at Melbourne, where I was presented with a Lifetime Achievement Award. But his presence at the surprise party the teams threw for me at Indianapolis 2001, my last Grand Prix, touched me deeply. Tony Jardine, a great showman, masterminded it and was getting the many drivers who were there to take a card with the words of one of my bloopers on it and imitate me delivering it. He called Michael up to say, in my way, 'And here's Michael Schumacher, son of Ralf Schumacher. Now the boot is on the other Schumacher!' I stoutly contest that I ever said it, mind you, but that's another story.

Michael was mystified. 'What do I have to do?'

'Say it like Murray did!'

'But I wasn't there – I was in the race.'

'Here, Michael,' I said, 'Let's do it together.'

I put my arm round his shoulders and we did a duet that brought the house down. I was touched and delighted that he came at all, even more so by the fact that, on the eve of the race, he stayed for the whole hour and a half, never mind being mightily impressed at his being prepared to have a go at the 'Murrayism.'

'Were you happy with what Tony did, Murray?' he asked afterwards.

'Yes, Michael, I was delighted, why?'

'I thought he lacked respect.'

'No, no, that was just a bit of fun.'

'Oh, was that your English sense of humour?'

'Well yes, I suppose it was.'

'Oh, I see.'

I don't think he did, because to him it must have seemed a very strange way of honouring someone. Afterwards he said he would like to be interviewed by me following the race and, from a bloke who just does not give interviews at the track, I regarded that as a true honour. It was the last interview I did and one of my best. With one of the very best. If not *the* best.

I've had a lot of fun with Bernie Ecclestone, too. Bernie's image is of a hard, ruthless, immensely wealthy and enormously powerful business tycoon and you certainly don't get to where he is from nowhere without being an awesomely competent and adventurous entrepreneur who takes no prisoners. 'I do deals,' says Bernie. Deals which started in his childhood and progressed through a motor-cycle business into cars, property and Formula 1.

He was a racer himself, from 500cc single-seaters up to Grand Prix standard, before he decided he was better at managing than driving and looked after two of Grand Prix racing's greatest naturals, Stewart Lewis-Evans, who was tragically killed before he could realize his full potential with Vanwall, and Jochen Rindt, Formula 1's only posthumous World Champion. Bernie then bought Brabham and made a double World Champion out of Nelson Piquet in 1981 and 1983. The world knows him now, of course, as the unchallenged boss of Formula 1. Nothing happens without Bernie knowing and approving and through his audacious wheeling and dealing he has made himself an immensely wealthy man. In the process he has made Formula 1 what it is today – a worldwide sport that nations vie with each other to host. A sport for which, at immense personal expense, he has created his own digital TV empire, a sport whose TV ratings are only exceeded by the Olympic Games and the World Cup (which happen once every four years compared with Formula 1's 17 races a year), a sport that the world's car manufacturers are eager to support and which has made a lot of team owners multi-millionaires.

Of course he is as tough and demanding, hard and determined, as you'd expect him to be but he is also razor sharp, incredibly quick-witted and, when people least expect it, extremely kind and thoughtful. His standards of presentation are obsessively high and years ago when I asked him if I could go to his Brabham premises at Chessington to interview his gifted and talented designer Gordon Murray he said, 'No, no, I don't want your lot dragging their cameras along the walls.' But he relented when I gave him my personal guarantee that we'd all respect his building. Gordon sat in a corner of the design office with windows to the left of and behind him and when the cameraman went to adjust the vertical blinds that controlled the natural light he said 'They don't move.'

'Yes they do,' said the cameraman. 'You just pull this chain here.' Which he did, only to find that indeed they didn't move.

'Mr Ecclestone didn't like the angle we had them at so they've been bolted up solid,' said Gordon.

Then there's the other side to Bernie. In 1988 BBC *Grand*

Prix celebrated its 10th anniversary at the Monaco GP so we took a special cake with us and arranged for all the team bosses – Ron Dennis, Frank Williams, Ken Tyrrell, Jackie Oliver and Co. – to form a semi-circle round me while I did my bit to camera. 'OK, gentlemen,' I said, 'here's the deal. When I've done my words I'm going to cut the cake and I want you all to shout out together "Happy Birthday *Grand Prix*". Got it? Good. Let's do it.' As I got ready to do a take I noticed Bernie quietly going down the line speaking to the talent. I should have known. When I finished my lines to camera and started cutting the cake they all shouted, as one, 'BOLLOCKS!'

The Spanish Grand Prix that year was at Jerez and it was Herbie Blash's birthday. Herbie is one of Bernie's trusted lieutenants from way back. Bernie took the whole of the first floor at a restaurant near the circuit and threw a colossal party. When Herbie's cake came in, the party rapidly deteriorated into a massive no-holds-barred cake-throwing and water-fight extravaganza started by Nelson Piquet and with Bernie directing operations. To this day I have a vivid image of him, in his usual immaculate white shirt and knife-edge-creased black trousers, dodging behind a very big chap as a bucket of water was thrown at him. The bloke ducked and Bernie got the lot. 'What a great party!' everyone was saying as they made their way home, soaking wet and smothered with cake, past the bemused, up-market Spanish diners on the ground floor. Funny lot, we British. Heaven knows what the Spanish thought of us.

Bernie masterminds everything at Grands Prix from a sinister grey, custom-built coach, commonly known as 'The

Kremlin', from which he can see you without you seeing him. I was looking for him one day and got in, to find it full of compartments which were seemingly empty. 'Anybody here?' I shouted. 'It depends who wants to know!' came Bernie's voice from the back.

About ten years ago I was walking round the circuit at Monaco on the Wednesday before the race to see whether there had been any changes since the year before when a Fiat with smoked windows drew up alongside me. The back window went down a few inches, a pair of heavy black, horn-rimmed, glasses looked out at me and I was offered a lift.

'Thanks, Bernie', I said, recognizing him instantly.

'Where are you going?'

'Only to the paddock.'

When we arrived Bernie took a wad of tissue paper out of his pocket and said, 'I was passing a jewellers in Bond Street the other day and saw this. I thought you might like it.'

I unwrapped it and there was a gold lapel-pin reproduction of the old eight-sided BBC table microphone. I was pole-axed and as I spluttered out my very sincere thanks he said, 'Well, you *are* the BBC, aren't you?'

Undeserved praise but I was, and am, immensely grateful. I suspect, incidentally, that I wouldn't have got the ITV job if Bernie hadn't said he was happy for me to do it. In 2001 I was the very proud recipient of one of the first four 'Bernie' awards, a sort of Formula 1 Oscar in the form of a gold statuette of the man himself. Mine was a Lifetime Achievement Award and the other three went to Michael Schumacher, Professor Sid Watkins and Jenson Button for his magnificent rookie year in 2000. So I was in very good company.

All good things come to an end and in 2001 they came to an end for me at Indianapolis. My wife Elizabeth's first Grand Prix with me was my last and on race day Bernie said to me, 'You're taking your wife on to the grid.' Now going on to the grid is something that only appropriate team members and VIPs are allowed to do, so it was a real privilege. But I couldn't do it.

'No, I'm not, Bernie,' I said. 'I've got to go to the commentary box right now but thank you for the offer.'

'Oh well,' he said, 'I suppose I'll have to take her myself.' So from way up at the top of the multi-tiered grandstand I watched Elizabeth strolling through the two lines of cars, doing her own version of the Martin Brundle pit walk, and I felt very proud. Bernie had been at the fantastic surprise party that had been thrown for me in the Paddock Club the previous evening and in front of all the guests he'd said, 'You're not retiring. You've got 10 years left in you. You're going to work for me.' But, for once, he was wrong.

CHAPTER FOURTEEN

I *Am* Very Much Mistaken

At the first Australian Grand Prix in 1985 a man came up to me in the paddock at Adelaide holding something in his hand. 'Hi, Murray! Me and my mates are big fans of yours. We've had this made and if you don't mind we're all going to wear one in the Grandstand on Sunday.'

'Oh, right,' I said. 'What is it?'

'It's a T-shirt,' he said, opening it up to reveal a big cartoon drawing of myself with the words MURRAY WALKER FAN CLUB.

'Thank you,' I said simperingly, 'I don't see how anyone could object to that. I think it's terrific. I'm very flattered.'

'Great, Murray. Glad you like it. Now I'll show you the back.'

In big letters it said: UNLESS I'M VERY MUCH MISTAKEN . . . YES, I *AM* VERY MUCH MISTAKEN!

I thought it was great and not only did Ozzie and his chums

wear them on raceday but David Hill, the Channel 9 producer, filmed an extremely well-endowed girl in one. He opened all the commercial breaks with her getting everyone's attention as she walked towards the camera and closed them with her walking away, to give the viewers both messages. That got me off to a flying start in Australia, with people in the street shouting, 'Unless I'm very much mistaken!' at me, but my reputation had obviously preceded me.

'Murrayisms' they're called – those verbal bloopers with which I became irretrievably associated. Words coming out in the wrong order or thoughts getting jumbled in my enthusiasm to verbalize what was happening before my very eyes. They didn't worry me unduly. Sports commentating shouldn't just be about facts, history and what-is-happening-now. It should involve enthusiasm, spontaneity and a bit of fun, or at least I think so. The viewers want to be entertained, not just informed. Formula 1 is a fast-moving sport that calls for passionate and engaging description. So get your foot down and give it all you've got. Reach out to them as friends. *Involve* them. I was told time after time that I should engage brain before operating mouth but I was often too fired up for that to happen. What I said came from the heart, even though it was sometimes flawed.

I know my style used to annoy some people, but luckily for me most of them seemed to enjoy it and regard it as my distinctive trademark. I wasn't ashamed of it, I wasn't self-conscious about it: it was *me*. I was delighted and felt good about the fact that people liked what I did and, to be honest, I've done very well out of my reputation because I've used my banana-skin deliveries in after-dinner speeches that raise a lot of laughs and keep the wolf from the door. I sometimes got a bit depressed when articles headed, '20 THINGS MURRAY WALKER WISHED HE'D NEVER SAID' presented me as a bumbling idiot who continually got things wrong, but I like to think the fluffs were very much the exception rather than the rule.

We all make mistakes. My problem was that mine were made on an electronic medium which immediately transmitted them to millions of people all over the world. In the never-ending heat of the action I either didn't realize what I had said or, if I did, couldn't correct it because things had moved on. I used to shrug it all off by saying, 'I don't make mistakes. I make prophesies that immediately turn out to be wrong!' But I have to admit that there were a few of them which Martin, bless him, would usually gently put right for me.

With the benefit of hindsight, plus years of experience of opening my mouth and putting my foot in it, I have carefully analysed my problem areas which I feel can be categorized under these five headings:

Well, there's a surprise!
Maybe I should rephrase that?
If you see what I mean . . .
Appearances can be deceptive . . .
I really do not believe I said that . . .

So let's review them.

Well, there's a surprise!

I think this is the biggest category of all – the ones which, looked at afterwards, state the blindingly obvious as though it was a brilliantly perceptive flash of inspiration. I could explain a lot of them, which might make them seem more sensible than they sound, but don't ask me, in cold blood, why on earth I said them. They just came out. Try these for size:

'And now Laffite is as close to Surer as Surer is to Laffite!'

'There's nothing wrong with the car except it's on fire.'

'With half the race gone there is half the race still to go.'

'I imagine the conditions in those cars are totally unimaginable.'

'Tambay's hopes, which were previously nil, are now absolutely zero.'

'Either that car is stationary or it's on the move.'

'There's no doubt in my mind that if the race had lasted for 46 laps instead of 45 it would have been a McLaren first and second but it didn't so it wasn't.'

'You can't see the digital clock on your monitors because there isn't one.'

'Keith Ripp's in trouble – *real* trouble!' (A masterpiece of understatement. Keith's Rallycross Mini was rolling end over end at Lydden, disintegrating as it did so.)

'It's raining and the track is wet.'

'We're now on the 73rd lap and the next one will be the 74th.'

'This is an interesting circuit because it has inclines and not just up, but down as well.'

Murray: 'And there are flames coming from the back of Prost's car as he enters the swimming pool!'
James Hunt: 'Well, that should put them out then!'
(Prost was entering the swimming pool *section* at Monaco.)

'The gap between the two cars is 0.9 seconds – that's less than a second.'

'He's in front of everyone in this race except for the two in front of him.'

'Into lap 53, the penultimate last lap but one.'

'He's obviously gone in for a wheel change. I say obviously because I can't see it.'

Maybe I should rephrase that?

'Do my eyes deceive me or is Senna's car sounding a bit rough?'

'I can't imagine what kind of a problem Senna has. I imagine it must be some sort of a grip problem.'

'Here they come – Haas first!' (Werner Haas was NSU's top rider at the 1954 250cc TT.)

'Speaking from memory I don't know how many points Piquet's got.'

'Alain Prost is in a commanding second place.' (I was talking about the Championship rather than the race at the time.)

'What a fabulous race! Barry Sheene's riding his Suzuki as though he's married to it.'

'Only ten of the drivers who started this race are left. I make no apologies for their absence, I'm sorry they're not here.'

'Prost can see Mansell in his earphones!'

'I've just stopped my startwatch.'

'And we've had five races so far this year – Brazil, Argentina, Imola, Schumacher and Monaco.'

If you see what I mean . . .

'A mediocre season for Nelson Piquet, as he is now known, and always has been.' (Piquet's full name is Nelson Piquet Souto-Maior. When he started racing he dropped his surname in an effort to stop his parents knowing. It didn't work but he stayed Nelson Piquet.)

'The first four cars are both on the same tyres.'

'And the first five places are filled by five different cars.' (By which I meant cars from five different *constructors*.)

'That was exactly the same place where Senna overtook Nannini that he didn't overtake Prost.' (I knew what I meant but did they?)

'As you look at the first four the significant thing is that Alboreto is fifth.' (Because that meant he was earning two Championship points.)

'And this is the third-placed car about to lap the second-placed car.' (Don't ask!)

'Here's Giacomelli, driving like the veteran he is not.'

'The battle is well and truly on if it wasn't on before, and it certainly was.'

'Two laps to go, then the action will begin. Unless *this* is the action, which it is.'

'And there's a dry line emerging in the tunnel.' (Wet patches had developed in the tunnel at Monaco after a chip pan fire in the hotel kitchen overhead activated the sprinklers.)

Appearances can be deceptive . . .

'And it's Mansell, Mansell, Mansell, Nigel Mansell!' (It was Alain Prost in an identical Ferrari.)

Murray: 'There's a fiery glow coming from the back of the Ferrari!'
James Hunt: 'No, Murray, that's his rear safety light.'

'Damon Hill is coming into the pit lane, yes it's Damon Hill coming into the Williams pit, and Damon Hill is in the pit – no, it's Schumacher.'

Murray: 'Bernie, it's some 17 years since you bought McLaren. You've had some good times and bad times. What do you remember best?'
Bernie Ecclestone: 'I don't remember buying McLaren!' (It was Brabham.)

'Piet Dam wins as he looks through a completely clear windscreen which is, of course, the advantage of being in front.' (As I said this he drove straight into a grass bank.)

'For real action watch *this*!' (Malcolm Wilson left the line at Esgyr Daffyd in his Ford Escort, developed a mammoth tank-slapper and flipped the car upside-down.)

'Let's watch this typical Formula Ford start.' (It was anything but. They all drove into each other.)

'It is clear at this stage of the race that Nigel Mansell is *not* going to make a pit stop.' (Of course he did.)

'Here comes the gallant little Frenchman Alain Prost, almost home for his sixth Grand Prix win – nothing can stop him now!' (He hit a wet patch, spun into the barrier, lost a wheel and retired.)

I really do not believe I said that . . .

'It's a sad ending, albeit a happy one, here at Montreal for today's Grand Prix.'

'The young Ralf Schumacher has been upstaged by teenager Jenson Button who is 20.'

'Andrea de Cesaris, the man who has won more Grands Prix than anyone else without actually winning one.' (I think I meant to say *competed* in more Grands Prix.)

Taken out of context they sound pretty weird. A lot of them sound pretty weird *in* context but, on the other hand, there were things I said that made me quite pleased with myself for plucking them out of thin air in the heat of the moment. People used to accuse me of dreaming them up beforehand, writing them on the commentary box wall and then waiting for the right moment to say them. Not true. They really were spontaneous. Honestly. Ask Martin. He was there beside me for a lot of them. These are the ones I like the best:

'Unless I'm very much mistaken . . . !

'GO! GO! GO!'

'Spin! Spin! Spin!'

'Fire! Fire! Fire!' (Good things obviously come in threes.)

'The atmosphere is so tense you could cut it with a cricket stump!'

'And now the boot is on the other Schumacher!'

'Anything can happen in Formula 1 – and it usually does!'

'If Mika Hakkinen's going to do well he needs to pull his great big woolly Finnish socks up.'

'IF – that's F1 spelt backwards.'

'There's only a second between them. "ONE". That's how long a second is!'

'And now excuse me while I interrupt myself!'

'He's shedding buckets of adrenalin in that car.'

'And I've got to stop now because I've got a lump in my throat.' (When Damon Hill crossed the line at Suzuka in 1996 to win the race and the World Championship.)

There were, of course, many others and doubtless you will have your favourites – those are just the ones I'm not too embarrassed to recall.

The atmosphere in the commentary box was often highly charged, and with live transmission whatever was said went out instantaneously. In 1995 at Adelaide my co-commentator was the blunt and outspoken Alan Jones, Australia's World Champion of 1980. As Jean Alesi and Michael Schumacher collided in a fracas about track position I said, 'What *was* Alesi thinking of?

'I can hazard a guess,' said Alan, 'He was thinking, "You're not going to pass me you arrogant little Kraut!"' At which point I changed the subject.

In 1979 I had to commentate from my open grandstand position at Monaco while, around and over me, two foreign commentators, one on my immediate left and the other on my immediate right, had a violent fight. At the same time the pictures I was supposed to be talking about completely disappeared. Needless to say the viewers at home knew nothing of this and wondered why the incompetent idiot of a commentator wasn't telling them about what they could see. Nor did it help that I wore headphones through which the producer talked to me in mid-commentary. In fact in the BBC days there were *two* producers, one at the *Grandstand* gallery in London and the other with me in the commentary box, and they both used to talk to me through my headphones.

While I was commentating from, say, Hockenheim, Ken Burton alongside me would say through my headphones, '*Grandstand* left us 20 minutes ago for the 2.30 at Haydock Park, Murray. They'll be back in one minute. While they've been away Prost in the lead came in for tyres and rejoined fifth. Mansell took the lead but came in a lap later and now he's fourth. When they come back update things and give us the top six.'

While he was spouting all this into my ears I'd be talking to the viewers everywhere else in the world, but I'd somehow remember what he said and update them with the current race situation. At which point the *Grandstand* producer in London, John Phillips, would say (while I was still talking), 'You haven't said anything about Martin Brundle, Murray. Where is he?'

Now I wouldn't have the faintest idea where Martin was so I'd look down at the lap chart that Mike Doodson kept for me. Martin was number 12 and when I spotted it on the chart I'd see that he was eighth. While all this was happening and I'd been looking away from the monitor the viewers had seen the new leader's car shoot off the track into the armco and burst into flames while the driver got out and punched a marshal. 'Here's something interesting,' I would say. 'Martin Brundle is now in eighth place!' And the poor viewer would think I'd lost my marbles.

CHAPTER FIFTEEN

Out With a Bang

At the end of 2000 I'd long been retired from my 'proper' job and had been broadcasting for 52 years. I was very fit, in command and loving every second of my Formula 1 life on the box but, at the age of 77, was starting to worry about my continued ability to do the job properly.

It is a very demanding existence, physically and mentally: 17 races a year between March and October, all but one outside Britain, including six with tiring long-haul flights, and each for a minimum of four long days of non-stop, high-pressure activity. I was convinced that in the not too distant future, for either mental or physical reasons, my competence would start to fade and I wouldn't be able to keep up. Age withers and it was going to wither me. I passionately wanted to go on until I dropped and liked the job far too much to stop willingly, but I was appalled by the thought of losing my edge, not being able to beaver energetically for facts and gossip, stand in the commentary box for at least two hours at a time, giving it my enthusiastic best or be unwilling to attend evening functions for fear of being like a wet rag the next day. Like Jackie Stewart, I'd always resolved to stop when I felt I was still at the top of the tree rather than tumbling down it, and I was determined not to hang on for the sake of a year or two with the risk that I'd deteriorate and lose my grip. My pride was at stake – better by far to stop a little too soon than a little too late.

I wonder, though, to what extent journalist Mike Davidson's attack on Formula 1, Martin Brundle and myself in the *Daily Mail* of 31 July 2000 ('*Wheels come off for Steptoe and Son*') subconsciously affected my decision. It was triggered by a ludicrous and inexcusable mistake I made at the start of the 2000 German Grand Prix, when I said that Rubens Barrichello, a lowly 18th on the grid, had gone off – when it was actually front-row starter Michael Schumacher. The criticism was entirely justified but, to me, its sneering and plain nasty tone was not.

'The Steptoe and Son of the asphalt track have learned to live off scraps and invent drama where there is none,' it said. 'So when the genuine article unfolded before their eyes at Hockenheim they panicked.'

The next day under the heading, '*Should Murray Walker do a runner and retire?*' and subheading, 'He has been doing this job since 1949 . . . and it is beginning to show', Davidson opened with very generous comments about my broadcasting career and achievements before developing his belief that, 'Murray has become a trifle flat, a tad more repetitive. His cock-ups have begun to irritate rather than entertain . . . the unpalatable truth is that he finds himself fronting an inferior product bland enough to suit his fading talents.' Good provocative stuff without a doubt, which was then exploited by the appropriately named *Daily Mirror*. The mini-saga lasted for six days and caused a bit of an uproar with ITV sending an official letter of protest to the *Daily Mail*.

Like all these things it died down very quickly with no real harm done but I'm a sensitive soul who would never have made a politician and, even though readers' polls in both papers gave me overwhelming votes of confidence, it created a feeling of disquiet in my mind. I like to think I am my harshest critic and I knew the identification mistake I had made in Germany was a major one. I had been criticized in the past and rightly so but, allied to my feeling that I was nearing the end of the road anyway, maybe this was a warning shot across my bows. *No smoke without fire* was the thought that went through my mind: *It's time to go*.

So I talked to my friend, guide and boss Brian Barwick, ITV's Head of Sport, whose decency, experience and straight-shooting personality I very much respect, to thrash the whole thing out. 'I've always told you that *you'd* make the decision,' he said. '*I'm* not saying you should stop. You've still got it and I'm sure you could go on, but it's your life and you must do whatever you think is right. There's a lot to consider though – when to do it, how to do it, who's going to succeed you . . . and a whole lot more.'

I was originally intending to finish at the end of 2000 but Brian, sage advisor that he is, had a much better idea. 'Do another year, Murray, and let's all try to make it a great finale. Do most of the races but wind down a bit by missing a few. That would also give me time to think about who's going to take your place and to try them out at race weekends. And we'll give you a bumper send-off!' We shook hands on it, Brian was true to his word and the result was the best year I ever had in my long career behind the microphone. The die was cast, but much as I was undoubtedly going to miss the fun, the friendship, the travel, and the sheer joy of talking about the sport I love, I knew I'd done the right thing.

My swansong year, 2001, was one of enormous emotion, capping an unforgettable career of mainly colossal highs in Formula 1. In telling you about the recognition I was lucky enough to achieve over the years I hope I don't come across as vain or boastful; it's just that I'm enormously proud of what happened to me and I'd like you to know about it – starting with the biggest occasion of all. It was in 1996, my last year with the BBC when, on 12 December, I received the OBE from Her Majesty the Queen.

I had been told of the award ('For services to Broadcasting and Motor Sports') seven months earlier in a letter from the Prime Minister's Office, which notified me, in strict confidence, that my name was to be submitted to the Queen with a recommendation that I be appointed an Officer of the Order of the British Empire, and would I assure them that this would be agreeable. *Agreeable*? I couldn't get to the writing paper fast enough. As a flag-waving patriot fiercely proud of his great country and its monarchy, this was something I had never envisaged happening to me in a thousand years. I could hardly contain myself but I had to do so until the end of the year – amid all the turmoil of Damon Hill's great battle for the World Championship and my imminent departure from the BBC.

Eventually though, on Investiture Day, I drove into the inner courtyard of Buckingham Palace with Elizabeth and walked, awestruck, past the Life Guards in full ceremonial dress and into the gallery, where I was briefed with the rest of the recipients on when and where to walk and what to say by one of her Majesty's Colonels. (I nearly stood to attention and half expected him to inspect the backs of my jacket buttons.) 'If Her Majesty continues to talk to you after congratulating you, you first address her as "Your Majesty". Thereafter you do so as "Ma'am" as in "Jam", *not* "Marm" as in "Jarm", and after she has shaken your hand you get on your bike. All clear?'

Later as Her Majesty hung the medal on my lapel she said, 'I seem to have been listening to you for a very long time!'

'I'm delighted to hear that, Your Majesty.'

'How long have you been commentating now?'

'48 years, Ma'am.' (As in 'Jam'!)

'That *is* a long time!'

Her Majesty was right and I am very conscious of it. In some quarters these days there is a lot of criticism and complaining about the British Honours system but, unsurprisingly, I totally disagree with it. The people who regard it as elitist and somehow degrading ought to have been at the Investiture I attended, which, I am sure, was typical. There were people from all walks of life, factory workers to managing directors and commoners to noblemen, and they were all clearly delighted and immensely proud to be there and to have been honoured for their very different achievements, which covered an amazing range of human endeavour. With the superb and historic location, the military band playing from the gallery and the mingling in the courtyard afterwards it was a truly memorable occasion – and so was the very happy celebratory lunch that Elizabeth and I had afterwards. To me, being honoured by your country for doing something that gave you so much happiness and satisfaction was the ultimate achievement I could have hoped for.

I have always regarded myself as a pretty ordinary chap who is lucky enough to have had a good education, albeit with absolutely no academic distinction. No GCSEs back then – even O and A levels didn't exist when I went to Highgate School. Most of us aspired to the then O-level equivalent, the School Certificate, while the brainier ones went for the Higher Certificate. One of my chums at school, a boy named Eddie Bartholomew, was so bright that he passed his Higher Cert at the age of 13 and then successfully took it again every year until he left, but plodders like me reckoned we were doing well if we got the right number of credits and distinctions to achieve the School Cert Matriculation level. I did well at things like History and English but was a complete duffer at Maths. There was certainly no thought of my going to university, partly because in the late 1930s you had to be well-connected and well-off to do so and partly because, at that time, you went into the forces as soon as you could to fight the Germans and Japanese.

I was therefore astounded when in May 1997, some 60 years after I had left school, I was awarded an Honorary Degree of Doctor of Arts by Bournemouth University. To my even greater amazement and delight I was later approached by De Montfort University, one of Britain's largest with over 31,000 students, who similarly awarded me an Honorary Degree, this time as Master of Letters. I was genuinely overwhelmed by two such impressive accolades.

'The Doctor of Arts degree is conferred on persons of high intellectual and cultural distinction,' said the De Montfort citation. It isn't quite how I would have described myself but I was flattered that somebody thought the cap fitted. On 4 September 1998 I walked in procession through the streets of Bedford, wearing the long gold academic robe and black velvet floppy hat, behind the Pro Chancellor, the Pro Vice Chancellors, the Governors, the Academic Board, the Professors and Academic Staff, to the Hall where the presentation was to be made in front of all the graduating students who had qualified the hard way through years of study. I made a speech, received my Honorary Doctorate and Diploma and felt as though I was in some kind of a dream.

Two months later it was Bournemouth's turn for a delayed presentation at the magnificent Bournemouth International Centre, and this ceremony was even more impressive and emotional for me because it took place on 11 November, Armistice Day, when the nation remembers the dead of two terrible world wars. My father had fought and been wounded in the first, I had fought in the second, and my war years were the most impressionable of my life. The two-minute silence was held just prior to my conferment ceremony and I had to make my speech shortly after Professor Nicholas Grief had delivered my citation. It was all very moving and it is at times like this that my emotions can take over, particularly if the war is involved. The solemnity of the occasion, allied to the gravity of the silence and the reason for it, deeply affected me as I started to speak. I suddenly felt my eyes fill with tears and my throat tighten and I stood there for about 15 seconds totally unable to say anything while I fought to get control of myself – an almost unique experience for me. It seemed to last forever but happily no one appeared to notice and once I started the speech itself went very well.

I truly appreciated (and still do) those awards and the kindness and generosity the universities showed in granting me them. Occasionally I get letters addressed to Doctor Murray Walker, MA, and my immediate reaction is that the postman has delivered them to the wrong chap!

Time goes fast when you lead a busy life and before I knew where I was it was 2001, the year I'd decided was going to be my last as a commentator, although hopefully not as a broadcaster. It hurtled by in a cloud of euphoria amid emotional occasion after emotional occasion – so much so that it was actually difficult to do my job at times. I was determined not to be distracted and to concentrate on what I was really at the Grands Prix for – to commentate on qualifying and the race and to do background pieces for ITV. I wanted so much to go out with my head held high and was determined not to get so caught up in the 'Murray's last year' atmosphere that the commentaries would suffer. It wasn't easy though, because almost everywhere I went there were major ego-boosting farewell events, starting at the first race of the year in Melbourne.

Nowhere, but nowhere, does it like Australia. The only thing I don't like about the Australian GP is that it is the first race of the year. When it used to be in Adelaide it was the last and everyone looked forward to a great climax to the season in a wonderful country. You could even squeeze in a fabulous holiday in the Southern Hemisphere between it and the preceding race in Japan, to miss some of the English winter, but when the race moved to Melbourne it became the first of the season. 'A great place for the race' the publicity claims, and much of that is down to the enthusiastic leadership and entrepreneurial flair of the commanding Ron Walker, businessman, politician, organizer and promoter *extraordinaire,* who towers over the whole event and whose flair and drive has made it the best of the year.

For me 2001 certainly started with a bang. Typically, Australia was the first country to have a Grand Prix Ball and theirs is still the Daddy of them all. It is held in the magnificent ballroom of the high-rise Crowne Plaza complex that towers over the Yarra River and is a very grand affair. Steve Bracks, the Premier of the State of Victoria, was there, as was motor-racing fan Prince Michael of Kent and most of the Grand Prix world's big-hitters. (Elizabeth and I sat with Prince Michael, Ron and Mrs Walker, Michael Schumacher, Rubens Barrichello, Jean Todt, Flavio Briatore and Naomi Campbell. Heady stuff!). Unsurprisingly, they do it differently in Australia with long intervals between courses for socializing. Between the first and main courses Ron made a welcome speech, accompanied by Prince Michael, and then he called me up to the stage. I genuinely didn't know why and was almost in tears when Prince Michael presented me with a Lifetime Achievement Award from the Australian Grand Prix. It wasn't just the honour and the occasion that overwhelmed me, it was the award itself: a replica of the winner's trophy, a magnificent Australian silver dish with a centre of Australian gold carrying a very generously worded inscription, surrounded by a replica of Jack Brabham's 1959 Cooper steering wheel. I know the details because I met the Australian brothers who made the original trophy at the first Melbourne GP in 1996, and I cannot think of a greater compliment to have received.

There was more to come though. On race day my friend Stuart Sykes, one of the prime movers of the Australian Grand Prix media team, asked me to be on the starting grid when the drivers' parade formed up. There were 24 superb vintage cars, each of which was going to carry one of the race drivers on a lap of the Albert Park circuit for the crowd to cheer. Hold on, no, there were 25 – and the 25th was for me. A magnificent boat-tailed two-seater of the 1930s Bentley tradition, and I sat up high on the fuel tank while we slowly paraded round the 3.3 mile circuit absorbing the cheers and waves of the enormous crowd. They were applauding their heroes, the Michael Schumachers and Mika Hakkinens of this world, but I got the tail end of it and, just like Silverstone 1996, it was a really heart-warming experience. The race, tragically marred by the death of race marshal Graham Beveridge, set the pattern for Michael's fourth World Championship-winning season and I left Australia very unwillingly, fondly hoping that I would be there again.

Malaysia was great after Elizabeth and I had stayed at the superbly restored Raffles Hotel in Singapore, travelled the length of Malaysia and up into Thailand to Bangkok on the fabulous Eastern and Oriental Express train, and then driven back to Kuala Lumpur from Penang. But with no great regret I gave Brazil a miss. I know I'm biased and that there are a lot of wonderful places there but I haven't seen any of them. Sao Paulo certainly isn't one – a great circuit at Interlagos most certainly and many excellent hotels and restaurants, but the infrastructure, the overcrowding, the violence, the hideous poverty-stricken *favelas* and general air of Third-World dilapidation made me almost glad to be sitting this one out.

Eight races later and well into the season, with Michael Schumacher now only two races from clinching his fourth World Championship in Hungary after a season of utter domination, it was the British Grand Prix, the one nearest to my heart. I'm proud to be British, I always know so many people at Silverstone, the crowd is like no other in terms of enthusiasm and friendliness and the atmosphere is fabulous. Silverstone and I go back a long way together, to its beginning in fact, for I was at the ex-RAF bomber base in 1948 for the first post-war Grand Prix in Britain, where Luigi Villoresi was victorious in his Maserati. In 1949 I did my first ever broadcast at the Silverstone British Grand Prix, won by Baron Toulo de Graffenried, and in 1950 I attended the first ever

Formula 1 World Championship event, the 'Royal' British Grand Prix before King George VI and Queen Elizabeth, our late and much-missed Queen Mother. I've been to every British Grand Prix there since and so many of them were spellbinding, starting with 1951 when the mighty Alfa-Romeo 158s were first defeated by Ferrari. I've seen and commentated on almost every wheel-based sport there, cars, trucks and bikes alike. It is where I drove the Formula 1 McLaren, where James Hunt and I so nearly came to blows, where I was the BBC's Number Two to my beloved father for so many years, where I excitingly flew the circuit at low altitude in Tommy Sopwith's helicopter and where I had the thrill of a lifetime behind Martin Brundle in the McLaren two-seater. The memories just keep coming and they are all good ones. In 2001 I was to add to them at my last British Grand Prix for ITV with a weekend I will never forget.

One of my proudest achievements is to have become a member of the British Racing Drivers' Club. You may think that's a bit odd for a chap who has never driven four wheels competitively on the track but in 1985 I was invited to become an Associate Member. The BRDC is not only Britain's elite motor sport organization but it owns Silverstone, home of the British Grand Prix, which, without a penny of state aid, it has consistently improved over the years. It has a magnificent clubhouse and has done so much to bring on young talent with its special awards. On 13 July, prior to the Grand Prix Dinner, Jackie Stewart (yet to be knighted) presented me with the Club's Gold Medal. In its long history only four had previously been presented – to Bernie Ecclestone, Frank Williams, Ken

Tyrrell and Stirling Moss – so I could hardly have been in more illustrious company. I returned to my hotel walking very tall indeed.

I wasn't there for very long though, for the one blot on Silverstone's reputation (which they are putting right) is that it takes ages to get in. As ever I had to set off in the early hours for the 2001 qualifying and race days but it was well worth it. What an experience they were! ITV were promoting a competition for the best 'Murray Walker' banner at the circuit so the whole place was awash with them and literally everywhere I went people were stopping me for a chat and to wish me luck when my commentating days were over. In the ITV coverage just before the race there was a feature of clips from my past which, for me, was immensely moving as I watched it in the commentary box and, to cap it all, the RAF Falcons Parachute Display Team culminated their incredible display with a vertical stack of them floating down under their multi-coloured parachutes with a massive banner reading, 'GOOD LUCK MURRAY FROM THE RAF FALCONS.' Then, with minutes to go, Jim Rosenthal handed over to me from the studio.

'Are you ready?' I said. 'Because this is the big one!' And it was. A brilliant comeback victory for Mika Hakkinen, who hadn't won since Spa 2000, some 15 races before, and a wonderful send-off for me. I'll see Silverstone again, but never like that.

By contrast, Monza in September was a sad and gloomy place, filled with foreboding after the appalling terrorist attacks in the USA on 11 September, only five days earlier. Several of the drivers, especially the Schumacher brothers, were very reluctant to take part and nobody anywhere, particularly Americans, wanted to fly. It was a deeply depressing day but in my opinion it was absolutely right to hold the event. Mine may seem a hard-nosed and even callous attitude, probably nurtured by my war years, but what good would it have done to cancel it? Respect for the dead? Yes, of course, but the respect that already existed could not have been greater and, to me, not to have held the race would have been giving in to terrorism. Even after something as shocking as that, life must go on. It was, of course, an immensely sombre and low-key occasion but, almost embarrassingly, it ended with a joyous atmosphere for me with a wonderful in-flight party in one of Paul Stoddart's European Aviation BA 111s.

Paul is like no one else I've ever met and the sort of person who makes Formula 1 such a challenging and exciting environment in which to work. He is a self-made, self-starting, free-wheeling and enormously successful Australian who is also an entirely normal, very friendly, cheerful, self-effacing and all-round Grade A super chap. As you may have gathered I like him very much, as I do his charming partner, Sue Aston. Paul has made himself a very wealthy man by building up a worldwide, 24-hours-a-day aircraft parts business, as well as numerous other enterprises ranging from aircraft leasing and seats to building right-hand drive Austin Maestros from new parts that were originally intended for assembly in Bulgaria. He is, in short, like Bernie Ecclestone, a wheeler-dealer, an entrepreneur who has the courage to have a go at almost anything, but he is also a Formula 1 fanatic. No mean racing driver himself and a successful competitor in the historic single-seater BOSS series, he tried to buy the Tyrrell organization when Ken decided to stop, only to be frustrated by BAR. Nothing daunted, he bought everything from the team that he could to add to his already impressive collection and now owns something like 75 Formula 1 cars and their support vehicles, all of them runners and in immaculate condition. It was Paul Stoddart who, in 2000, bought the Minardi team and is now working tirelessly to make the team competitive. Amongst his many business ventures is his European charter airline, a fleet of planes that flies everyone from the Pope to the Rolling Stones. Paul used it to part-sponsor his friend Ken Tyrrell's team by flying it to and from the European races and that was the happy band I was invited to join.

What a fabulous experience it was. First with Tyrrell, then Arrows, Jordan and later with Arrows again and Minardi. It was certainly first-class travel – I was picked up at my Hampshire home and driven right to the steps of the all-first-class-accommodation BA 111 at Bournemouth Airport. No customs, no immigration hassle, just straight to the plane where Amanda, Kerry, Leslie and Belinda, the charming hostesses, would greet me with champagne at my seat. Maybe there would be one or two other privileged people like me but maybe there wouldn't. Either way there was no delay – door shut and straight off to Coventry to collect the others. More champagne on the way and then a full English breakfast before landing at an airport close to the track, rather than somewhere like Barcelona with all the usual frenetic hassle.

Into one of Paul's fleet of cars, which met us at the airport, and straight to the circuit. On Sunday evening after the race it was the same thing in reverse and I was usually in my own bed by midnight. Travelling with European was not only a joy in terms of convenience but a delight because it was always such fun. I was straight into the Formula 1 environment from the moment the team got on the plane and with such lovely people. It was like family.

My last 'working' flight with European was one I will never ever forget. Monza 2001 was my final Formula 1 commentary in Europe and the return flight from Bergamo was to be my swansong with the airline. There was just my last ever Formula 1 commentary at Indianapolis to look forward to before I hung up my microphone. As ever I travelled to the airport with Paul and Sue in one of the Citröen Picassos, but for a change it was an uneventful trip. No Italian policewoman levelling her pistol at Paul as, against her repeated orders, he tried to muscle into the traffic; no 100-mile detour into the mountains because the road was blocked; no filling of the diesel-powered Picasso with petrol and having to drain it all out against the clock; no thundering up the wrong autostrada for mile after mile or 100mph-plus storming of the autobahn, in and out of traffic lanes while Paul simultaneously drove and organized complicated air movements on his mobile phone. No, this time it had been a breeze and all the team people, the journalists, the photographers and Paul's guests left the departure lounge to get on the plane in good time. But not Paul, Sue, myself and a couple of others. I should have known.

'No hurry, Murray. We're just waiting for them to get

settled in and then we'll be on our way.' Soon afterwards we got into our own coach and drove to the plane on the far side of the airport. It was dark by now but as we got closer I could see dozens of people lined up in two rows at the plane's steps, all of them in white tops.

'Hey, Sue,' I said, 'look at all those people. I wonder what the hell they're doing?' I soon found out, for as we stopped I saw that they were wearing T-shirts emblazoned with the words, 'Thanks for the memories, Murray!' The people inside them were all my friends who had left us earlier.

It was to get even better though. I thought, 'This is great. I'll do the departing dignitary bit and shake everyone's hand and say a few encouraging words as I walk to the steps', but as I did so I saw that on the side of the fuselage was an absolutely enormous picture of me at the wheel of Stirling Moss' 1955 Mille Miglia-winning Mercedes-Benz, alongside the words 'Thanks for the memories, Murray!' Wow. Up the steps and there was the lovely Amanda. 'We want you in the middle of the plane, Murray.'

As I said, the whole thing is done out to First Class standards and in the middle there is a big mahogany table. On that table was a massive iced cake with the words, guess what, 'Thanks for the memories, Murray!' The whole plane was decked out in balloons and streamers carrying the same message, there were party-poppers and champagne and we had the most fantastic two-hour inflight party, which included a whole lot of things that my natural introversion and airline regulations inhibit me from describing. Let's just say that for me there's never been anything like it and I'm sure there never will be again. I do, however, seem to remember someone who looked very much like me serving drinks and meals dressed in a European stewardess' uniform, and very fetching it was too. I've got the pictures to prove it because top-snapper Keith Sutton and his men were firing away non-stop, as was our ace ITV cameraman Andy Parr. I'll be paying them hush money for the rest of my life. I have, too, got the superb Andy Kitson painting of the very BA 111 we were in, flying above a 1998 Tyrrell, a 1999 Jordan, a 2000 Arrows and a 2001 Minardi, which Paul emotionally presented me with in mid-air and which now faces my study desk constantly to add to the wonderful memories that Formula 1, Paul and my countless other friends have given me.

Formula 1 calls its Drivers' and Constructors' contests 'World Championships' but it's rather an exaggeration when America, the largest sporting nation on the planet, takes little part. Formula 1? They've never heard of it. From 1959 to 1991 there were American Grands Prix at numerous locations but even the longest-lasting of them, Watkins Glen, petered out, and several of them happened only once. 'They average 80 miles an hour?' someone in Detroit once famously said of its twisty, street-circuit Grand Prix, 'Our cabs go faster than that.'

So there is obviously a massive educational and promotional job to be done in America if Formula 1 is to become a true World Championship. To his eternal credit, that is exactly what Bernie Ecclestone has been trying to do for years, and now it looks as though he may have cracked it, with a major deal to hold the United States Grand Prix at the fabled Indianapolis Motor Speedway. If it doesn't work there it won't work anywhere, for the IMS is the Holy Grail of motor racing in America, with the history, traditions and facilities to attract the punters who, if they like the show, will come back for more time and time again. I firmly believe that, at Indianapolis, the United States Grand Prix will at last become a major American sporting fixture because although the existing States-wide fan base is thinly spread, it is big in numbers. Already, in my experience, there is nothing like it and with the charisma of Indianapolis, promoted by its enormously experienced and capable boss Tony George, it can only get better.

ITV went to Indianapolis in mid-February 2000 to do our Grand Prix season preview and I was knocked out by what it was clearly going to be. I had been there in 1993 of course, when Nigel Mansell had so nearly won, but this was something else. Completely new garages were being built specifically for Formula 1 plus a magnificent new control tower, new pit-lane, new grandstands and, of course, the brand spanking new Grand Prix circuit, which was going to run clockwise, the opposite way to the Indy 500, turning off the main straight just before Turn Four and winding its way through the infield, past the in-track championship golf course, to rejoin the Super Speedway between Turns Two and One. It was bitterly cold as Martin Brundle and I recorded our pieces to camera standing on the hallowed Yard of Bricks, the symbolic last remaining part of Indy's original all-brick surface, but as the workmen swarmed around us we were obviously there at the start of something big. It was a huge success, with over 250,000 present on race day. They loved the noise of the massed V10s and the sight of high-speed racing in the wet (oval races in America are rightly stopped if it rains) but how many of them had liked what they saw enough to come back again?

The answer would come in 2001. However, America was grief-stricken, traumatized and didn't want to go anywhere, for the second United States GP at Indianapolis was to be held on 30 September, just 19 days after the mind-numbing terrorist attacks in New York and Washington. As at Monza, there was serious talk of cancelling the race but fortunately wisdom prevailed and it went ahead. America rallied, took a deep breath, showed two fingers to terrorism and turned up – on race day over 200,000 people poured through the gates of the vast stadium, nearly twice as many as at any other Grand Prix, a courageous and heartening sign that there was a firm foundation to build on. It looked as though Bernie and Tony's adventurous gamble was paying off. Everyone who entered was given a little American Stars and Stripes flag to wave and mine now lives on my study mantelpiece as a memento of an unforgettable day. There was an outpouring of passion, defiance and national pride the like of which I had never seen anywhere and it was a great race, with victory going to Mika Hakkinen in a return to the Championship-winning form he had shown so often in the past but which had been singularly lacking for most of the season. For me, of course, Indianapolis was an emotional cauldron because it was to be my last-ever Grand Prix commentary, over half a century after my first.

Everything went normally until the Friday evening. During

the day several people had told me they were sorry they wouldn't be able to come to my party because they were working. 'Not a problem,' I replied, 'I'm not having a party!' I was trying very hard to have a normal Grand Prix weekend and to keep my eye on the ball but I suspected that something was afoot, especially after ITV's Paul Tyrrell said, 'I know you know that something's up, Murray. Let's go and find out what it is.'

Off we went to the Williams pavilion in the exclusive Paddock Club and when I walked in I was flabbergasted. At a time when I would have expected everyone to be working like mad, getting their cars ready for the next day's vital qualifying session, there were some 300 people sitting at tables drinking champagne and obviously waiting for something to begin. Drivers, team principals, sponsors, engineers, mechanics, media people, they were all there and I knew all of them. They had even been in to the city to collect Elizabeth. Tony Jardine was at a lectern in front of a cinema screen and Michael Schumacher was sitting at the side. So I went and joined him.

And then Tony took off with a brilliantly funny and endearing review of my life and times, illustrated by film clips of my most famous gaffes. Bernie Ecclestone was there, Flavio Briatore, Ross Brawn and Paul Stoddart, and so were David Coulthard, Eddie Irvine, Jenson Button, Rubens Barrichello and so many other Formula 1 notables that I had known for years. One by one Tony got them up to say some very pleasant things about my contribution to their world, but the best and by far the funniest was when he cajoled them into imitating my 'Murrayisms' the way I said them. David Coulthard, bless him, was prepared to do it but only if no one could see him, so he literally crouched down inside the lectern to read his piece. Eddie Irvine, whom I had always been more reluctant to approach than the other British drivers, warmed my heart and made me feel churlish about my previous attitude to him by recalling his time at Ferrari when the team would always review and analyse a finished race by looking at the TV tapes but with no sound or commentary. 'Jeez, Murray,' said Eddie, 'I never realised now dull some of them would be without your commentary.' At which point he turned to Bernie Ecclestone and said, 'We really ought to improve the show, Bernie!' Not perhaps welcome words for Bernie but they were music to my ears.

Then Bernie himself stepped up to say some wonderful things, including the fact that I'd be getting one of the rare and incredibly privileged Red Passes normally only given to past World Champions, and then Tony George appeared at the lectern. Now this was unbelievable for me – Tony is an action man of very few words. Compared with him the uncommunicative Mika Hakkinen is a charismatic chatterbox.

'Murray,' he said, reaching down into a box at his feet, 'we normally give one of these to the Indy 500 winner and that's about it but this one is yours.' It was one of the bricks which had formed the original 1909 surface of Indianapolis, to give it its name 'The Brickyard', varnished and beautifully mounted on a wooden base with an inscribed plaque carrying, under the famous IMS winged symbol, the words 'The Indianapolis Motor Speedway salutes Murray Walker, the voice of

Formula 1. September 2001.' I was overwhelmed, but now it was time for me to say something.

'I can't tell you how much I appreciate you all being here. You are all my friends and I've loved every second of working with you because ours is a wonderful sport and you are a marvellous lot. This is an incredible and genuinely unexpected occasion for me and Sunday is going to be very tough and emotional because it is going to be the last time I will see you all, doing what I love so much, but I'll be giving it my best shot. For now though we've all got jobs to do and I really appreciate you interrupting yours to be here. So off you go, with my heartfelt thanks for your company. Believe me, I will remember this for ever.'

Sunday's race and its unforgettable atmosphere made the whole thing more than worthwhile and that night we flew out of Indianapolis with British Airways. My commentating life was over.

So many splendid memories. Those wonderful years at the Isle of Man, first watching my father win the superb silver Mercury TT replicas time and time again and then seeing him finally win the race itself. Commentating, firstly with him and then on my own, in his place, on the deeds of the world's finest riders on the world's finest racetrack. Knowing Jimmy Guthrie, Stanley Woods, Mike Hailwood, Giacomo Agostini, John Surtees, Barry Sheene and so many other motor-cycle racing superstars. Then my fabulous car years. Watching races and working at the Nurburgring. Commentating at Le Mans in 1959, the year that Aston Martin won. Following the RAC

Rally for BBC TV through some of Britain's most glorious scenery. Being able to travel the world and see places that, ordinarily, I would never have been able to visit. Loving every second of the wonderful Goodwood Festival of Speed and Revival meetings. Being able to call Stirling Moss, Jackie Stewart, Nigel Mansell, Damon Hill, David Coulthard, Johnny Herbert and Bernie Ecclestone my friends. But most of all sharing a wonderful existence with so many kind and helpful people all over the world. I've been a very lucky man.

CHAPTER SIXTEEN

A Full-Time Passion

I suspect for a lot of men their job is a means to an end: something they do to earn a living and not something that fills them with enthusiasm. They lead predictable lives with regular hours. They go to work in the morning, come home in the evening, watch TV and have their weekends free for hobbies and other things which have nothing to do with their jobs. They have children and family interests, may or may not achieve their ambitions and retire on a pension to do things like play golf, develop their hobbies, travel or just switch off. Very nice too and good luck to them. It's a worthy existence and I'm not knocking it. But we're all different. I'm not like that and never have been.

Because I've been a high-profile motor-sport commentator in the public eye for so long, people assume that is all I've ever done. 'What a fabulous job with all that travel. But don't you get fed up with it? What passions do you have outside of the sport?' Well, the simple answers are that, no, I didn't get fed up with the travel and that, until I retired from my 36 years in the advertising business, my passions were motor sport and broadcasting. When I wasn't working at my 'proper' job I was working at another one which also happened to be my passion, and when I retired from the business my passion then became my full-time job as a result of the immutable law that work expands according to time available.

For the whole of my long working life it was usual for me to be working at weekends as well as weekdays. In my scrambling and rallycross years there were Boxing Day events to which I had to travel on Christmas Day and the Easter break was invariably spent covering some motor-cycle or car meeting. Travelling to interesting and stimulating places and enjoying life as much as I did, I never felt I wanted a holiday and I was more than happy to spend my very limited spare time at home. 'How appallingly selfish – what about his poor wife?' I hear you angrily cry. To which my reply is that Elizabeth mattered more to me than the job and if she had been unhappy with what I was doing I would have done something about it. She would have let me know quickly enough, believe me, for Elizabeth is a long way from being a downtrodden shrinking violet!

During the whole of my scrambling and rallycross years in Britain she went everywhere with me and did my lap scoring but that stopped when my Formula 1 travels started taking me overseas every fortnight. Being together at the meetings was no longer a realistic option so, like any other husband in the Formula 1 world, I went to the races while Elizabeth developed her many other interests. It's a life that would not suit everyone but it suited us and after I had retired from Masius I was home during some of the week although, to be honest, I still spent most it doing things like writing, after-dinner speeches and promotional work. I like working and I'm always happiest when I'm doing so. Luckily enough I have been able to fill my life with activity that may have been 'work' to most people but which was challenging, absorbing and rewarding to me. Going to work when I was in business was never a problem and the broadcasting world gave me a terrific buzz. I am the first to admit that my life has been dominated by an almost obsessive passion but, as a result, it has been one full of variety and satisfaction. It has meant that I have missed out on all sorts of things that matter to others, but I've no complaints.

Retiring altogether is something I've never wanted to do. Quite apart from loving what I do and wanting to keep on doing it I've seen too many men die not long after they stopped working simply because they had nothing to occupy them and exercise their brains. Playing golf, a favourite of many a retired man, is one of the many things I don't do – my hand and eye co-ordination isn't good enough and I don't have the patience to practice and become competent (and if I wasn't competent, I wouldn't want to do it: I wouldn't say I was a perfectionist but I do like to get things right). I was once sitting next to a rather surly chap at a lunch at my wife's golf club. 'What do you do?' I asked him.

'*Do?*' he replied grumpily. 'Nothing. I've retired.'

'Oh, have you? Then what *did* you do?'

'I was a company chairman.'

'Do you miss it?'

'Miss it? Of course, I bloody miss it. I was somebody there. I had a Rolls-Royce with a chauffeur and when I arrived in the morning I got respect, but all I do now is hoover the house for the bloody wife.'

He was a pathetic case and I wonder if he is still with us or whether he has snuffed it from sheer boredom. Thank God I'm not like him. I'm certainly not setting myself up as a paragon but, at nearly 80, I'm enjoying every second of still being able to work and hope to be able to go on doing so for some time yet. I've stopped commentating but now fill the time with lots of other things like writing, working for ITV as a pundit, appearing in videos, attending corporate functions, and making after-dinner speeches and commercials. Stirling Moss still makes a very healthy living 40 years after the massive accident that ended his great racing career and I'd like to be like him. I want to stay sharp, not vegetate, and I firmly believe that the way to do so is to keep in touch and be in competition with younger people.

Others do that through their children but Elizabeth and I never had any. I've no regrets on that score, incidentally. Some people's lives are frustratingly incomplete without children but what I've never had I never miss. To have a happy, loving and caring family must be the ultimate thing in the world but to have the opposite must be a living hell. Elizabeth and I were destined not to have either and fortunately for me neither of us were worried by it. I've been exceptionally lucky to have a tolerant and understanding wife who puts up with my lifestyle and I certainly appreciate it. I've seen lots of marriages in Formula 1 break up because the wife complained that she didn't marry only to be parted from her husband for the majority of the year.

But there's more. To lead the life I do I have to be physically fit. My commentating career was demanding and stressful with the workload, travel, frequent time changes and the constant need to combat a lot of very capable and much younger men who would have given anything for my job. I wasn't going to be able to stave them off if I wasn't fit so I joined the health club at the superb Chewton Glen Hotel near where we live. I still go there now, twice a week, for a 90-minute workout on the treadmill, step machine, cross-trainer and cycle followed by the various arm, stomach and leg resistance machines and 10 lengths of the pool. I really enjoy it: I'm not trying to be a muscle-bound freak, just fit enough to do all the things I want to do without being exhausted by them. Chewton Glen is also our social centre and Elizabeth and I make a very pleasant day of it, taking in lunch and talking to friends.

I don't smoke and never have. My mother pulled a psychological masterstroke by betting me a substantial amount of money when I was at school that I would have started smoking by the time I was 17. I won by proving her wrong and never subsequently started. Incidentally, I find myself ambivalent to tobacco sponsorship in Formula 1. While I admire the result of what the teams do with the enormous funding they get from it, I don't think much of the cigarette manufacturers for the addiction and misery their products cause. Why anyone smokes when they must know the possible consequences is beyond my comprehension.

I drink moderately, eat sensibly, and make sure I get plenty of sleep. I'm sure this all sounds incredibly dull and righteous but good health is the most important thing you can have and I want to keep mine. In 1992, though, I had a bit of a fitness crisis which would have stopped my career dead in its tracks with nine years still to go if I hadn't been able to do something about it. My left hip got more and more painful until I was having to hobble around on a stick in great discomfort and it was clear that it was packing up. I don't think it actually affected my performance in the commentary box but it certainly wasn't much fun standing up for over two hours at a time to do the job. Surgeon John Carvell told me it was worn out; my mother had had the same problem. I grimly stuck it out until the end of the season and then went into hospital and got a new hip joint. After eight days there, followed by about six weeks' convalescence, I was like a new man, walking around as though I had never had any sort of a problem. When I thanked John Carvell for having transformed my life he said, 'That's all right, old boy, I'm just a high-class carpenter! I've got the video if you'd like to see it.' As a hip replacement is literally a hammer-and-chisel job, with lots of bone removal, insertion of a prosthesis (metal joint to you and I), complicated skeletal geometry and buckets of blood, I could think of few things I'd like to see less! But it wouldn't have been the first time I had watched an operation.

When I was 15 years old, Bob Galloway, the surgeon father of Bill Galloway, my best friend at school and a keen motor-cycle trials sidecar competitor, invited me to stand at the end of the operating table in the North Middlesex Hospital while he conducted appendix removal operations on two of his patients. I put on the gown and mask and got through watching him pull intestine out of the incision and complete the operation the first time but was feeling distinctly woozy and unsteady halfway through the second when, to my great relief, the Theatre Sister quietly said to me, 'I'd go *now* while you still can'. I had apparently turned green. Years later, when I needed information about heart valve operations to write some advertising copy for my Smiths Industries client, I went to see a heart surgeon. 'An ounce of practice is worth a pound of theory,' he said. 'I'll arrange for you to watch a heart valve replacement.' I could hardly refuse so I stood and watched a Polish woman, who had been near death, having the job done, which involves opening up the chest by sawing through the rib cage to get at the heart. Not for the squeamish but I made it to the end and the next day she was sitting up in bed as bright as a button – incredible!

Seeing my own hip replacement didn't appeal at all though, so I declined Mr Carvell's invitation. Two years later I was back to have the other hip replaced and I thank my lucky stars that I was born into an era where this type of surgery is possible. I could have been shuffling around on a Zimmer frame for the last decade and missed my wonderful final years of Formula 1.

Because of what I do I must have seen more of the world than most people. Formula 1 currently takes you to 17 events a year in 15 different countries (Italy and Germany have two races per season and why Britain, which is more important in worldwide motor sport than either of them, does not do so too is beyond me), and over the years I have been to many more through my motor sport and advertising work. So going abroad for the sake of it holds no great appeal for me. We have a very nice home in the New Forest with open country surroundings, a trout river and our own woodlands inhabited by deer, foxes, countless squirrels and a regiment of rabbits. It's a very nice place to live in and I enjoy just being there amid the peace and quiet.

I was also very happy at our previous home at Hadley Wood in Hertfordshire, which was 50 minutes away from my office in St James's Square but which overlooked open countryside and whose garden ran down to the first tee at the excellent golf course. However, when I retired from the business one of the first things that Elizabeth said to me was, '*Now* can we live in the country?' As far as I was concerned we were virtually living in the country already but I agreed on condition she found somewhere we both liked. At the time it made little difference to me whether I was not at home at Hadley Wood or not at home somewhere else. About a year later, when I'd forgotten all about it, Elizabeth said, 'I think I've found somewhere you'll like, dear, and I've seen it twice now. Can we go and look at it together?'

'Oh yes, sure,' I replied, 'but I'm a bit busy at the moment.'

'I've looked at your diary and you're not doing anything on Tuesday – can we go then?'

'Oh, er, yes. Yes, sure!'

So on Tuesday we got in the car and I said, facetiously, 'Where are we going then? Inverness? Penzance? Bristol? Kings Lynn?'

'Drive as though we were going to see your mother.'

That's odd. My mother and Elizabeth, who were totally different in character, had one thing in common – very strong personalities that tended to result in an explosive atmosphere when they were together. So why would we be going in the direction of Beaulieu where my mother lived? It all became clear when we arrived for it was a gem of a house and still is. The moral of the story? Never underestimate the power of a woman.

So holidays have to be a bit special to get us out of the house. We found the ideal to be holiday cruises and we've both become enthusiasts. We got the bug when Cunard invited me to do a series of talks on the magnificent *QE2*, for which I recruited some of my motor sport mates to form a panel: Formula 1 journalists Alan Henry and Nigel Roebuck, McLaren's Jo Ramirez and sportscar star John Fitzpatrick, who was also the Secretary of the British Racing Drivers' Club. It was a great success and I subsequently did similar trips on the fine P&O ships *Victoria, Arcadia* and *Oriana* whilst Elizabeth and I also took journeys together. It is a great way to take a holiday, for if you pick the right ship it is a five-star floating hotel with unique benefits. No constant packing and unpacking, every facility you could possibly want from health centres and restaurants to clay pigeon shooting, shops, library, stage shows and cinemas – plus the interesting places you can visit. We've gone on cruises in the Caribbean, the

Black Sea, the Mediterranean and to New York, and I never tire of them. I hope to do a lot more now that I have some free time on my hands, but there are so many other things to take in as well. I love Australia and want to explore the whole country; New Zealand, too, because I've yet to go there despite several invitations which I had to turn down because they clashed with other commitments; and I've still to see the Antarctic and the Norwegian fjords. The motor museums of the world beckon me, especially those in America, Fangio's place at Balcarce and the Schlumpf Collection in Alsace Lorraine. The Targa Tasmania rally is something I'd love to compete in. So much to see and do!

But of one thing I'm sure. Motor sport hasn't seen the last of me and, hopefully, neither has broadcasting. They both mean too much to me. Now I'll be able to go back to the Isle of Man and catch up with what has been happening at the TT since I was last there. World Championship Rallying is a wonderful sport which I loved working on for BBC TV and which I'd like to see a lot more of as it evolves into something even more impressive and exciting under the new control of Dave Richards and his colleagues. ITV are continuing to use me in an 'elder statesman' role in their Formula 1 coverage and if they continue to do so it would be a marvellous way for me to maintain contact with the sport I love. Old soldiers never die, they only fade away, and I want to do so with dignity, keeping the light burning brightly until my time comes. I'm told there is a life after Formula 1 and I intend to prove it with races still to see, jobs yet to be done, new friends to make, reminiscences to be shared and places yet to visit.

It's a great life if you don't weaken and I hope not to do that for a while. I'll be mindful of those words of my mother, 'Always remember, dear, when one door closes another opens' – and I look forward to walking through it.

Career Appendix

Born: 10 October 1923, Birmingham, christened Graeme Murray Walker
Parents: Graham and Elsie
Wife: Elizabeth, married in 1959
Family home: Enfield, Middlesex
Education: Highgate School

World War II service (1944–47)
Royal Scots Greys (Tanks)
Demobilised as Captain (Technical Adjutant, BAOR AFV School, Belsen)

Advertising career
Dunlop Rubber Company (1947–54): Advertising Executive (Tyre Division); Advertising Manager (Dunlopillo, Dunlop General Rubber Goods Division and Dunlop

Special Products); Public Relations Manager (Dunlop Group).

Aspro-Nicholas (1954–56): Advertising Manager (Home and Overseas).

McCann Erickson (1956–59): Account Executive (Esso).

Masius Wynne-Williams (1959–82): Main Board and Management Committee Member; Account Director (British Rail, Beecham, The Co-op, Mars Confectionery, Petfoods Ltd, Dornay Foods, Vauxhall Motors, Bedford Trucks, Dunlop Tyres, Simoniz, Ever Ready, Eastern Electricity. Remained on Board of Trustees until 1992.

Competition career

Trials riding: Gold Medal and Club Team Prize, International Six Days Trial 1949.

First Class Award, Scottish Six Days Trial 1949.

Southern Experts Trial 1949.

250cc and 350cc motor-cycle races at Brands Hatch and Cadwell Park.

Broadcasting career

First commentary: 1948 Shelsley Walsh Hill Climb, Worcestershire. Public address for Midland Automobile Club.

First radio commentary: 1949 British Grand Prix at Silverstone for BBC, won by Baron Toulo de Graffenried in a Maserati 4CLT.

First TV commentary: 1949 Knatts Valley motor-cycle hill climb for BBC.

First Isle of Man TT commentary: 1949 BBC Radio: Junior TT, won by Freddie Frith on a Velocette.
First Formula 1 television commentary: 1978 Monaco Grand Prix, won by Patrick Depailler in a Tyrrell-Ford.
Long-term TV co-commentators: James Hunt (BBC: 1980–93), Jonathan Palmer (BBC: 1993–96) and Martin Brundle (ITV: 1997–2001).
Final Formula 1 TV commentary: 2001 United States Grand Prix, Indianapolis, 30 September, won by Mika Hakkinen in a McLaren-Mercedes-Benz.

Broadcasting highlights

Isle of Man TT (1949–78): Commentated on over 200 Isle of Man TT and Manx Grand Prix events.
Motor-cycle trials (1949–50): BBC Radio.
Motocross (1957–85): ITV *World of Sport* and BBC TV *Grandstand* events including British Motocross Grand Prix and Motocross des Nations.
Rallycross (1968–94): BBC TV *Grandstand* series and British Rallycross Grand Prix.
Powerboats (1980–85): BBC TV *Grandstand* Formula Johnson series; Embassy Grand Prix, Bristol Docks; South African Nashua Grand Prix, Johannesburg; Thames Powerboat Grand Prix.
Truck Racing (1988–89).BBC TV *Grandstand* series.
Karts (1983–85) TVB Hong Kong: HK International Kart Grand Prix.
Touring Cars: (1988–97): British Touring Car Championships (BBC TV); Bathurst 1000 Australia (Channel 7); Australian

Touring Car Championship (Channel 9); Guia Touring Car Race (Macau TV). BBC coverage and commentaries also syndicated around the world, especially to Australia, New Zealand, South Africa and Sweden.

Other categories (1976–97): Speedway, Rallying (including RAC Rally), Sportscars (including Le Mans), Formula Ford, Formula Vauxhall Lotus, Formula 3 (including Macau Grand Prix), Formula Atlantic, Formula 2, Formula 3000, Formula 5000.

Formula 1 (1969–2001): BBC TV: continuously from 1978–96 plus individual races for BBC radio from 1969–78. ITV: 1997–2001.

BBC/ITV coverage and commentaries also taken by Australia, New Zealand, Canada, South Africa, Hong Kong, Singapore, India, Pakistan and 19 Middle East and African countries.

Commentated on over 350 Formula One Grand Prix events from 12 European countries, Argentina, Australia, Brazil, Canada, Japan, Malaysia, Mexico, South Africa and the USA.

Other commentaries

White City Tattoo

Serpentine Regatta

Great Britain versus The Commonwealth Weightlifting Championships

BBC TV *Driving Force* series.

Awards

OBE from Her Majesty the Queen 1996

Honorary Degree: Doctor of Letters, De Montfort University 1998

Honorary Degree: Doctor of Arts, Bournemouth University 1998

British Racing Drivers' Club Gold Medal 2001

British Automobile Racing Club Gold Medal 1996

BAFTA Lifetime Achievement Award 2001

Royal Television Society Lifetime Achievement Award 2000

Australian Grand Prix Corporation Lifetime Achievement Award 2001

Television and Radio Industries Club Special Award 1997

Autosport Gregor Grant Award 1993

Guild of Motoring Writers Timo Makinen Trophy 1991

Guild of Motoring Writers Pemberton Trophy 1996

Index

INDEX

INDEX

INDEX

Photographic credits

Allsport 29t, 29c, 31b;
Andy Earl/F1 Racing 28tl
Belgrave Press Bureau 13tr
Brian Holder 13tl
Clifford Studios 10t
Colin Taylor 14c
Darren Heath 19c
Don Morley 7t, 7b, 8t, 8c, 8b, 11tl, 18t, 18b
Empics 30t, 32cl
F1 Magazine 28c
Formula One Pictures 27b, 32cr
George Schofield 5t
Gordon Francis 11tr
Grand Prix Library 17t
Jack Kay 15b
Jim Greening 12t
John Wynne-Williams 10cr
K G Jones 5c, 6c, 11b
LAT 5b, 12b, 19b, 22t, 29b, 30c, 30b, 31t, 32t, 32b
Mortons Motorcycle Media 3b
Northampton Mercury 15t
Paul Postle 20b
Press Association 26b
Ray Berghouse 24t
R C Vine 24c
Sutton Images 22b, 24b, 25t, 25c
Tank Museum, Bovington 27c
Ted Welch 25b
Temple Press 6b
The News Studio 27t

Every effort has been made to contact the copyright holders of the photographs included in this book. Where there have been omissions, the Publishers will endeavour to rectify any outstanding permissions on publication.

The Publishers would also like to thank Helen Smith, Eric Silbermann, Barbara Dixon, Cathie Arrington and Ingrid Lock for their work on this book.